Science for Children

Science for Children introduces readers to the pedagogy of primary and early childhood science education. It presents a wealth of science content across the birth-to-12-years continuum, demonstrating how science can come alive in the classroom.

The book pays special attention to the three strands of science, in accordance with the Australian Curriculum. It also uses the practice principles and learning outcomes of the national Early Years Learning Framework to present content for babies through to the transition into the Foundation year at school.

Science for Children explores various approaches to teaching and learning in science. It covers inquiry approaches in detail; makes explicit links to the 5Es; critiques longstanding approaches, such as discovery approaches and a transmission approach; and explores Indigenous perspectives and a Vygotskian framework. This allows the reader to make informed choices about when to use a particular approach in primary classrooms and early childhood settings.

Designed to prepare future educators for practice, *Science for Children* challenges students and offers practical classroom-based strategies for their science teaching careers.

Science for Children includes a single-use six-month subscription to *Cambridge Dynamic Science*, providing access to interactive content to support complex science topics. Additional resources for instructors are available online at www.cambridge.edu.au/academic/science.

Marilyn Fleer is the Foundation Chair of Early Childhood Education at Monash University.

Science for
Children

Marilyn Fleer

CAMBRIDGE
UNIVERSITY PRESS

University Printing House, Cambridge CB2 8BS, United Kingdom

One Liberty Plaza, 20th Floor, New York, NY 10006, USA

477 Williamstown Road, Port Melbourne, VIC 3207, Australia

314–321, 3rd Floor, Plot 3, Splendor Forum, Jasola District Centre, New Delhi – 110025, India

103 Penang Road, #05–06/07, Visioncrest Commercial, Singapore 238467

Cambridge University Press is part of the University of Cambridge.

It furthers the University's mission by disseminating knowledge in the
pursuit of education, learning and research at the highest international
levels of excellence.

www.cambridge.org
Information on this title: www.cambridge.org/9781107548701

© Cambridge University Press 2015

First published by Prentice–Hall Australia 1996
Second edition published by Pearson Education Australia 2001
Third edition 2007
First published by Cambridge University Press 2015 (version 8, January 2022)

Cover designed by Marianna Berek-Lewis
Typeset by Newgen Publishing and Data Services
Printed in Australia by Ligare Pty Ltd, December 2021

A catalogue record for this publication is available from the British Library

*A Cataloguing-in-Publication entry is available from the catalogue
of the National Library of Australia at www.nla.gov.au*

ISBN 978-1-107-54870-1 Paperback

Additional resources for this publication at www.cambridge.edu.au/academic/science

Contents

Science for Children and Cambridge Dynamic Science

Cambridge Dynamic Science harnesses the power of interactive digital technology to deliver a comprehensive online resource for teaching and learning in the science classroom.

Purchasers of *Science for Children* are provided with a single-use, 6-month subscription to *Cambridge Dynamic Science*, which contains interactive content to support complex science topics. Your unique access code is printed on the inside front cover (ebook purchasers should follow the instructions provided on page ii).

Relevant interactive activities are identified throughout the book with this icon. The relevant Year, Module and Units are listed with the icons.

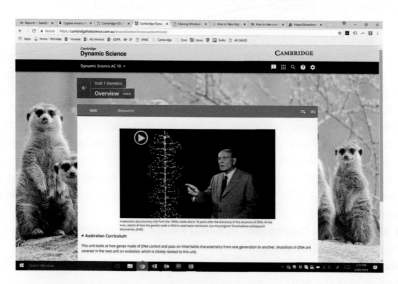

Login/access instructions

1. Go to www.cambridge.edu.au/activate and enter your activation code.
2. Accept the terms of use, then click the 'activate' button.

Acknowledgements

I wish to acknowledge the foundational co-author of the first edition of *Science for Children*, Dr Tim Hardy, and the subsequent co-author Rev Dr Beverley Jane for editions two and three. Their contributions to the ideas and directions of the previous editions have provided a strong foundation from which to prepare this book. In addition, I would like to thank Nina Sharpe for her untiring belief in the value of this publication and in her unwavering support in bringing this book to press. Special acknowledgement is made to all the individuals who have contributed to specific chapters. Details are provided in the relevant chapters.

Cambridge University Press is grateful to the following individuals and organisations for permission to use their material in *Science for Children*.

Web icon: © shutterstock.com/veronchick84; **Figure 2.3** (clockwise from top): © shutterstock.com/SoRad; © shutterstock.com/Piyato; © shutterstock.com/RATOCA; © shutterstock.com/Ramona Kaulitzki; © shutterstock.com/Panaiotidi; © shutterstock.com/MaKars; **2.4** (clockwise from top): © shutterstock.com/ufuk sezgen; Newgen Publishing and Data Services; © shutterstock.com/Miroslava Hlavacova; © shutterstock.com/S.V.Art; © shutterstock.com/Tribalium; © shutterstock.com/Alemon cz; © shutterstock.com/T-Kot; © shutterstock.com/Ramona Kaulitzki; **2.5–7** (magnifying glass): © shutterstock.com/Mega Pixel, (image) © shutterstock.com/Olesya Feketa. All Shutterstock.com images 2015 are used under licence from Shutterstock.com.

All material identified by (ACARA <year>) is material subject to copyright under the *Copyright Act 1968* (Cth) and is owned by the Australia Curriculum, Assessment and Reporting Authority 2015.

For all Australian Curriculum material except elaborations: This is an extract from the Australian Curriculum.

Elaborations: This may be a modified extract from the Australian Curriculum and may include the work of other authors.

Disclaimer: ACARA neither endorses nor verifies the accuracy of the information provided and accepts no responsibility for incomplete or inaccurate information. In particular, ACARA does not endorse or verify that:

- The content descriptions are solely for a particular year and subject;
- All the content descriptions for that year and subject have been used; and
- The author's material aligns with the Australian Curriculum content descriptions for the relevant year and subject.

You can find the unaltered and most up to date version of this material at http://www.australiancurriculum.edu.au. This material is reproduced with the permission of ACARA.

Every effort has been made to track and acknowledge copyright. The publisher apologises for any accidental infringement and welcomes information that would redress this situation.

PART 1

Research Foundation for Developing a Personal Approach to Teaching Science

In this first section of the book you are introduced to science as a human endeavour. Chapters 1 and 2 present a range of perspectives on how science can be thought about. We begin with a child's perspective, followed by an institutional perspective through the eyes of teachers, and conclude in Chapter 2 with a personal and cultural perspective on finding out how children work and think scientifically from birth to 12 years. As you read through the first two chapters, continually reflect upon the question of 'What does science mean for your community, for you as a teacher and for children?'

CHAPTER 1

Science as a human endeavour

Introduction

In this book we introduce you to the pedagogy of primary and early childhood science education. We pay special attention to the idea of science as a human endeavour in the context of the Australian curriculum – Science (ACARA 2014). This overarching idea:

- frames the *Science Understanding* strand
- supports the *Science Inquiry Skills* strand
- contributes to the development of an understanding about the *Nature of Science*.

Similarly, the *practice principles and the learning outcomes* of the national Early Years Learning Framework (EYLF) (Australian Government 2009) are used to frame content for babies through to the transition into the Foundation year at school.

Each of the chapters that follow gives details of different approaches to teaching and learning in science, with a special focus on the development of science concepts for children aged from birth to 12 years.

In this chapter we specifically focus on the *nature of science* where we highlight science as a human endeavour through the topic of energy and the EYLF outcome for the development of skills and processes, such as problem solving, inquiry, experimentation, hypothesising, researching and investigating (Australian Government 2009).

We begin this chapter by looking at how science is perceived by children, followed by a case example of a multiage group of children and their teachers learning about the *nature of science* through researching matter and energy. Through studying 'What are the discoveries in energy that have made a real difference in our world', the children in the case study came to recognise that science is a human

Figure 1.1 Australian Curriculum – Science: science knowledge helps people to understand the effect of their actions.

endeavour that changes the quality of their lives as well as shaping how they live, learn and work in their communities. We finish this chapter with a discussion of what a quality science interaction looks like for infants, toddlers and preschoolers working and playing scientifically. We specifically draw out curiosity, cooperation, confidence, creativity, commitment, enthusiasm, persistence, imagination and reflexivity as discussed in EYLF.

As you read through this chapter, document what you believe constitutes the characteristics of science as a human endeavour.

REFLECTIONS 1.1: IMAGINE A SCIENTIST

Close your eyes for a few moments and imagine a scientist.

What did you see in your mind's eye?

A man in a white coat? With glasses? With a beard? Surrounded by scientific instruments?

With books and filing cabinets nearby? Perhaps some experimentation? Perhaps you heard a 'eureka!'?

If you 'saw' and 'heard' all this in your imagination, you have a well-defined, stereotyped image of a scientist!

Figure 1.2 EYLF: Children develop a range of skills and processes such as problem solving, enquiry, experimentation, hypothesising, researching and investigating.

RESEARCH ACTIVITY 1.1: WHAT IS A SCIENTIST?

When children are asked to respond to the question, 'What is a scientist?', by drawing a group of scientists and discussing their thinking, a range of representations emerge. The picture in Figure 1.3 was drawn by Nicola and shows the stereotypical 'scientist': white lab coat, beakers, test tubes and working in a laboratory, alone, carrying out experiments. The stereotype is a male scientist, so Nicola's drawing of a female scientist is not entirely stereotypical.

When you talk to children about what is a scientist, you may find that some similar stereotypical representations emerge. As in the famous description of Lord Byron, many children saw scientists as being *mad* or *bad* (see over) …

Draw a group of scientists

Figure 1.3 Nicola's drawing of a scientist alone in the lab.

Mea: Scientists knock down walls with a big hammer. They make people drink potions.

They are bad people and they where [sic] tall boots.

And dangerous to know.

Chloe: They make stuff like potions.

Researcher: What are these potions used for?

Chloe: They turned a man into a llama and then he needed another potion to turn him back into a person.

Researcher: Why do you think that?

Chloe: I saw it on *The Emperor's New Groove!*

Some children think that scientists are mostly men.

The research has also shown that some children realised that they themselves were scientists, and said: WE ARE SCIENTISTS! We worked together to explore!

We came up with theories! We were researchers! We discovered! We had fun! But not all children have these views, where they conceptualise the work of scientists and themselves as inquiry-based. For instance, the stereotypical images that are evident when children are asked to think about or draw pictures of scientists tend to reflect:

- lab coat
- spectacles
- facial hair (beards, moustaches, very long sideburns)
- laboratory materials and equipment, such as fizzy reactions, test tubes
- books and reports
- technological products of science
- captions – eureka, bam, formulae, chemical equations, etc.

These representations by primary children are in line with what has traditionally been represented across a broad range of literature. For instance, in Germany, Markic, Valanides and Eilks (2005) evaluated 104 science student teachers' conceptions using a modified version of the Draw-A-Science Teacher Teaching Checklist (DASTT-C). The study found that secondary chemistry and physics student teachers hold conventional and teacher-centred views on science teaching and learning. In contrast, biology student teachers and 'even much more primary science student teachers have a more open, student-centred and constructivistic view on teaching their respective subject' (Markic et al. 2005, p. 1). While the findings of this study are encouraging for primary science, Nicola's drawing, as shown here, indicate that we need to do more to dislodge the stereotypical views of scientists that some children hold. The stereotypical images influence how children perceive science, and the negative images of scientists can affect the choice of careers by minority groups and female students (Carter 2007).

Zapata (2013) has also shown that when student teachers studying to be primary teachers were asked about their perceptions of scientists, they too responded like the primary students illustrated in the examples mentioned. She found that 58 per cent of the student-teachers perceived scientists to be male, supporting the belief that 'messages received in science classrooms position men as the ones who have shaped the world and the ones recognized as thinker and so, naturally science is presented from a seemingly male perspective' (p. 784). When Zapata (2013) interviewed the pre-service teachers, this was highlighted, for example:

Valarie: This scientist does stem cell research. He also is a professor at a university. During his free time he likes to read about different topics in science. He also loves to teach his students what he learns from his research. He hopes to find the cure for cancer through his many hours of hard work and research (p. 788).

Angie: My scientist is an older, very bright intelligent man that enjoys doing experiments and solving science problems. He enjoys working with elements on the periodic table and reading books to further his science knowledge. He works in a lab all day long in the hopes of solving some major science mysteries (p. 789).

The examples above show particular beliefs and constructions of science and scientific activity by scientists. Zapata (2013) suggests that 'the pervasive elitist view of science along with a staunch claim to objectivity that presents the illusion of science is separate from an individual's history and how that history influences ones' knowledge of the world' (p. 797). Typically, scientists have a shared set of values, including objectivity, respect for evidence and a rigorous systematic approach to the scientific enterprise. Zapata (2013) argues that we need to recognise 'that knowledge is constructed through social acts'. He argues that it is also '"culturally embedded" and must give the opportunities for the experiences of women, minorities and currently marginalized members of society to present their views as resources for research' (p. 797). The nature of science therefore must be viewed more broadly in the general community, so that perceptions of what science is and what scientists do includes the perspectives of others. Cheng (2013) used the same tool as Zapata (2013), but with Year 2 and Year 5 children from Australia and from China, and found that science was deemed important for their everyday lives, but because the Chinese students had not learned science formally at school and were unsure of what science was about, half of the Chinese children in Year 2 (but none in Year 5) said they would like to be inventors in the future, while none of the Australian children interviewed wanted to be scientists. Cheng (2013) suggested that one way to introduce and put forward the positive side of science to children, rather than the stereotypical images, would be to use the biographies and stories of scientists, alongside real-world connections by presenting a clearer image of how science is used in everyday life. An example follows.

Leading change in science

Jumping genes: www.dnaftb. org/32/ animation. html

Year 7, Module 1, Unit 1
Year 10, Module 1, Unit 1

Barbara McClintock (1902–92) won a Nobel Prize for her pioneering work in the field of genetics in 1983. She introduced the idea of the 'jumping genes'. Through her corn breeding experiments she was able to show how the unstable mutations of the variegated streaking on cobs of corn occurred at the genetic level. Each kernel in a corn cob is an embryo that is produced from an individual fertilisation. Each cob can produce hundreds of offspring, making it an ideal plant for the study of genetics. McClintock found that an organism's genome was not stationary, but rather was subject to alteration and rearrangement. At the time, her findings were highly criticised, not only because she challenged the established thinking in genetics, but also because of the method of her research.

In the biography of Barbara McClintock, Fox Keller (1983) wrote that 'Good science cannot proceed without a deep emotional investment' and expansive imagination (p. 197). She states that McClintock had an '"exceedingly strong feeling" for the oneness of things' (p. 201), where she projected herself inside the microscope joining the chromosomes she studied. But this understanding came from looking down a microscope and also by being in the field studying the corn crops closely.

This approach 'both promotes and is promoted by her access to the profound con-nectivity of all biological forms – of the cell, of the organism, of the ecosystem' (p. 201). This approach to science was not respected at the time, nor were the find-ings. Yet, her work changed the course of research in genetics, and laid a new foun-dation from which all other scientists in genetics have worked.

Looking inside the classroom

In the case study that follows we see how values play out among children as they work together exploring big ideas in science, alongside studying the people who made important scientific discoveries that changed everyday lives.

A case study of a Year 3/4 classroom

Our children's inquiry question: *What are the discoveries in energy that have made a real difference in our world?*

At Princes Hill Primary School the teaching–learning spaces are arranged into neighbourhood communities, where teams of teachers work with multi-aged groups of children. The spaces are expansive, with a variety of nooks available for group and individual projects (see Chapter 6 for another case study of a multi-age group). In this space the learning inquiries feature predominantly, as shown in Figure 1.4.

Figure 1.4 The learning spaces for science inquiries in the Year 3/4 neighbourhood community.

The teachers actively work together in teams to research, plan, implement and develop the learning inquiries. The class documentation presents the pedagogical and learning journey, and is presented here as a case study of learning and teaching in the Year 3/4 neighbourhood community.

We wanted to ensure that the 'small' ideas developed from studying particular topic of interest would build to form 'bigger' ideas which connected to fundamental laws, systems and cycles. We wanted children to be able to link new experiences to what they already knew. It meant that teaching and learning needed to be sufficiently flexible to allow for differences in children's thinking processes and the range of ways they would construct meaning from the experiences.

We needed to acknowledge different starting points, and despite working towards common goals, we thought the children would want to build their own pathways to these goals in different ways.

We wanted an idea that could be:

- applied to many aspects of science – physical, chemical, biological and technological
- developed through a variety of expressions – traditional science experimentation through to exploring with dance and their bodies.

Year 8,
Module 4,
Unit 9

The big idea that we decided upon was: *The total amount of energy in the universe is always the same, but energy can be transformed when things change or are made to happen.*

We knew that each experience needed to engage and connect with existing understandings, while at the same time providing for multiple pathways for exploration.

Teacher research into science concepts

As part of working as a teaching team, the teachers decided that it was important to research the concepts themselves. A group approach helps build confidence and competence to teach science because teachers can help each other, and draw on the collective research of the group to support implementation of a unit of science.

In order to create these understandings in our students we had to develop our own knowledge through teacher research into what was key to building the conceptual understandings for the children.

What we identified in our research were:

1 Many processes or events involve change and require energy to make them happen.
2 Energy can be transferred from one body to another in various ways.
3 Energy cannot be created nor destroyed.

We broke these ideas down into key concepts.

1   Many processes or events involve change and require energy to make them happen:
    - heating things requires energy and produces a range of changes.
    - there is a range of energy forms such as electricity, magnetism, solar, etc.

2   Energy can be transferred from one body to another in various ways:
    - energy makes things change (e.g. ice to water, water to steam, chemical energy to electrical energy)
    - in the process of change, energy is transformed from one form to another
    - an object which transfers energy to something else is called a source of energy
    - objects have energy because of their chemical composition (as in fuels and batteries), their movement (e.g. spring), their temperature (e.g. hot water bottle), their position in a gravitational or other field (e.g. tides), or because of compression or distortion (e.g. elastic)
    - potential energy is stored energy
    - kinetic energy is the energy of motion.

3   Energy cannot be created nor destroyed:
    - when energy is transferred form one object to others the total amount of energy in the universe remains the same
    - the amount of energy that one object loses is the same amount of energy that the other object gains.

What was important for the teachers in their research was finding out that words in science have specific meanings and the meanings may be different from how they are used in everyday life (we take this up further in the next chapter). For instance, the words energy and force are not interchangeable. They are not the same as each other. Push and pull are often used to explain force. A force can generally be demonstrated and felt. However, energy is a slightly more abstract concept. We measure energy in joules and we measure force in newtons. It was decided that the topic of force would not be covered.

Teacher research into the curriculum

The teachers from the neighbourhood communities also examined the Australian Curriculum – Science closely to find out more about the key idea of 'What are the discoveries in energy that have made a real difference in our world'. They wanted to connect this to the idea of science being a human endeavour. In doing so, they found two key sub-strands to consider at the Year 3–6 level. They were:

Year 7,
Module 5,
Unit 13

- use and influence of science
- nature and development of science.

This led to further analysis by the teachers of the curriculum content for science as a human endeavour, and what this might mean for them and the children in the neighbourhood community – as shown in Table 1.1.

Table 1.1 Science as a Human Endeavour 3–6

Years 3–4	
Nature and development of science	**Use and influence of science**
Science involves making predictions and describing patterns and relationships.	Science knowledge helps people to understand the effect of their actions.

Children's research

The teachers worked with the children on their group inquiries, which together fed into the key idea of 'What are the discoveries in energy that have made a real difference in our world'.

We began with a research phase where the emphasis was placed on finding out the reasons behind why scientists go about making discoveries. These discoveries are connected to the needs of societies.

The children were involved in conferencing with a teacher to demonstrate that they had sufficiently researched the discovery, the life and activity of the scientists, while considering their ideas on what led to the discovery. Aspects of teamwork where also featured.

In the second phase, as a teaching team we decided to select working groups for the students to extend their interpersonal skills through working with a range of others who were not in their friendship group. The teams were mostly mixed gender, age and interests. This raised issues of cooperation and collaboration, equity of workload and roles and engagement, all of which challenged groups to manage themselves. This was also valuable for talking about how scientific teams form and work together.

Students were also conferenced frequently on their progress in their project; this included reflections on teamwork, sharing of roles, and equity in their contribution. It was during this time that the teachers decided the work needed more focus and purpose, and together with the children they explored the idea of having a school expo, to share their findings with the community.

The third phase focused around creating an experiment or demonstration and being able to explain, as a group, how that experiment would help the visitors to the expo to understand what their learning was about and how it connected to the discovery they were investigating. Where possible, teachers would model the idea of the documentation of process before, during and after the demonstration/experiment.

We needed to be explicit about what a scientist would do if something did not work. We discussed how scientists would go back and analyse the reasons for the failure and re-plan the experiment (children were mostly changing the variable without analysis). Students mostly elected to do this by filming what they were doing in stages.

Figure 1.5 What do scientists do?

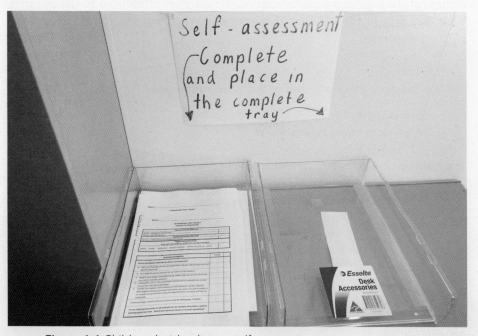

Figure 1.6 Children decide when to self-assess.

Students devised a list of possible questions about content, process and teamwork. They practised the method of delivery and presentation of their learning through conferencing of the different stages of the brief with a teacher. Conferences focused on the teamwork aspect of the groups too. We have focused on reflection as a genre, process writing through a series of drafts based on reflections of working within their group. The students at different phases of the inquiry completed a self-assessment proforma which was used for teacher–child conferencing of learning outcomes.

REFLECTION – BY ISABELLE

At the start I felt it was a bit of a challenge working with different people and not having an idea what fossil fuels were, but now I have a much better understanding of fossil fuels. Sometimes I felt that my group could concentrate a bit more. I still think we can try a bit harder so we all work together as a group. I think this experience has made me better friends with the people I have been working with.

My favourite part of this experience was making the model of the coal power station because I like making things. I also enjoyed finding out who discovered oil because I like finding out all the information about Edwin Drake.

Next time when I get put into a group without my friends, I will be more confident because I have done it before.

To ensure that the children's thinking focused on the content area of energy in the context of the big discoveries in science, the teachers introduced to the children, what they called 'provocations'. These are shown below in the context of how the children responded.

The key questions that were used as the 'provocation' were:

1   What is energy?
2   Where does energy come from?

The learning objectives that were shared with the children were:
- To be able to say what energy is and what it can do.
- To begin to think about where energy comes from.

What is energy?

Brainstorm ideas. Think of sentences that have the word 'energy' in them. What do you think it means?

Discuss the ideas you have come up with.

Can you think of something that uses energy in the neighbourhood? At home? Anywhere else?

BRIGID'S THINKING ABOUT ENERGY

'I think energy looks like fruit because when you eat it you get energy.'

'I think a slide gives you energy because sometimes you can get electric shock.'

'I think lightning gives you energy because when you get struck by it, it's like a big electric shock.'

'I think electric poles give you energy because it sends energy to everyone's house.'

'I think that a trampoline gives you energy because when you sit or lie down on it you can get electric shocks.'

Teacher observations of children: observing how children collaborate in these new situations

Teachers observed and recorded student interactions through photographs and video footage. These were then analysed during team meetings. The groups were also provided with a photograph of their team working together. This was used to make an evaluation of their progress as a team. Many workshops were provided to the students to build specific skills, strategies and vocabulary in science. But the students also needed support in the development of teamwork skills and effective collaboration.

Figure 1.7 Collaborating in science.

The science expo

The teachers and the children decided that it was important to showcase the outcome of 'What are the discoveries in energy that have made a real difference in our world?'

The children created advertisements for letting families and the community know about scientific discoveries on energy. Examples of the children's 'TV advertisements' are shown on the *Science for Children* website.

Showcasing science through an expo is one way to share with families what children are learning in science at school, particularly when the learning is about presenting science as a human endeavour. The Australian Curriculum – Science advocates that from Year 3 onwards children should have opportunities '... to investigate how science understanding has developed, including considering some of the people and the stories behind these advances in science. They will also recognise how this science understanding can be applied to their lives and the lives of others. As students develop a more sophisticated understanding of the knowledge and skills of science they are increasingly able to appreciate the role of science in society' (p. 8). But, understandings about the nature of science must go beyond a conception of just Western science. The role of science in society must be conceptualised in relation to the cultural communities that make

Children's TV advertisements: www. cambridge. edu.au/ academic/ science

Figure 1.8 Designing advertisements for a school expo on 'Discoveries that have made a real difference in our world'.

up that particular society. For instance, we know from the research of Aikenhead and Michell (2011) that understandings develop across and within societies. For example, Aikenhead and Michell (2011, p. 116) show how ideas about the world are formed and how we come to understand the world through particular scientific or Indigenous lenses:

Table 1.2 shows the common ground for knowledge construction in communities – often within just one local community. The case study of the Year 3/4 children focused on science as a particular form of knowledge. The unit could also have included the knowledge of local elders, so that valuable Aboriginal and

Table 1.2 Ideas about how to understand the world, and what those ideas are based on

Themes	Indigenous ways of living in nature	Common ground	Eurocentric sciences
Empirically based			
Ideas about how to understand the world, and what those ideas are based on.	'Experiments' rely on natural environmental changes over many generations and involve collective wisdom.	Experimental.	Experiments are undertaken by humans over relatively short periods of time.
	Source: both material and non-material (monism).	Observing.	Source: material world only (dualism).
	Relationship-based.		No relationship exists between the observer and object.
	What is the world?	Questioning.	How does the world work?
	Who is that? How are they related? Who is doing that? What do they do?	Classifying.	What grouping does that fit? What are similarities/patterns that can arbitrarily define a group?
	To balance interrelationships in Mother Earth.	Predicting.	To explain and predict natural events.
	A myriad of representations of wisdom-in-action.	Models.	Mechanistic, often amenable to quantification, many are visual.
	Conducted by everyone, incudes personal experience.	Monitoring.	Conducted by professionally trained experts and technicians.
	Appropriated tools and processes from modern technology.	Technological tools and processes to investigate nature.	Advanced technologies and scientific processes approved in paradigms.

Torres Strait Islander understandings could have been investigated and included as important knowledge construction for children to understand (see Chapter 9 for further discussion and an example). Similarly, the knowledge construction of other cultures, such as giving voice to Asian worldviews or particular African perspectives of community leaders, could have been investigated. What other perspectives could have been considered? In this way the children could have considered a broader range of forms of knowledge held by elders and community leaders. Martin (2013) has argued that, 'people are not dualistic but have multiple subjectivities across cultures. This is a tenet of the Aboriginal worldview when one evolves through life's experiences to make conscious the many roles and therefore identities one will enact' (p. 29).

The work of scientists across cultures has been conceptualised by MacDonald, Miller, Murry, Herrera and Spears (2013) in what they call a biography-driven instruction (BDI) approach that acts as a cultural guide for gaining insights into cultural forms of science knowledge, and seeks to make visible cultural forms of scientific knowledge held by children. Similarly, Hamlin (2013) provides a methodology for finding out about traditional forms of knowledge. The building of trust for a respectful exchange of knowledge sharing is foregrounded in her work. She argues that a teacher should begin this process by observing and participating in his or her local community. Once relationships have been built and a sense of trust established, then the teacher should begin sharing what has been observed, and in so doing should ask for clarification – firstly beginning with 'what questions' and later 'how questions'. This positions the Indigenous elders and others in the community as those with knowledge about their community. Further details on this methodology are provided in Chapter 2 and also Chapter 9.

The Australian Curriculum – Science also encourages teachers and their students to take a culturally sensitive approach to gaining insights into local knowledge about culture, country and nature. Science as a human endeavour captures this idea. By following this method, as suggested by Hamlin (2013), teachers can investigate how science understandings develop within the communities in which they are teaching. Here the stories of people who are the holders of important localised knowledge can be respectfully gained. In addition, the ways of constructing knowledge, how knowledge is passed on from one generation to the next and how these knowledges have informed and advanced communities can then be revealed as valued funds of knowledge that are used to support everyday life. This is also an example of science as a human endeavour.

Looking inside an early childhood setting

What is a quality interaction for supporting science learning?

Selecting topics and science content that does not restrict the development of children's scientific thinking is important for the study of science in early childhood.

For instance, in Chapter 7 are examples of four-year-old children working with electricity, and in Chapter 5 we see examples of infants and toddlers learning about the biological sciences. These chapters show how very young children can and do think scientifically about their world. It is often the limitations of adults, rather than the competencies of children, that restrict the development of scientific thinking. Cowie and Otrel-Cass (2011) argue for a 'sustained focus on "big science ideas" with young children' (p. 285). What is key here is creating the right conditions for science learning for infants, toddlers and preschool children so they can engage with the big ideas in science.

Throughout this book are a detailed range of pedagogical approaches for promoting young children's thinking and acting in science. With the exception of Chapter 4 (A discovery-based approach to learning science), teachers are primarily positioned as taking an active role in supporting sustained shared interactions for developing scientific thinking and acting (see Fleer and Pramling 2015). This is in line with the EYLF, which advocates for intentional teaching.

Intentional teaching: involves educators being deliberate, purposeful and thoughtful in their decisions and actions. Intentional teaching is the opposite of teaching by rote or continuing with traditions simply because things have 'always' been done that way. (Australian Government 2009, p. 45).

However, not all teachers feel comfortable to take an active role. Blake and Howitt (2012) in their research have shown how in early childhood settings, children's experiences can be thought about as:

- satisfying curiosity
- guided play
- lost opportunities.

For instance, *satisfying curiosity* related to space and time enables children to follow their own individual pursuits in science – they give the example of a three-year-old child in a playgroup setting who is making a skateboard from wooden blocks (cylinders) and a box. The skater boy prepares a prototype, stands on it to test it, then adjusts the number of 'wheels' (cylinders), and then re-tests the skateboard by standing on it. We can see many examples of children exploring materials in early childhood settings. By observing them closely, we notice if and how they satisfy their curiosity.

Guided play has been described by Blake and Howitt (2012) in an example of two children aged three years in a childcare centre having access to, but not using, a table filled with seeds and other natural materials. As the resources were not being used, the researcher invited the children over to the table and supported them to begin experiencing the materials. As the children became engaged with what was on the table, a great deal of discussion could be heard, as they sorted, classified, problem solved. The adult was pivotal in guiding children in their play. The educator took a key role in highlighting the science and building a quality scientific interaction.

Lost opportunities is captured by Blake and Howitt (2012) through the example of a whole group experience of making popcorn, where the children initially discussed what they knew about popcorn, then they observed the popcorn being made, and finally they were invited to comment on what they noticed. It was only later that they had the opportunity to compare cooked and uncooked popcorn. After the activity, the children were free to play in the centre. Blake and Howitt (2012) argue that this experience was full of promise, but represented a lost opportunity because they were not practically engaged in the experience, and had to sit for a long period of time. They state that 'Treated as a one-off science activity, little scientific learning occurred as a consequence of not following up the corn activity' (p. 296).

It has been suggested by Siry and Kremer (2011) that science opportunities become evident in relation to what interests children. As such, children's interests act as a resource for supporting the informal teaching–learning process. Hedges and Cullen (2005) have argued that often teachers just pride open-ended experiences as part of their play-based programs for the learning of content knowledge, believing learning occurs through osmosis (i.e. discovery learning – see Chapter 4) rather than through formal teaching. In addition, Edwards and Cutter-Mackenzie (2011) have found that in play-based settings there tends to be three pedagogical approaches for supporting environmental education – modelled play, open-ended

Figure 1.9 Elvin makes *discoveries that are important in his world.*

play and purposefully framed play – for supporting the conceptual development of young children. As with Wood (2007), they note that a mixed approach supports 'specific skills and concepts' (p. 58).

Tu (2006) has shown in her research that the preschool environment is full of rich science opportunities for children, such as force when riding a bike. However, she argues that teachers simply provide the rich environment, and do not always recognise the science possibilities. That is, they don't talk to the children about the science concepts that could help explain, for example, why they are experiencing difficulties with riding their bike in the sand. Recognising science possibilities represents a kind of 'science attitude' or 'sciencing' as described by Tu (2006). Tu (2006) noted that science in early childhood settings could be thought about as:

- *formal sciencing*: planned science activities that are deliberately organised by the teacher
- *informal sciencing*: teacher might organise a space within the centre for promoting scientific interactions and explorations
- *incidental sciencing*: interactions that occur between children and the teacher as a result of an occurrence in the centre (e.g. rainbow appears).

Fleer, Gomes and March (2014) also found formal, informal and incidental sciencing prevalent when researching in Australian preschools. They noted that teachers also created opportunities for using science purposefully. But they found additional categories to those of Tu (2006):

- sciencing as part of the constant areas within the preschool
- building science infrastructure into the centre
- using science in everyday life in the centre.

As part of the constant areas within preschools, sciencing supports what children do, such as learning concepts of force in the context of block building. This would be evident through sustained shared science conversations. Some examples include:

- water trough, with equipment such as tubes, waterwheels, etc. (force)
- swing and see-saw (force)
- digging patch, where sand adheres when wet (force).

Building science infrastructure into the centre would be seen occurring through providing and having regular science conversations in:

- a vegetable garden (plant care)
- sensory shrubs (herbs – use, growth and care)
- flower beds (plant growth).

RESEARCH ACTIVITY 1.2: WHAT SCIENCE IS AFFORDED IN YOUR EARLY CHILDHOOD SETTING?

On your next field placement, take photographs and field notes of the early childhood environment and analyse it for:

1   Formal sciencing opportunities.
2   Informal sciencing opportunities.
3   Incidental sciencing moments.
4   Sciencing as part of the learning areas (e.g. special area just for science).
5   Science infrastructure.
6   Using science in everyday life.

What do you notice? Compare your findings with your peers. What opportunities are available to the children? How might more science be afforded by just changing the environment? Examine what you find in relation to the EYLF and the Australian Curriculum – Science. How might the EYLF and the Australian Curriculum – Science inform how you might change the environment to give more affordances for science learning?

Science in everyday life can support a purposeful engagement in science in early childhood settings (Vygotsky 1987). The research of Fleer, Gomes and March (2014) found that the teacher regularly used the website of the Bureau of Meteorology (BOM) for accessing the radar of her community to determine the weather, and together with the children discussed what they could do on that day. The teacher included in the outdoor area a rain gauge and a windmill. These tools were used for noticing weather patterns in the preschool environment. The children engaged in weather watching. Their activities were scientifically supported through the use of the prism to refract light. The prism allowed the children to observe (and create) rainbows inside the preschool. In the preschool community environment, the children regularly observed rainbows. Using a prism to create a rainbow in the preschool allowed the teacher to connect the introduced science with the children's everyday lives. Preschools can introduce science to support the everyday activities of the centre. The approach to science adopted by the teacher used the BOM as a resource for showing scientific ways of thinking and acting for the organisation of the day. The lived experiences of the children where the actual weather conditions could be compared with the predictions of the Bureau of Meteorology generated a lot of discussion. The children's science was real and meaningful to the children. It was more than incidental science, because the science was ongoing

Figure 1.10 Elvin's teacher builds upon the *discoveries that are important in his world –* expanding his everyday experiences of harvesting and eating strawberries, to reading about how 'the hungry caterpillar likes to eat strawberries too'.

as part of everyday life in the centre for the children. The weather conditions were important for making decisions about if and how long the children could play in the outdoor area, or if they might spot a rainbow. The purposeful inclusion of science in the everyday lives of the teachers and children supports the view that science is a human endeavour that makes a difference to the quality of children's life and play.

Fleer, Gomes and March (2014) were able to show that teachers with a sciencing attitude think about how to draw out the science possibilities that are available in the preschool environment. In these contexts teachers draw on the preschool infrastructure to support learning science (see Chapter 8 for a deeper discussion of this, under the topic of conceptual play).

When children experience these rich interactions in a science context, where the teacher has a sciencing attitude, then infants, toddlers and preschoolers are able to work and play scientifically in ways that develop curiosity, cooperation, confidence, creativity, commitment, enthusiasm, persistence, imagination and reflexivity (Australian Government 2009). The EYLF advocates for these important inquiry skills outcomes, and this connects well with the Australian Curriculum – Science strand of Science as a Human Endeavour. In the Foundation to Year 2 level, the 'Nature and development of science' sub-strand within the Science as a Human Endeavour strand also focuses on scientific inquiry, enabling transitions from the early childhood period to the Foundation year of school. The Australian Curriculum – Science, suggests that children begin to make clear connections between the 'inquiry skills that they are learning and the work of scientists' (ACARA 2014, p. 8).

How we feel about science matters

When you think about your own experiences of science, what comes to mind? Record your thoughts.

Do you feel like Child 1 who wrote about science as 'being okay' but not really his 'favourite subject' or like Child 2 who has found science to be useful for satisfying her curiosity?

Child 1: I think some of Science is okay. It is not my favourite subject. It is third bottom on my list of favourite subjects.

Child 2: I think Science is fun because you learn things that you never thought existed. Did you know that the first horse was about 20cm?

As a teacher of science, how you feel about teaching science matters. For instance, Aguilar-Valdez, LopezLeiva, Roberts-Harris, Torres-Valasquez, Lobo and Westby (2013) found that when teachers from a range of cultural backgrounds discussed how they felt about science, an easiness surrounding how some learned science became evident.

JEAN

Background: I grew up as a half Cuban, half Panamanian in Miami, in a working-class family with traditional Latin@ values. Entering into the world of academic science was, for me, like stepping onto another planet – a total culture shock (Aguilar-Valdez, LopezLeiva, Roberts-Harris, Torres-Valasquez, Lobo and Westby 2013, p. 846).

Bridges: In learning how to speak not only the language of science, but the language of this Anglo and male dominated world, I found new ways to exist within them … I learned how to cross those bridges and persevere' (Aguilar-Valdez, LopezLeiva, Roberts-Harris, Torres-Valasquez, Lobo and Westby 2013, p. 846).

Teaching science: I found the actual *doing* of science – the curiosity, problem-solving, inquiry, and the real messiness of science – became an act of healing for my students, who before this had been struggling … with traditional content-knowledge of science … My students told me at the beginning of the year how much they hated science, because it was all difficult words and memorization. But by openly walking this path of *doing* science with my students in a way that acknowledged and spoke in their language(s), honored their culture, and developed family and community along the way, we forged new ways of being Latin@ scientists, and overcame science-phobia' (Aguilar-Valdez, LopezLeiva, Roberts-Harris, Torres-Valasquez, Lobo and Westby 2013, p. 846).

The hidden pain of learning science becomes clearly evident here. What might you do to create a positive experience for the learners of science? What ideas do you have? Chapter 9 gives some insights into how to avoid the scenario of Jean being reproduced in other classrooms or early childhood settings. Did you identify in any way with Jean? Do you have stories of learning science that reflect this level of trauma? Maybe your experiences are more positive, and the learning of science may be more comfortable for you. What is key here is how Jean used the messiness of science to forge ahead and create for herself and her children a different way of working and thinking about science. The particular inquiry-based way of learning science for building bridges across knowledge constructions is also evident in the example of Diane.

DIANE

When I began teaching, I went through a phase that was informed by formal Eurocentric teaching models and found they helped a little, but did not really help me [to] connect with my students in ways that improved their learning. I found I was more successful as a teacher when I worked to help students understand and comprehend context and content in their native language and in English. As an elementary school teacher, I found that science was a magical space where only curiosity and inquiry mattered. Doing inquiry with hands-on science leveled the playing field for all students, including bilingual students and students with disabilities (Aguilar-Valdez, LopezLeiva, Roberts-Harris, Torres-Valasquez, Lobo and Westby 2013, p. 848).

What we learn is how the nature of science and science teaching are both personal and cultural, and in the case of Jean and Diane, they also allow for maintaining and strengthening children's agency and identity.

By being able to take your culture with you into the classroom and early childhood setting, your ways of knowing and doing are respected. As Jean says in quoting a Francisco Alarcon poem: 'I carry my roots with me all the time, rolled up I use them as my pillow' (Aguilar-Valdez, et al. 2013, p. 847).

Being able to take your own culture into the classroom means that both the teacher and the learner feel more confident and competent to teach science. How you feel about teaching science is important because this underpins your level of confidence and competence for the teaching of science. However, building science competence and pedagogical confidence to teach science is a journey. The content of this book has been designed with this journey in mind.

Summary

Your pedagogical journey

At the beginning of this chapter we invited you to document the characteristics of science as a human endeavour. Now that you have read this chapter, what view have you formed?

In the context of the Year 3/4 children who studied 'What are the discoveries in energy that have made a real difference in our world' and through the sciencing attitude of the teacher in the early years, it was possible to see how children have the ability to develop conceptions about the *nature of science*. This is an important dimension of science as a human endeavour.

The Year 3/4 children learned to work in teams exploring the nature of scientific discoveries and the people behind them, and developing competencies in science communication (preparing for their science expo). We also saw how the early childhood teacher used the Bureau of Meteorology with her children as a tool for predicting when to play outside, thus showing how science is useful for everyday life.

Together, these case examples show how 'Science involves making predictions and describing patterns and relationships' (ACARA 2014, p. 5). The children in the case examples were able to explore a range of ways in which scientists gathered evidence for their ideas and, work towards developing explanations. This helped them to consider how 'science knowledge helps people to understand the effect of their actions' (ACARA 2014, p. 5).

As argued in the Australian Curriculum – Science: 'Science is a dynamic, collaborative and creative human endeavour arising from our desire to make sense of our world through exploring the unknown, investigating universal mysteries, making predictions and solving problems' (ACARA 2014, p. 5). In this way science helps children and the community at large to 'improve their understanding and explanations of the natural world' (ACARA 2014, p. 5).

Science as a human endeavour positions knowledge as involving the construction of explanations based on evidence. In different communities, different forms of evidence may be drawn upon, and different sets of knowledge generated. But what is key here is that the knowledge generated must position science as influencing 'society by posing, and responding to, social and ethical questions, and scientific research is itself influenced by the needs and priorities of society' (ACARA 2014, p. 5).

Science as a human endeavour also considers science as a 'unique way of knowing and doing' where it must be acknowledged that 'making decisions about science practices and applications' take into account 'ethical and social implications' (ACARA 2014, p. 5), particularly for the diverse cultural communities that make up Australia's culturally and linguistically diverse society.

References

Aguilar-Valdez, JR, LopezLeiva, CA, Roberts-Harris, D, Torres-Valasquez, D, Lobo, G, Westby C 2013, 'Ciencia en *Nepantla:* The journey of *Nepantler@s* in science learning and teaching', *Cultural Studies of Science Education*, vol. 8, no. 4, pp. 821–58.

Aikenhead, G, Michell, H 2011, *Bridging Cultures: Indigenous and Scientific Ways of Knowing Nature*, Toronto: Pearson Canada.

Australian Curriculum, Assessment and Reporting Authority 2014, Australian Curriculum – Science. Available at http://www.australiancurriculum.edu.au/Science/Curriculum/F-6. (Accessed September 2014.)

Australian Government Department of Education, Employment and Workplace Relations 2009, *Belonging, Being and Becoming. The Early Years Learning Framework for Australia*, Canberra: Commonwealth of Australia.

Blake, E, Howitt, C 2012, 'Science in early learning centres: Satisfying curiosity, guided play or lost opportunities?' in KCD Tan & M Kim eds, *Issues and Challenges in Science Education Research: Moving Forward*, Dordrecht: Springer, pp. 281–98.

Carter, L 2007, 'Sociocultural influences on science education: Innovation for contemporary times', *Science Education*, 1–17. (DOI 10.1002/sce.)

Cheng, H 2013, 'What can we learn from Chinese and Australian primary school students' perceptions of scientist and science learning' in C Redman ed., *Successful Science Education Practices. Exploring What, Why and How they Worked*, New York: Nova Science, pp. 39–70.

Cowie, B, Otrel-Cass, K 2011, 'Exploring the value of "horizontal" learning in early years science classrooms', *Early Years: An International Journal of Research and Development*, vol. 31, no. 3, pp. 285–95.

Edwards, S, Cutter-Mackenzie, A 2011, 'Environmentalising early childhood education curriculum through pedagogies of play', *Australian Journal of Early Childhood*, vol. 36, no. 1, pp. 51–9.

Fleer, M, Gomes, J, March, S 2014, 'A cultural-historical reading of scientific concept formation: Affordances for science learning in preschools', *Australasian Journal of Early Childhood*, vol. 39, no. 1, pp. 38–49.

Fleer, M, Pramling, N 2015, *A Cultural-historical Study of Children Learning Science. Foregrounding Affective Imagination in Play-based Settings*, Dordrecht: Springer.

Fox Keller, E 1983, *A Feeling for the Organism. Life and Work of Barbara McClintock*, New York: Freeman.

Hamlin, ML 2013, '"Yo soy indigena": Identifying and using traditional ecological knowledge (TEK) to make the teaching of science culturally responsive for Mayua girls', *Cultural Studies of Science Education*, vol. 8, no. 4, pp. 759–76.

Hedges, H, Cullen, J 2005, 'Subject knowledge in early childhood curriculum and pedagogy: Beliefs and practices', *Contemporary Issues in Early Childhood*, vol. 6, no. 1, pp. 66–79.

MacDonald, GL, Miller, SS, Murry, K Herrera, S, Spears, JD 2013, 'Efficacy of ACA strategies in biography-driven science teaching: An investigation', *Cultural Studies of Science Education*, vol. 8, no. 4, pp. 889–903.

Markic, S, Valanides, N Eilks, I 2005, 'First-year science student teachers' images of science teaching in Germany', paper presented at the 5th European Science Education Research Association Conference, Barcelona (Spain), 28 August – 1 September.

Martin, KL 2013, '"At a loss: scared and excited": A response to Jonathan Silin', *Contemporary Issues in Early Childhood*, vol. 14, no. 1, pp. 29–31.

Siry, C, Kremer, I 2011, 'Children explain the rainbow: Using young children's ideas to guide science curricula', *International Journal of Science Education and Technology*, vol. 20, pp. 43–55.

Tu, T 2006, 'Preschool science environment: What is available in a preschool classroom?', *Early Childhood Education Journal*, vol. 33, no. 4, pp. 245–51. (Retrieved from DOI 10.1007/s10643-005-0049-8.)

Vygotsky, LS 1987, 'Thinking and speech' in LS Vygotsky, *The Collected Works of L.S. Vygotsky, Vol. 1, Problems of General Psychology*, RW Rieber & AS Carton eds, N Minick trans, New York: Plenum Press, pp. 39–285.

Wood, E 2007, 'Reconceptualising child-centred education: Contemporary directions in policy, theory and practice in early childhood', *Forum*, vol. 49, nos 1 & 2, pp. 119–33.

Zapata, M 2013, 'Substantiating the need to apply a sociocultural lens to the preparation of teachers in an effort to achieve science reform', *Cultural Studies of Science Education*, vol. 8, pp. 777–801. (DOI 10.1007/s11422-013-9513-8.)

Acknowledgement

Special thanks to the children at Red Hill Primary School and the student teachers involved in the Primary Science Curriculum unit who provided the data for the research reported here. Thank you also to Mr John Gipps for his initial paper and data analysis for this research. Also special thanks to my colleague Dr Liang Li for providing the infant photos in this chapter. Finally, the work samples, the rich teacher documentation and photographs taken of Princes Hill Primary School on the nature of science are also acknowledged.

CHAPTER 2

Researching children's understanding and ways of learning

Introduction

In the previous chapter we considered the nature of science and how science contributes to our everyday lives in positive ways. We also took a look at how the learning of science has not always been a positive experience for children or teachers. In this chapter we take a closer look at the learner and examine a range of ways of researching how a child thinks and acts in science in the context of everyday life.

In this chapter we specifically look at a case study of magnetism to illustrate the need for going beyond a personal representation in science, and to consider an institutional perspective of science, in addition to a community and societal worldview.

We also research what children think about living and non-living, and the classification of animals and plants, with a view to questioning a *one-worldview perspective* of nature and living.

Children's understanding

Rowan: Who will be Father Christmas when he is dead?

Adult: Umm … he is not going to die.

Rowan: Why doesn't he die?

Rowan's thinking about the mortality of humans is extended to something important to him – Father Christmas. We can find out a lot about children's thinking by listening to them. Children's understanding of the world is influenced by their daily experiences, as well as by direct encounters with information from books, their families, teachers and other children. Knowing what and how children think is important for understanding how concept formation in science can take place.

Rowan continues to share his thinking:

Rowan: If I ever die and someone pokes it, it will be gone.

Adult: Pokes what?

Rowan: The bubble in my head.

REFLECTIONS 2.1: HOW DO YOU FIND OUT WHAT CHILDREN THINK?

Before proceeding, record what you make of these comments by Rowan. *What is occurring here in terms of Rowan's understanding? How could you research what children think in relation to a range of science concepts?* What might have influenced Rowan's thinking? In general, where do you believe children get their ideas from? Make a list of the different ways children may be influenced? Now look at the photographs of Em at 13 months and Ivy at 23 months (Figures 2.1 and 2.2). *What might they be thinking? How might you begin to find out?* Record your ideas.

A great deal of research has been done over the years into children's thinking about science concepts, such as magnetism. Much of this research is presented in the chapters that follow. These studies reveal that children between the ages of seven and 15 years have different views about almost every scientific concept considered in school. Less is known about children below the age of seven, and even less is known about infants and toddlers (Sikder and Fleer 2014). The volume of research that has been conducted on young children's understandings of scientific phenomena tends to lead to two conclusions: first, that children have different views about scientific concepts to those of a Western scientist; second, that those views influence how they interpret the scientific experiences that are organised by their teacher. This literature tells us that:

- children develop mini-theories about their environment, based on their own cultural or everyday experiences (often called 'everyday explanations', 'alternative views' or 'misconceptions')

Figure 2.1 Em at 13 months. What might Em be thinking? How can we find out?

- children's existing ideas may or may not match those of Western school science
- children make sense of science ideas or lessons in relation to the existing views they hold
- differences in children's everyday or cultural ideas and Western school science cause variations in how children make sense of science activities (see the discussion on cultural border-crossing later in this chapter), and
- some children's ideas do not change as a result of science education.

We can reflect upon this summary of the accumulated literature and ask: Are these really mini theories? Consider how they are named, such as – everyday explanations, alternative views or misconceptions? Should these terms be used? How might these labels position children?

It is paramount that, as a teacher, you find out what children think about the scientific concept that you have decided to introduce, before you start teaching. The children probably hold quite different views from those you expect. But this is not so easy to do. The younger the child, the more challenging it is to find out their thinking. How did you respond to Reflection 2.1? Did you have a way of finding out Em's thinking?

Figure 2.2 Ivy at 23 months. What might Ivy be thinking? Do we use the same techniques for finding out about Em's thinking at 13 months?

Finding out children's understandings

When is an animal an animal?

The following extract is an example of an interview with a five-year-old boy (Nicky) about his understanding of animals. Note how Tim, the interviewer, focuses Nicky's attention and draws from him his view of whether or not the item in the picture is classified as an animal. The cards being used are shown in Figure 2.3.

In the second section you see that Tim goes back to each card and tries to elicit, once again, from Nicky more information about his criteria for 'animal'.

SECTION 1

Tim: Now see those six pictures, Nicky … Now, I want you to tell me whether you think they are an animal or not an animal. What's that, do you think?

Nicky: A cow.

Tim: Would you say that's an animal?

Nicky: Yes.

Tim: That's an animal. What do you think that is?

Nicky: Grass.

Tim: Is that an animal?

Nicky: No.

Tim: It's not an animal. What's that?

Nicky: A spider.

Tim: And what would you say that is? Is that an animal or not an animal?

Nicky: It's kind of an animal.

Tim: It's kind of an animal, is it?

Nicky: Yes.

Tim: Why do you say 'it's kind of an animal'?

Nicky: I just do.

Tim: I see. Okay. And what's this animal here do you think?

Nicky: A whale.

Tim: Is that an animal or not an animal?

Nicky: An animal.

Tim: What's this here?

Nicky: A worm.

Tim: Is that an animal or not an animal?

Nicky: It is an animal.

Tim: And this is a boy, is that an animal or not an animal?

Nicky: Yes, it is an animal.

 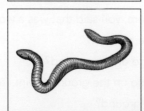 

Figure 2.3 Pictures (as cards) used to find out the meaning of the word 'animal'.

SECTION 2

Tim: That's an animal. Now you say that a cow is an animal, why do you say a cow is an animal?

Nicky: Because it gives milk.

Tim: Yes. What else about a cow, why is it an animal?

Nicky: Nothing else.

Tim: Now grass, what did you say about grass?

Nicky: It's not an animal.

Tim: Why did you say it's not an animal?

Nicky: Because it doesn't have eyes …

Tim: Yes … It doesn't have eyes.

Nicky: And it doesn't have ears.

Tim: It doesn't have ears, yes.

Nicky: And because it has roots.

Tim: It has roots, and animals don't have roots?

Nicky: No.

Tim: And what about the spider, is that an animal or not an animal?

Nicky: Kind of an animal.

Tim: Kind of an animal, yes.

Nicky: Because it feeds through its mouth.

Tim: Yes, and that makes it an animal, does it?

Nicky: A kind of animal.

Tim: Umm, but a cow is an animal, but what did you say about the spider? A kind of animal, is it really an animal or not?

Nicky: A kind of animal.

Tim: Umm, and what about the whale, you said that's an animal didn't you?

Nicky: Yes.

Tim: Why did you say that's an animal?

Nicky: Because it has eyes.

Tim: Yes. It has eyes does it? What else does it have that makes it an animal?

Nicky: It has fins.

Tim: What about this thing here, you said that was a worm. Why is that an animal?

Nicky: Because it goes on the ground.

Tim: Yes, and do all animals go on the ground?

Nicky: No. This one doesn't go on the ground (points to spider).

Tim: Spiders don't go on the ground?

Nicky: No.

Tim: Do they sometimes go on the ground?

Nicky: Yes.

Tim: And what about the boy? Is a boy an animal?

Nicky: Yes, 'cause people are animals!

Tim: Are they?

Nicky: Yes.

Tim: Why do you say they are animals?

Nicky: Because you say they are.

Tim: Oh I see, but what do you believe?

Nicky: You.

Tim: But what do you think, are they really animals?

Nicky: Yes.

Tim: Why do you think they are animals then?

Nicky: Because they are just a kind.

Tim: Just a kind, a kind of animal then?

Nicky: Yes.

Nicky's response to the task is quite sophisticated for a five-year-old child. Mobility and human-like characteristics, such as ears and eyes, are most important in his categorisation of what is an animal. The absence of these features means it is not an animal. He also knows that people are animals – although in everyday language the term 'animal' is not usually associated with humans (e.g. 'no animals allowed on the freeway'). As a result, scientific taxonomies or classification systems often cause confusion for children.

RESEARCH ACTIVITY 2.1: LIVING AND NON-LIVING

We noted the challenge of finding out Nicky's ideas about an animal or a non-animal. To take this further, we invite you to try interviewing children about their understandings of living and non-living. Individually interview three girls and three boys of approximately the same age about their understandings of the concepts of 'living' and 'non-living' things.

Make up a set of small pictures for the interview. Use the images of the cards provided in Figure 2.4. Try to keep the cards simple, for example, use line drawings without other features, or photographs of just the item, so as not to distract the child.

Before interviewing the children, record what you understand by 'living' and 'non-living' and go through the cards and categorise them into 'living or 'non-living' things. Then make some predictions about what the children will understand and how you expect them to categorise the cards. Note these predictions. This helps to tune you into the children's thinking. For younger children you could use the words 'alive' and 'not alive'.

During the interview, ask each child to:

1   Name the object on the card.
2   Think about whether the object on the card is living or non-living.
3   Put the card into one of three piles: living thing, non-living thing, or not sure.
4   Tell you why they've put that object into that pile.

Record:

1   The child's name, age and year level.
2   The reason(s) for each placement given by the child (recording his or her exact words – if you cannot capture all of them, then record the key words and phrases; a digital recorder can be useful).

Figure 2.4 Interview cards.

REFLECTIONS 2.2: REFLECTING ON THE DATA COLLECTED

CAMBRIDGE DYNAMIC SCIENCE

Year 7,
Module 1,
Unit 1

Reflect on and record:

1 What happened during the interviews?
2 Comment on interesting aspects of the data gathered (e.g. were your predictions confirmed?).
3 What you have learned from the experience?

Now compare what you have recorded with the following results (Table 2.1) gathered by a student teacher. The student used different cards.

Some interesting realisations about children's thinking can occur when they are interviewed. Did that happen for you? You may have noted from your data that:

- children might confuse deciduous trees with 'dead' trees
- movement is an important variable in classifying something as living (e.g. 'a bicycle is alive because it moves')
- static pictures of living things are deemed to be 'dead' (e.g. the kangaroo is not alive because 'it was found at the side of the road')
- human characteristics, such as eyes, are important in classification (e.g. 'it is alive because its eyes are open' or 'it's not alive because it does not have eyes, ears and a mouth').

Now consider some of the responses made by children who were interviewed by second-year Bachelor of Education student teachers who had done the 'living and non-living' task with young children, using the cards shown in Figure 2.4.

MICHELLE

I had six Year 2 children, four of them were seven and two boys were eight. I found that almost half of the responses they made were based on the criterion of movement, which is pretty much in common with everybody else.

They said kangaroo, child and the Sun were alive, because the Sun comes up in the morning and it goes down at night, and also the waves come onto the sand.

The fire they were not sure about. One of them said that it was not alive because you cook stuff in it. Most of them said it is not alive, but also they said they were not sure, because it is sort of alive because it grows and moves, but they ended up putting it in the not alive category anyway.

The bike and the computer were not alive. One girl said, 'The computer is not alive because it has a memory, but it's not like a human memory, it stores lots of things, but it can't remember all by itself.' She had a pretty good idea of what was going on there. Then she went on to explain how the computer stores things, but she was blundering around for words, and then she said, 'Because it's got lots of wires and that's why.'

There was one girl who had really good responses. She said, 'The kangaroo was alive because it had babies and it was a mammal', and this is a seven-year-old. Then she said, 'The tree was alive because it drinks water into its roots and it breathes in carbon dioxide and breathes out oxygen.' I thought that was really incredible for a seven-year-old girl.

The Sun really confused her. She said, 'The Sun is a star and it has fire, and a fire is not alive.' I then asked her to explain that a bit more and she got all flustered and said, 'It's just not alive, okay.'

TANIA

I asked one girl (age five years) if she was alive and she said, 'No, I am too little'. She also thought that a computer was alive when it was on and not alive if it was switched off.

I was talking about the Sun, and I said, 'Oh, the Sun moves around the Earth' and this five-year-old girl told me, 'No, it doesn't', she said. 'The Earth moves around the Sun.' She knew all about planets and things like that.

What is interesting to note about the responses reported by the student teachers is that, first, there is a wide range in understanding; second, the age of the child does not always correlate with better understanding; third, some children apply one criterion for sorting things (e.g. the relationship of the object to themselves); finally, many children already hold quite sophisticated views of living and non-living things. You may like to add a brief summary of the main ideas to Table 2.1 for easy reference and for later planning.

Have you been challenged in your own views about what is living and non-living as a result of this exercise? Quite often, student teachers have that experience, and sometimes they feel less certain about the distinction being black and white. For instance, is a branch that has just been cut from a tree a living thing or a non-living thing? What about a packet of seeds? And what about viruses in a crystalline form: are they living or non-living? Reflection on such questions might suggest that scientific ideas are not always clear-cut. As a further challenge, try out the interview exercise with some adults – you might be surprised by their responses.

Finding out what children think in group settings prior to teaching them concepts in science can be achieved through a range of strategies, such as asking children individually or in small groups to:

- draw pictures of what they know about something
- prepare a mind map

Table 2.1 Interview results for a different set of cards – how do your results compare?

Interviewed child	Tree	Boy	Bicycle	Car	Spider	Seagull	Fire	Fish
Jenna, five years.	Alive. Grows.	Alive. Walks.	Not alive. Doesn't walk or swim.	Not alive. Doesn't walk.	Alive. Crawls.	Alive. Flies.	Not alive. Doesn't walk or swim.	Alive. Swims.
Natasha, six years.	Not alive. Dead – leaves have come off.	Alive. Nothing is hurting him.	Alive. Nothing can make it break.	Alive. Nothing can make it die.	Not alive. It's dead. Something stepped on the spider.	Not alive. It's dead, been shot.	Not alive. It's gone out.	Not alive. Someone has cut the fish.
Hannah, six years.	Not alive. Leaves have fallen off. But some are alive, if they grow they're alive.	Alive. Moves like us.	Not alive. Hasn't got eyes, mouth like we have.	Not alive, but can move around same as bicycle.	Alive. Catches food and eats food.	Alive. They tweet.	Not alive.	Alive. Lives in water. Can breathe in water. Feed them.
Sarah, four years.	Not alive. Got no legs. Can't move.	Alive. Move.	Not alive. You can make it move.	Not alive. Doesn't have mouth, eyes, nose.	Alive. Got legs for its walking.	Alive. Has wings and feet. Its eyes are open.	Not alive.	Alive. Eyes are open.
Ryan, six years	Alive. Grows higher. Water, it gets bigger.	Alive. Walks.	Not alive. A person rides it.	Alive. Moves. Makes a noise.	Alive. Wriggles around.	Alive. Flies and eats. Eats food to get energy so it can fly.	Alive. Steams up. Doesn't eat.	Alive. Swims and eats to get energy.
Patrick, six years.	Alive. Drinks water and grows.	Alive. Drinks water and grows.	Not alive. Has a handle, wheels and flag.	Not alive. Has an engine. Not in a shape.	Not alive. Dead. Can't move.	Alive. Have air and fly, eats flowers and warms.	Not alive. Doesn't move.	Alive. Swims, drinks water. If they don't they die.
Darren, six years.	Alive. Has roots and grows.	Alive. Drinks and eats.	Not alive. Because it drives.	Not alive. Because it drives.	Alive. Crawls. Stings. Eats.	Alive. Flies. Eats.	Alive. Makes a noise.	Alive.

- make a dough or clay figure about the topic and tell a story
- interview each other and write down their findings
- prepare a computer animation of their understandings
- video or audio record their thinking
- work with buddies from an older grade to document their thinking
- role-play their understandings.

Further ideas can be found throughout this book.

HAVE YOU EVER WONDERED ABOUT ...? CONTEXTS OF SCIENCE

Did you know that a sea sponge is actually an animal? A sea sponge has many of the characteristics of a plant. A group of three- and four-year-old children return from the summer holidays, bringing with them many of their treasures to show their early childhood teacher. Among the treasures from the beaches they have visited are a range of sea sponges. Sian draws and narrates a story about her holidays into her 'science thinking book' and the teacher shares Sian's book with the group of children. They know from reading Hugh's encyclopaedia that the sea sponge is an animal, but they grapple with this idea. The following discussion shows their thinking as they explore the idea of a sea sponge being an animal.

Teacher: This is Sian's first page in her book. And it says, 'The diver is looking at the sponge'. That's the sort of sponge that we have here in our childcare centre.

Her next page says, 'Another sponge. There are big waves in the sea. And the people are going to drown. But, the sponge won't drown because it's real, and the sponge sucks up animals.' Then it says, 'Maybe it finds air under the water.'

Teacher: How do you think it might find air to breathe under water?

Simone: Because there's a snorkel.

Teacher: Do you think the sponge would have a snorkel?

Children laugh and call 'No!!!'

Jarrad: It doesn't have arms.

Simone: And it can't buy a snorkel.

Alex: It can't move.

Teacher: But in Sian's story she said the people were going to drown, but the sponge is not. So we asked, 'Why is the sponge not going to drown?'

Alex: Because it stays in the ground and it can't go anywhere else.

Teacher: (The teacher repeats what the child says to support and encourage Alex.) Because it stays in the ground and it can't go anywhere else.

Simone: Because the sea pushes it.

Andrea: It can't hop out.

Simone: Because they are STUCK!

Andrea: Because they are planted.

Teacher: Because they are stuck and because they are planted. But how is it going to breathe?

Simone: Snorkel.

Teacher: Does it breathe? Do you think it has a snorkel?

Children: Yes, yes, yes, no, no, no. (Mixed response from the group.)

Simone: I think it can just breathe.

Chuck: I think it can just find a way to breathe.

Teacher: Chuck thinks it can just find a way to breathe. Now I don't know, and I just looked up in a book, and it didn't tell me. So Hugh can we borrow your encyclopaedia again please?

Hugh: Yes. I will bring it.

Teacher: And then we might know, we could read about it, because it has a lot of information in it about sponges.

How do we classify the world? We saw how children classify in Table 2.1, and we can see how Hugh, Andrea, Simone, Chuck and the teacher grapple with the scientific classification of animals and plants when discussing the characteristics of a sea sponge. There are many different ways to classify the world, and even more when we think about how children from a range of cultures classify the world. How we traditionally classify the world into animals and plants is socially constructed within cultures and may be quite different from the way some traditionally oriented Aboriginal and Torres Strait Islander groups would classify the world or some Asian communities. For example, some community groups use the seasons as a way of classifying living things (Ninnes 2000). Reflect for a moment on this, and consider the range of views that might be expressed across Australia within urban, remote and rural regions.

In relation to the classification system of plants, Aikenhead and Michell (2011) argue that:

> Eurocentric botanists use the Linnaen taxonomy system to identify plants anywhere on the planet, Elders [First Nation Canadian peoples] employ their community's place-based traditions that 'may include stories relations to [a plant's] use as a food source, its ceremonial uses, its complex preparation process, the traditional accounts of its use (as a purification ritual), its kin affiliations, and so on' (Snively and Corsiglia 2001, p. 11). Sources of wood can be named according to the amount of heat given off when burned, or according to the technology for which they are used (p. 73).

If we think about the cards we have created for the classification system of living and non-living and animal and non-animal, these represent a particular Western construction of knowledge. This in itself sets up an assessment situation that *only* measures Western knowledge – by this very action it excludes many other world-views. The assessment activity does not capture other ways of thinking about all the things that are on our planet. What is needed is other ways of capturing what children know and can do in science. This also highlights how we as teachers *must* interrogate all the assessment systems we use and take for granted, to ensure they allow for a diverse range of views to emerge. When we do, it is possible to see that Indigenous perspectives on plants and animals broaden thinking and enrich understandings when thinking scientifically: such as, plants have specific purposes, for medicine and food, or animal movement or plant growth are indicators of a change in seasons and migration of animals. Classification is different and can be based on 'use properties', that is what they are used for in cooking, medicine, ceremony, etc.

What are the narratives that embed and speak into existence knowledge about our world? Martin (2013) says that in 'Aboriginal epistemology that stories convey knowledge, information and meaning just as much as any textbook' (p. 29). What is the nature of knowledge construction within and across communities? There are many ways, as has been pointed out by Martin (2013). Knowledge tells us who we are, and how we are connected to each other, to community, and to nature. In Aboriginal and Torres Strait Islanders, connection to country is also central. This knowledge construction or epistemology, as discussed by Martin (2013), is foundational and is passed on (or contested) from one generation to the next, and usually in ways that go beyond European heritage approaches.

Leading change in early childhood education

Associate Professor Karen Martin is a Noonuccal woman from North Stradbroke Island (south-east Queensland) with Bidjara ancestry (central Queensland). As a recipient of the Barbara Creaser Memorial Award from Early Childhood Australia (awarded in 2005), she is an acknowledged pedagogical leader for the field of early childhood education. Her work, as discussed in the many parts of this book, gives insights and directions for early childhood educators, but also for primary teachers. She is known for her epistemological work in early childhood education, informed by conceptualising Aboriginal epistemology as knowing, being and doing (see Chapter 9 for details).

Moving through learning rather than to learning – new lenses

A cultural–historical perspective on science education moves the research lens away from simply the individual and what the individual thinks, to considering the whole group of children. This latter view sees concept formation as something held within a community of practice and enacted through social engagement. Rogoff (2003) has used three lenses to show how this may be considered. In Figure 2.5, the first lens is shown focusing on the individual and what that individual knows and

Figure 2.5 The individual as the focus of analysis – what do the children and I know about magnets and magnetic force?

can do. The example illustrated is a student teacher making fridge magnets with a small group of children. Here, she is trying to determine the children's prior experiences and knowledge of fridge magnets.

MAGNETISM AS A CONCEPT

Children's thinking:

1 Children know about what magnets do, but do not understand magnetism.
2 Sometimes children will say that it is the Earth that acts like a magnet when explaining gravity. Other children think that magnetism is a form of gravity. Some children think that air is needed for a magnet to work. Size is thought of as an indication of magnetic strength.
3 Recognising the magnetic effect of the flow of electricity is difficult for children. Often young children pay attention to the wire only and not the current. They believe it is the wire that causes the magnetic effect.

Scientists' thinking:

1 A magnet exerts a force on magnetic materials. The south pole of one magnet and the north pole of another magnet attract one another. But two south poles repel one another, and two north poles repel one another. Magnetism can act at a distance.

2   The Earth behaves like a big magnet. A magnet when free to move always aligns in a north–south direction.

3   The flow of electricity has a magnetic field. This magnetic field can magnetise any material (that is magnetisable) in the space around it. An electromagnet is a coil of wire carrying electricity. The coil of wire is wound around a core of 'soft' magnetic material. Soft magnetism describes some magnetic materials that lose their magnetism when removed from the effect of a magnetic force.

Year 7,
Module 4,
Unit 10

Finding out what children think about particular science concepts 'tells us nothing of how the child operates with the concept in the real-life process of solving a problem, of how he [sic] uses it when some real-life need for it arises' (Vygotsky 1987, p. 123). The second lens (Figure 2.6) focuses on how the group of learners are interacting, and how understanding is being developed across the community of learners. In the example below, children discuss how to make the most effective use of the magnetic material so that their fridge magnets will work. Here, the children are supporting each other as they discuss how the fridge magnets can work best.

Figure 2.6 Interpersonal focus of analysis – the children are collectively trying to make a set of fridge magnets.

The third lens (Figure 2.7) draws our attention to the less obvious, but equally important, factors, such as the context that has been organised to introduce the science concept, the cultural background of the children, the rules and regulations as well as the expectations of education systems for framing and assessing learning. When focusing on science concepts, it is important to introduce the science within an experience that is meaningful to the children. For example, if the children in Figures 2.5–7 were from a rural community, they would have had many experiences with farm equipment. The teacher could then draw upon this knowledge of the community and introduce books that feature many different kinds of machinery, tools and non-fictional information about magnets.

Figure 2.7 Cultural–institutional focus of analysis – tools and materials that support learning about magnetism.

We now show these three lenses together for making judgements about the child's thinking and learning in science (see Figure 2.8). Table 2.2 shows assessment of children using the three lenses as discussed by Rogoff (2003) in the context of assessing and preparing for teaching and learning that follows accepted understandings as outlined in the Australian Curriculum – Science (ACARA 2014).

Using three lenses invites us to ask different questions to giving children cards to sort and classify. We ask:

1 What do these children already know about the concept?
2 How do these children work together?
3 What kinds of contexts are meaningful?

Children use many everyday concepts in their everyday practice – such as putting up notices or artwork on the fridge with a magnet. We know from research that children will use magnets, but many may not think about magnetism or even have scientific understandings to draw upon. For instance, children are likely to use words such as 'the magnet sticks to the paper and/or metal'. What Vygotsky (1987) argued for was seeing the everyday concept of 'sticking' and the scientific concept of 'magnetism' and 'magnetic force' as two sides of the same coin. He suggested that everyday experiences, such as children playing with and using fridge magnets, laid important foundations that work their way upwards, while teaching scientific

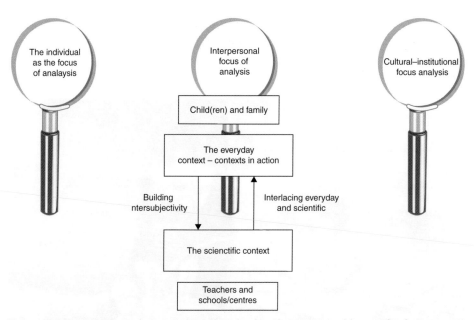

Figure 2.8 Using personal, interpersonal and cultural–institutional lenses for framing our analysis of children's thinking in science.

Table 2.2 Using three lenses for making judgements about children's thinking and acting in science

Lens (Rogoff 2003)	Preparation for children	Preparation for self	Organising learning
The individual as the focus of analysis. (Figure 2.5)	What do these children already know about the science concept?	What do I know about the science concept that I wish to teach? What do I need to find out?	Group orientation for: thinking, documenting and assessing.
Interpersonal focus of analysis. (Figure 2.6)	How do these children work together?	How can I work with families to find out what the children do and know about the science concept?	Interaction patterns that are culturally known and valued.
Cultural–institutional focus of analysis. (Figure 2.7)	What kinds of contexts are meaningful for children?	What kind of context do I need to create so that the concept can naturally arise? What cultural dimensions do I need to consider (e.g. the ways learning is organised in families; the beliefs about science, religion and other worldviews important to families)?	Authentic context – it looks like something people in the community do (e.g. professional, family or community roles). Culturally situated – children's ideas and ways of learning follow that of the cultural community. Ideas are introduced as *another* worldview, not *the* worldview.

concepts laid foundations that work their way downwards. Through knowing about magnetism and magnetic forces (i.e. the concept being conscious and available to the child), children's experiences with the everyday practices of using or playing with fridge magnets could be transformed. For example, knowing about magnetic force would mean a child would think differently about buying or selecting magnets – he or she would not simply buy or use the 'biggest', but would test for the strength of the force. The child would know that magnets only attract certain metals and would not assume that he or she could use magnets on all metallic things. Being consciously aware of magnetism means that children can act differently in their everyday lives. Vygotsky's (1987) theory of concept formation concentrates upon the dynamic interaction between the use of everyday concepts and the introduction of scientific understandings in meaningful everyday problem situations and life events. This is discussed further in Chapter 8.

This broader view of children's thinking in science (as individual, interpersonal and cultural–institutional) allows for other worldviews to be understood. Rogoff's (2003) three lenses help us to better understand children, to look for concepts in action, and to ask questions about culture, religion, interactions, child-rearing practices and institutions (rules and routines). For example, in discussing the concept of living and non-living introduced previously, Aikenhead and Michell (2011), in their review of the literature, found that a holistic conception of the world was held by many First Nation Canadian elders. They give the example that 'There is no animate/inanimate [living/nonliving] dichotomy. Everything is more or less animate [alive].' (Blackfoot Elder and scholar Little Bear 2000, p. 78, cited in Aikenhead and Michell (2011, p. 75). 'Thus everything in the world is alive: animals, plants, humans, rocks, celestial bodies, natural forces, etc' (Aikenhead and Michell 2011, p. 75). That is, all are linked in the world, all play a part in the holistic relational nature of the world.

Through a holistic worldview we do not lose sight of the individual and what he or she thinks, but we do build better understandings of the child and what he or she knows when we foreground interpersonal, cultural and institutional factors (see Australian Government 2009).

Knowledge construction through research

Consider the range of views expressed in the first part of this chapter about living and non-living, and animals and non-animals. They have been named as alternative views (see Chapter 7 for further details). These views were framed from a Western worldview. When we think about children's alternative views, we must ask, 'alternative to what?' Clearly, it is alternative to a Western worldview. Our research paradigm has embraced a Western orientation to framing what knowledge we look for and value. For example, in investigating children's ideas about night and day, we may only look for Western views and not Aboriginal and Torres Strait Islander views. Through using only Western lenses, we may not have allowed for broader forms of knowledge or understandings to emerge. As teachers, we must be actively thinking about children's views – not simply from a Western framework but also from a local Aboriginal and Torres Strait Islander framework, or other cultural orientation that may be likely, given the culturally diverse nature of Australia today. For example, if we ask about and look for understandings about the night sky based only on the Hercules constellations, how will we allow the emu and kangaroo constellations and storytelling that are a feature of some Indigenous cultures within Australia to emerge? See Chapter 8 for further insights into this important area.

A further example is cited by Jegede and Aikenhead (1999), who detail how, in 'some African cultures, a *rainbow* signifies a python crossing a river or the death of an important chief' (1999, p. 276, my emphasis). In Western science terms, this would be conceptualised as the light refracting as it hits the water molecules. These are many views of the same phenomenon being observed. The findings not only add to the growing body of research into children's thinking in science, but demonstrate the complexities associated with children's thinking and the need to think beyond Western worldviews.

Aikenhead and Michell (2011) argue that Indigenous ways of living in nature best describe the science of Indigenous peoples. Science knowledge and way of living in nature must be experienced through being:

1   In a particular place (it is place-based).
2   In the context of multiple relationships with nature and other people.
3   In the pursuit of wisdom-in-action for the purposes of survival (p. 70).

Aikenhead and Michell (2011) describe the process of coming to know as a personal, participatory process of gaining wisdom-in-action.

REFLECTIONS 2.3: MAPPING AND REPRESENTING WORLDVIEWS

Glossary: www. cambridge. edu.au/ academic/ science

It is argued by Aikenhead and Michell (2011) that knowledge systems, such as Western science and Indigenous ways of living in nature, should never be viewed as a dichotomy – that is, as against each other. Two examples of a dichotomy are 'girl – boy' or 'hard science – soft science'. They suggest there are fundamental differences in worldviews of peoples, and they use the term Euroscience to signal when thinking focuses only on Western science. They also use the term Indigenous ways of living in nature instead of the word science. They believe Indigenous ways of living in nature better reflects the knowledge system of Indigenous peoples. Below we summarise the differences between Western science and Indigenous ways of living in nature from this literature. They should not be read as a dichotomy, but rather as frameworks or worldviews that should be valued. We invite you to take these 11 principles and create your own map, model or framework for representing these key ideas so they are not dichotomous. Use the glossary provided in the Appendix and on the *Science for Children* website to help you with the complex terms being used.

1   General perspective: monistic, spiritual, relational and intuitive descriptions/explanations of nature, found in the wisdom tradition of thinking, reflecting, living and being – *compared with* dualistic, materialistic, comparatively non-relational, and often mechanistic descriptions/explanations of nature, found in the critical, independent, intellectual tradition of thinking.
2   Societal goals: communal wisdom-in-action for the survival of the group – *compared with* an individual's scientific credibility and many other social goals defined by the context of the scientific work, such as medical advances, environmental crises and progress in a Western capitalist society.
3   Assumptions: Mother Earth is mysterious and in continual flux – *compared with* nature as knowable and constant.
4   Intellectual goals: coexistence with the mysteries of Mother Earth by celebrating these mysteries through the maintenance of a host of interrelationships – *compared with* describing and explaining nature in ways acceptable to a community of scientists.
5   Fundamental value: harmony with Mother Earth by balancing a web of interrelationships for survival – *compared with* power and domination over nature.
6   Association with human action: intimacy, subjectivity, morality and ethically related to human action with respect to previous generations and those to come – *compared with* descriptions of human action against norms.
7   Notion of time: a cycle of life with no beginning or end – *compared with* rectilinear view of time.
8   *Concept of knowledge*: place-based, holistic and relational – compared with generalisable, reductionist, objective and anthropocentric.
9   *Type of validity*: content validity, based on thousands of years of survival – *compared with* predictive validity, based on reductionism through experimentation.
10 *Learning goals*: a holistic view of learning which includes, emotional, spiritual, intellectual and physical – compared with understanding a repository of knowledge, often linear and abstract.
11 *Socio-political contexts:* has been devalued and destroyed as a result of colonisation, global oppression or political revolution – *compared with* an icon of privilege, prestige and power (comparison of Indigenous ways of living in nature and Eurocentric sciences summarised from Aikenhead and Michell 2011, pp. 110–1).

Investigating cultural constructions of knowledge in science is important for building shared understandings and respect across and within cultures. Ensuring that non-Indigenous students have access to, for example, Eastern, Western and Indigenous worldviews is as important as Aboriginal and Torres Strait Islander children accessing Western, Eastern and non-Indigenous worldviews. Through providing insights into other ways of thinking, we build respect and provide a range (rather than one view) of ways of conceptualising our world.

Border-crossing in science education

Aikenhead and Michell (2011) have labelled the movement in thinking from an Indigenous worldview to a Western school science view by Indigenous students as *border-crossing*. They argue that how children negotiate the differing cultural borders – borders of Western school science and lived everyday experiences – will significantly influence their success in science education. When a child's everyday lived experiences and worldview are similar to that of Western school science, the transition for the child is harmonious and without difficulty. We can argue that Western school science will then support the child's view of the world because there is alignment.

When the border-crossing experience leads to the child abandoning his or her worldview, assimilation has taken place. Assimilation can alienate children from their culture, thereby causing various social disruptions; or, alternatively, attempts at assimilation can alienate children from science, thereby causing them to develop clever ways (school games) to pass their science courses without learning the content in a meaningful way, as expected by the school and community. In the long-standing research of Jegede and Aikenhead (1999) on border-crossing, the following categories were generated:

1 *Potent scientist,* whose transitions are *smooth* because the cultures of family and science are congruent.
2 *Other smart kids,* whose transitions are *manageable* because the two cultures are somewhat different.
3 *'I don't know' students,* whose transitions tend to be *hazardous* when the two cultures are diverse.
4 *Outsiders,* whose transitions are virtually *impossible* because the cultures are highly discordant (Jegede and Aikenhead 1999, p. 5, original emphasis).

As children's border-crossing experiences will influence their success or failure in science, it is important to understand how children navigate border-crossing. Four key additional areas of learning have been identified as taking place during border-crossing:

- parallel
- simultaneous
- dependent
- secured.

These categories should be thought about as located along a continuum.

Parallel collateral learning occurs when children have a scientific and a commonsense understanding, but will apply the scientific understanding only to the school context, and the commonsense understanding to their home or everyday context. For example, children will talk about the rainbow at home in relation to its cultural significance – that is, the python crossing the river or an elder passing away. In the school context they will discuss the refraction of light producing the rainbow.

Simultaneous collateral learning describes the way children can hold in their minds two different ways of explaining a science concept; for example, knowing that electricity is conserved in the battery as a Western science explanation described at school, but also when at school believing that when a battery 'goes flat' the energy is squeezed out – a toothpaste theory of electricity. They hold these views simultaneously, noting, but not questioning the contradiction in the explanation.

At the other end of the continuum is *dependent* and *secured collateral* learning, where children do not necessarily have the same levels of contradiction. They have developed ways or justifications for holding onto differing views or, in fact, do not hold opposing views – rather, their thinking is more closely aligned to the accepted scientific perspective.

Clearly, then, border-crossing is a treacherous path, as the mindset that must be negotiated to engage in Western science is exceedingly different from how many people think, feel and connect with their real world. For many Indigenous students, the border-crossing between home-lived experience and Western school science can be seen as more marked than it is for non-Indigenous children. For some children it can be viewed as *cultural violence*, as was noted in Chapter 1. Cultural violence is said to occur when Western school science is totally at odds with a child's view of the world (family belief system). For example, creationists could experience cultural violence when studying the evolution of humans. Do we recognise cultural violence when it is experienced by children? Do we notice when what they learn at home is so different from what they learn at school or in their early childhood setting?

Cultural violence has also been taken up by Martin (2013), but in quite a different way. In the context of early childhood education, she specifically addresses the idea of children dealing with difficult and painful events, such as death, and how educators avoid dealing with sensitive issues that we can see are related to science education:

> … we sanitise early childhood curriculum and pedagogy from parts of the constellation of characteristics when we only refer to positive ones and only provide positive experiences without equally referring to the real (including those experiences that are negative). How is it young children can learn about and become 'socially competent' and 'effective communicators' (two Learning Outcomes of the Early Years Learning Framework, Australian Government, Department of Education, Employment and Workplace Relations 2009) if the adults in their lives resolve their tensions, spare them of conflict and don't acknowledge loss in their lives? What are they missing out on, or being denied in being taught by early childhood educators who are only ever happy and are always striving to achieve happy early childhood programs and services? These are … the 'less obvious' questions about us, first as people and then as early childhood educators (pp. 29–30).

Do we as teachers deal with death, as both a cultural form of knowledge and as a scientific conception? For example, in Mexico, communities have a celebration of the dead. It is a whole community event that is joyous. In many other cultural communities it is a private and solemn event. How do we discuss and teach the concept of death? In Australia, do we sanitise the curriculum as suggested by Martin (2013), and avoid this scientific topic when it arises?

In returning to the work of Jegede and Aikenhead (1999) on border-crossing, they have suggested that the teacher can also act as a 'culture broker'. The culture broker is viewed as the person who will guide children between their 'life world culture' and the 'culture of science'. The culture of science is the principal site of investigation, and the teacher is positioned as someone who helps children by showing what to look for, and discussing how to use these ideas in their everyday lives outside of school.

The student as traveller: In this scenario, the teacher acts as a tour guide. For students who require less assistance with negotiating their travels through to another culture, the teacher will act as a 'travel agent' providing interesting activities for children.

If we act as a tour guide or as a culture broker, we must always be mindful of the worldviews that children hold. We need to appreciate the discontinuities that may exist between children's everyday view of the world and Western school science (Hernandez, Morales and Shroyer 2013). When science learning is presented as connected to children's experience, then they are more likely to transition between their worldview and Western school science. This results in more harmony and greater dignity. Valuing and respecting the diversity of worldviews that may arise within a single classroom or early childhood setting in a culturally and linguistically diverse Australian community is an important first step in planning for children's learning in science.

Martin (2005) has challenged educators to deal with different forms of knowledge construction (rather than just European heritage knowledge) that are unfamiliar, and explicitly confront how uncomfortable one may feel in coming to know difference at a more personal level. Martin (2013) argues that, 'Learning therefore requires the loss of some parts of the self in order to progress. This is exciting and scary' (p. 29).

Aguilar-Valdez, LopezLeiva, Roberts-Harris, Torres-Valasquez, Lobo and Westby (2013) state that the intention is for teachers of science to move away from what they call 'colour blindness'. That is, 'to acknowledge diversity and include it in an integrated way that will prevent the marginalization of ways of knowing, doing, and being a scientist and being a person' (p. 853). They argue that 'how students are perceived deeply affects the space we give to students' ways of knowing and student voice, or to the oppression of that voice' (p. 853). In thinking about how alternative views in science have emerged, they argue that this matching of thinking to Western science positions children as 'broken' rather than conceptualising them as achievers. They state, 'non-dominant cultures are not broken, and they do not need fixing', but rather teachers should 'work alongside students' who are 'caught in these in-between places' (p. 853) – that is, between Indigenous knowledge systems and the Western science knowledge system. Teachers need to think more broadly than European heritage or Western communities, because many communities are now made up of a range of culturally diverse families, many of whom will have Indigenous knowledge that they value and pass on to their children. Licona (2013) says 'Kris Guitierrez and Barbara Rogoff (2003) are working to remove obstacles for the culturally different by interrupting deficit thinking and suggesting research-based ideas to inform practice' (p. 871).

Ways of learning

Martin (2005) wrote about ways of being, knowing and doing. She developed a theoretical framework and methods for Indigenous and Indigenist research that are helpful to both primary teachers and early childhood teachers (see Chapter 9). In the process of finding out children's understandings, we are also acting as researchers, gathering data about children and their families. In research we must take responsibility for how we conceptualise our interactions, the kinds of questions we might ask, and the conditions we create that may or may not allow children to express themselves. In many cultures, there will always be accumulated knowledge and ways of constructing that knowledge that we do not have the right to know. Here we take the lead from Martin (2003), and consider research and the cultural construction of knowledge and the learning of that knowledge, as a process of understanding the ways of knowing, being and doing. These ideas are discussed further in Chapters 8 and 9.

Summary

We have now explored how children think about the things around them. In posing challenging questions to children, we begin to understand that they can have quite sophisticated ideas, as well as many views, beliefs and understandings that do not easily fit within a Western science curriculum. The criteria used by children in making judgments about their world may or may not be particularly helpful when the context is different (e.g. school, family or community). As teachers, we must listen to children so that we understand what they think about the concepts we are considering teaching. However, it is not enough just to find out children's views; we must also think about how we can move children towards scientific understandings so that border-crossing is a sensitive rather than a violent experience. We also have to consider where children get their alternative views of the world from culture, media, peers, etc. (Reflections 2.2). Return to the list you created. After reading this chapter, can you now add to your list?

What are the different ways that we can set up science learning experiences for children so we take into account their worldviews? In the chapters that following, we invite you examine a range of pedagogical approaches for the teaching of science. At the end of the book (Chapter 10) we ask you to think about which approach or approaches sit best with you and the communities in which you will be teaching.

References

Aguilar-Valdez, JR, LopezLeiva, CA, Roberts-Haris, D, Torrres-Valasquez, D, Lobo, G, Westby, C 2013, 'Ciencia en *Nepantla*: The journey of Nepantler@s in science learning and teaching', *Cultural Studies of Science Education*, vol. 8, no. 4 pp. 821–58.

Aikenhead, G, Michell, H 2011, *Bridging Cultures. Indigenous and Scientific Ways of Knowing Nature*, Toronto: Pearson Canada.

Australian Curriculum, Assessment and Reporting Authority 2014, Australian Curriculum – Science, http://www.australiancurriculum.edu.au/Science/Curriculum/F-6. (Accessed September 2014.)

Australian Government Department of Education, Employment and Workplace Relations 2009, *Belonging, Being and Becoming. The Early Years Learning Framework for Australia*, Canberra: Commonwealth of Australia.

Guitierrez, KD, Rogoff, B 2003, 'Cultural ways of learning: Individual traits or repertoires of practice', *Educational Researcher*, vol. 32, no. 5, pp. 19–25.

Hernandez, CM, Morales, AR, Shroyer, MG 2013, 'The development of a model of culturally responsive science and mathematics teaching', *Cultural Studies of Science Education*, vol. 8, pp 803–20. (DOI 10.1007/s11422-013-9513-8.)

Jegede, O, Aikenhead GS 1999, 'Transcending cultural borders: Implications for science teaching'. (Accessed at www.ouhk.edu.hk/cridal/misc/narst99.htm.)

Licona, MM 2013, 'Mexican and Mexican-American children's funds of knowledge as interventions into deficit thinking: Opportunities for praxis in science education', *Cultural Studies of Science Education*, vol. 8, pp. 859–73. (DOI 10.1007/s11422-013-9513-8.)

Martin, K 2003, 'Ways of knowing, being and doing: A theoretical framework and methods for Indigenous and Indigenist research' in K McWilliam, P Stephenson and G Thompson eds, *Voicing Dissent, New Talents 21C: Next Generation Australian Studies,* St Lucia, Qld: University of Queensland Press, pp. 203–14.

Martin, K 2005, 'Childhood, Lifehood and Relatedness: Aboriginal ways of being, knowing and doing' in J Phillips and J Lampert eds, *Introductory Indigenous Studies in Education: The Importance of Knowing*, Frenchs Forest: Pearson Education, pp. 27–40.

Martin, KL 2013, '"At a loss: scared and excited": A response to Jonathan Silin', *Contemporary Issues in Early Childhood*, vol. 14, no. 1, pp. 29–31.

Ninnes, P 2000, 'Representations of indigenous knowledges in secondary school science textbooks in Australia and Canada', *International Journal of Science Education*, vol. 22, no. 6, pp. 603–17.

Rogoff, B 2003, *The Cultural Nature of Human Development*, New York: Oxford University Press.

Sikder, S, Fleer, M 2014, 'Small science: Infants and toddlers experiencing science in everyday family play', *Research in Science Education*. (DOI 10.1007/s11165-014-9431-0.)

Vygotsky, LS 1987, 'Thinking and speech' in LS Vygotsky, *The Collected Works of L.S. Vygotsky, Vol. 1, Problems of General Psychology,* RW Rieber and AS Carton eds, N Minick trans. New York: Plenum Press, pp. 39–285.

Appendix

Glossary

Principle 1

Monistic: A philosophical view that suggests that things can be explained in terms of a single reality. That is, one foundational principle to explain reality.

Spiritual: In this context spiritual does not mean religion. Rather, all living things have a spirit and are interconnected. For example, humans do not own land, but rather the land owns the people. See http://www.creativespirits.info/aboriginalculture/land/meaning-of-land-to-aboriginal-people and https://www.academia.edu/670279/Aboriginal_spirituality_Aboriginal_philosophy_the_basis_of_Aboriginal_social_and_Emotional_wellbeing.

Dualistic: A philosophical view that suggests that things can be explained in terms of opposing principles. Reality is explained by contrasting one thing against another.

Materialistic: In this context, this term refers to the excessive focus on the acquisition of material possessions and physical comfort.

Mechanistic descriptions/explanations of nature: This refers to giving physical or biological definitions only for explaining nature.

Principle 2

Communal wisdom-in-action for the survival of the group: This refers to how groups of people draw upon each other as a valued source of information, support, comfort, aggregate knowledge base and intuition. A related example can be found at: http://www.preventioninstitute.org/about-us/our-approach/rooted-in-community-wisdom.html.

Scientific credibility: Scientific information or knowledge is valued only after it is put out for scrutiny within the scientific community. The process draws upon processes that the scientific community has sanctioned.

Western capitalist society: Refers to an economic system, where wealth is predominantly exchanged by individuals and private corporations (as opposed to state-owned companies).

Principle 3

Maintenance of interrelationships: This refers to focusing on supporting people and processes in a community to ensure that the nature of the established relations between things and people is maintained.

Power and domination over nature: A belief that nature can be controlled and dominated to serve human needs.

Principle 4

Subjectivity: This is a term that captures the nature of the person, their feelings, their beliefs and the power they have. Subjectivity constitutes a person's sense of reality. It explains what informs and influences their judgements about reality.

Morality: This refers to the system of values and principles held.

Ethically related to human action: This captures the way individuals are collectively bound to both the past and future generations. An action of an individual is interconnected with the past and the future.

Principle 5

Rather than conceptualising a cycle of life as having a beginning point to an end point, what is referenced in this principle is that a cycle does not have a defined beginning or end. It simply continues.

Rectilinear view of time: Time is conceptualised as occurring in a straight line.

Principle 6

Place-based: this usually refers to an intimate or intergenerational connectivity with a place, such as being spiritually connected to a river system, or geographical part of a country.

Holistic: where all parts of something are interconnected, and each part is referenced in relation to the whole.

Relational: In this context, relational means how, and the ways in which, things and people are connected to each other.

Generalisable: Means how findings and conclusions determined through research on a particular sample or situation are then applied to the population as a whole or to broader contexts.

Reductionist: A belief that a complex system is made up of parts, and these parts are what constitutes the whole. As such, the complex system can be understood by examining its parts.

Anthropocentric: This term names the belief that humans are the central and most important element of existence.

Principle 7

Validity: When something is factually sound or cogent.

Content validity: Refers to how well something (data, statement, image, etc.) represents what it seeks to measure. In this context, content validity is based on thousands of years of survival of particular communities.

Predictive validity: Predictive validity means how well a score or result can be used to predict. The prediction is based on reducing a complex system into parts and experimentation based on the parts rather than the whole system.

Principle 8

Holistic view of learning: Where the complex system of learning sometimes also includes emotional, spiritual, intellectual and physical dimensions (not just the cognitive dimensions).

Learning as a repository of knowledge: This signals that knowledge can be stored and retrieved, like a database. The method of retrieval is usually linear and abstract and not necessarily connected to everyday life, where the knowledge was originally developed.

Principle 9

Colonisation: Usually refers to another cultural group entering into the home community or Indigenous group and subjecting the Indigenous group to the invading group's beliefs and knowledge systems, often controlling and dominating Indigenous worldviews.

Oppression: Refers to unjust treatment of individuals or groups where the oppressor exercises authority and sometimes cruelty.

Political revolution: Where a government or significant organisation in a community is subjected to upheaval, and where the authority or leaders of that organisation are replaced or the original form of governing is altered.

Acknowledgement

Special thanks to my colleague Dr Avis Ridgway for providing the infant photos in this chapter.

PART 2

Transmission and Discovery Approaches to Teaching and Learning in Science

In this section of the book are two chapters that are completely different from one another. Each approach assumes a very different role for the teacher.

The chapters are: Chapter 3: A transmission approach to teaching science and Chapter 4: A discovery-based approach to learning science.

The approaches in these chapters conceptualise the role of the child in the process of learning in two different ways.

There are two continua for you to consider as you read these chapters. They are:

Teacher-centred ⟵——————————⟶ Child-centred
Focus on teaching science ⟵——————⟶ Focus on discovering science

Please plot on this continuum where you would locate the particular approach in terms of each of these.

As you read both chapters there are **key things to look for**. Think about what conditions the teacher creates for learning and why.

Things to think about are: What were the differences to what happened and what was learned when it was child-centred and when it was teacher-centred? What might be the strengths and what might be the limitations of each of these approaches for the learner and for you as the teacher?

CHAPTER 3

A transmission approach to teaching science

Introduction

A transmission approach (sometimes referred to as 'direct instruction', 'teacher lecture strategy', 'teacher explanation' or 'traditional teaching') places heavy emphasis on the science content to be learned. While the approach is readily criticised as being too teacher directed, a careful examination of this approach is essential so that we can decide when to use it appropriately in teaching science. The effectiveness of the transmission approach for children's learning will depend on the care and creativeness of the teacher, who may incorporate this strategy within part of a lesson (Regan 2013).

In this chapter we will examine a transmission approach to teaching science, drawing on the science understandings of *Earth and Space Sciences* as presented in the Australian Curriculum – Science (ACARA 2014).

A case study of children learning about *Earth and Space Sciences* is presented. We begin with a curiosity. This sets the context for the case study.

HAVE YOU EVER WONDERED ABOUT ...?
CONTEXTS OF SCIENCE

Have you ever wondered about why we look out into the night sky and talk about the 'Southern Cross' or the 'Emu in the sky'? What are the stories told about the night sky that join up the dots, spark our imagination, and make it easy for seafarers to cross the oceans, navigating by the stars? What are the maps that are narrated through stories of the night sky? What stories are told to explain the many wonders of the night

Through Our Eyes – 'Dhinawan (Emu) In The Sky' with Ben Flick: www.youtube.com/watch?v=LzFYFutiwoA.

Figure 3.1 The joys of finding out new things.

See examples here: www.thenational.ae/news/world/americas/still-visible-after-40-years-the-last-footprints-on-the-moon

sky and our planet Earth? Share one story that was told to you by your family or by a friend with someone in your group. If you do not have a story to share, then click on the YouTube link provided in the margin.

Maybe you wondered why the footprint of the first astronaut on the moon was still visible years later?

Could it have something to do with the absence of an atmosphere?

Follow this link for some things to consider: www.space.com/14740-footprints-moon.html

See also: www.space.com/12846-apollo-moon-landing-sites-flags-footprints.html.

Looking inside a classroom and early childhood setting: a transmission approach

A Year 2 group of children participated in a unit called 'night and day'. This unit focused on the differences between night and day. The children drew in their booklets and wrote about what they had seen in the sky at various times throughout the day and again at night. They observed their own shadows on the playground surface and discussed how these changed in length and direction during the day. The children also observed shadows in the classroom.

The teacher invited a group of children to the front of the class to view a large globe, where she had attached a small figure called 'Mary' to the map of

Figure 3.2 Transmitting *Earth and Space Science* in the classroom.

Australia. A strong light was shone on one side of the globe. Initially Australia was on the shadow side.

Teacher: What is it like for Mary? She is in Australia.

Brenden: It's dark.

Sonya: It's night time.

Teacher: That's right. What would she see if she looked up into the sky?

Paveena: She'd just see a dark sky and the Moon.

Teacher: Yes, Paveena. Now I am going to start moving the Earth. Look closely at what's going to happen.

The teacher begins to rotate the globe.

Bountieng: It's still night time there.

Teacher: Yes it is, Bountieng. Now watch.

The head of the figure just comes into the light.

Teacher: Ah ha!

Paveena: The Sun is shining on her face.

Brenden: She'll get blinded!

Teacher: Yes, Brenden! Mary had better turn her head a bit! What is she seeing now? Can you imagine what it's like? You had all better come over near Mary and look from where she is.

The children move nearer to Mary.

Sonya: I think it would be like the beginning of morning.

Teacher: Yes, Sonya! And what do we call this time of the day?

There is no answer from the children, who shrug their shoulders and make other non-verbal gestures, indicating that they do not know the answer.

Teacher: It's the dawn, isn't it? That's when the Sun comes up, and you can see the sunlight is just reaching Mary. Now what do you see happening?

Bountieng: There's a shadow on the ground.

Brenden: It's a little shadow.

Teacher: Now as I turn the Earth more, look at what's happening.

Brenden: The shadow is getting longer.

Sonya: That's what happened to our shadows outside!

Teacher: Yes. That's right, Sonya. Now you can see the light is right over Mary and her shadow is tiny. Can you tell me what's going to happen next?

Paveena: Mary's shadow is going to get bigger again.

Brenden: Now it's on the other side.

Teacher: Yes. It is on the other side of Mary. She is in a different position now she is moving away from the Sun. It's like when you moved the torches over those pencils, isn't it, and the shadows changed direction and shape?

Sonya: Look how long the shadow is now!

Teacher: And what time of the day is it, Sonya?

Sonya: I don't know.

Teacher: It's now the time the Sun sets, isn't it? It's sunset. We say the Sun is going down, don't we? But it's the Earth that is spinning around, and the Sun is really still. But it just looks like it's the Sun that is moving across the Earth.

Bountieng: How do you know the Sun is still?

We will stop our observation at that interesting point. Consider what happened in this group with the teacher.

REFLECTIONS 3.1: THE ROLE OF THE TEACHER

Record what you think was being done in this situation by (a) the teacher and (b) the children.

What were positive aspects of the teaching and learning? What were negative aspects of the teaching and learning? If possible, compare your views.

In this situation there was a high level of control by the teacher, and she asked many questions of the children in a focused way. You might have noted that there was little interaction between the children. However, the children appeared to be involved in the learning situation, making comments and at the end asking their teacher a relevant question.

What has been portrayed in the situation is an example of a transmission approach to teaching. To you, it might not have seemed like direct transmission of knowledge. Maybe you immediately think of a lecturer or a teacher dictating notes when you think of 'transmission'. These situations would be included within a broad notion of a transmission approach, but it can be quite varied. It is an approach that is very easy to stereotype and criticise because we have all experienced a great deal of transmission in our schools and tertiary institutions. Transmission is widely used with large groups, it is seen to be relatively easy to use, and the teacher usually has a sense of control with the approach.

It is easy to recall examples of poor transmission, but here we want to focus on the positive aspects of a transmission approach, while pointing out potential problems with it. We contend that, whatever our approach in teaching, inevitably it will contain elements of transmission. Furthermore, we believe that the approach, when developed effectively, has a valid place in teaching science.

Transmission in everyday life

When we consider a typical day in our lives, we soon recognise that we are often in contexts that involve the transmission of knowledge.

REFLECTIONS 3.2: TRANSMISSION IN YOUR DAILY LIFE

Think about your activities in a typical day at home, work, university and in other settings. List and identify transmission elements in those activities, as both a 'receiver' and a 'transmitter'.

How effective are the experiences of transmission, especially when you are 'receiving' the transmission? What are the factors that make the experience effective?

As a final part of this activity, consider how dependent you are on transmission in your everyday life.

You have probably concluded that there is a significant amount of transmission of knowledge going on every day and that we are all highly dependent on this for many of our activities. Perhaps you have also noted that much of it is ephemeral, and we do not take much notice of some of the information that is directed at us – television advertising is a good example. Sometimes the transmission is unsuccessful because it is of poor quality, or because, in that particular context, we have little need of the knowledge.

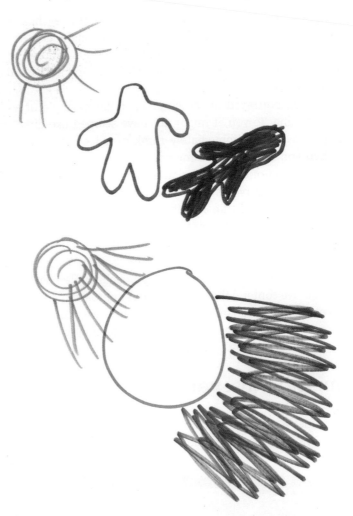

Figure 3.3 Shadows in the playground – making us think about the Sun (Year 2).

Figure 3.4 Silvana at 18 months is learning from her father about how to brush her teeth.

What assumptions underpin a transmission approach to teaching science?

The nature of science

A transmission approach to teaching emphasises the idea of science as a body of knowledge that has been generated over many centuries of investigation and theorising. Science is a complex accumulation of facts, concepts, theories and laws, as a result of a rigorous investigation of the world. The approach fosters the misleading view that the production of this knowledge is the preserve of highly skilled and specialised scientists.

We can see (from Chapters 1 and 2) that there are challenges to the notion of science as the linear development of objective knowledge about the world. Some teachers using a transmission approach may take such criticisms into account and describe scientific knowledge as being impermanent and always subject to change, which is certainly not the case.

Teaching

The fundamental challenge for a teacher of science using this approach is to select and modify the science content so that it is suitable for the learner. This means that the teacher must ensure that the scientific knowledge is at an appropriate level and couched in language that is understandable by the children. In the example provided at the beginning of this chapter, the key role for the teacher was to use her expertise to mediate between the scientific knowledge and the child. The teacher is seen to be at the centre of the teaching–learning process.

The most important learning outcome sought in the transmission approach is the learning of scientific knowledge – that is, its facts, concepts, theories and laws – rather than practical skills in doing science. However, the approach is likely to assume that some elements of scientific thinking are important; in particular, logical and critical thought are desirable outcomes.

This approach to teaching directly raises the question: What knowledge is of most worth? The teacher or curriculum developer who supports the transmission of specific content should answer this critical question carefully. The approach does not allow for significant control by children over content in the science curriculum. A transmission-focused teacher would not necessarily consider the question of content as problematic. In this case, the teacher might not be sufficiently aware of the changing and complex nature of scientific knowledge. One of the problems with this approach is that the teacher might select content based on personal preference, or what he or she was taught in science, rather than a comprehensive and balanced coverage of science or science that connected with what was of interest to the children.

What is a shadow?
- It stops the light.
- We stop the light from going on the ground.
- It doesn't show your eyes, nose or mouth.
- They are dark.

Figure 3.5 Checking for understanding – understandings can be gained during group discussions about night and day (Year 2).

REFLECTIONS 3.3: CONSIDERING THE CONTENT

Consider the following content areas that a teacher might teach:

- dinosaurs
- structure of a flower
- the Solar system
- rocket flight.

Are these topics appropriate for young children? What justification would you use for their inclusion? Are they topics that might readily be taught through a transmission approach?

Children's learning

A teacher using this approach is less likely to find out what children already know about the science concept before teaching the topic. In Chapter 2 we discussed the importance of finding out about children's scientific understandings before teaching science. In a transmission approach it is usually assumed (incorrectly) that the child's pre-existing knowledge is deficient or almost non-existent. Why is it important to find out about children's scientific understandings before teaching science? An effective transmission approach teacher would attempt to build bridges to earlier teachings. The teacher in the case study was trying to do this.

An important assumption in this approach is that children's learning is maximised if teaching is tightly focused and carefully structured.

Strategies for developing effective teaching and learning

Some teachers who lack confidence in teaching science might resort to a transmission approach because it appears to them the most straightforward strategy and one that will give them a high level of control over children's learning. Unfortunately, teachers who adopt this approach may not be particularly effective. There are many potential negative outcomes from using a transmission approach, including failure to motivate children, a lack of authentic participation in learning and promoting a view of science as a static body of knowledge that can be developed only by remote experts in science. However, this approach may be useful in some contexts, and it is important that we understand how we can work towards developing effective elements in the approach.

A transmission approach to teaching is not based on any one learning theory. Variations of the approach include the 'exposition model' and the 'direct instruction' approach. Some educational researchers claim that there is good evidence for the efficacy of highly structured and teacher-centred approaches. Some describe this approach as a 'teacher lecture strategy' that has three components: focus (usually teacher-to-whole-class routine), presentation (series of teacher-explanations and teacher-led discussions with the whole class) and application (individual or group tasks).

An approach to teaching that is basically one of exposition can involve:

- narration – recounting a succession of events
- explanation – showing the interdependence between events
- practice – repeatedly using new knowledge and skills
- feedback – providing information to pupils about the adequacy of their knowledge and skills.

Another way of conceptualising the pedagogy can involve:

- meaningfulness – examples used are known to pupils, or are consistent with their experiences
- clarity – a high level of correspondence between key elements in the examples and the subject matter being explained
- variety – several examples are used to explain an idea
- interest value – children find ideas relevant and stimulating
- simplicity – complex subject matter is broken into parts and each is illustrated with simple examples
- concreteness – examples using physical objects, pictures and models provide visual imagery.

When we apply these ideas to the teaching context presented at the beginning of this chapter, we see a teacher using a range of strategies to increase the effectiveness of her transmission approach. Through directed questions and explanations, she builds a picture of the interdependence between the spinning of the Earth and shadows during the day. The teacher simplifies the complexity of this relationship and uses concrete models to demonstrate the ideas. Her teaching has meaning for the children when they relate what they are seeing to earlier observations of shadows in the playground. Throughout the transcript we see that the teacher provides continuous feedback to the children about the accuracy of their ideas.

REFLECTIONS 3.4: USING NEW KNOWLEDGE

A transmission approach improves in effectiveness if we give children the opportunity to apply and to practise using new knowledge.

Suggest some activities that the teacher could set for the children that would allow the group to apply their newly acquired knowledge.

The place of transmission in the teaching of science

Transmission can be justified in the following situations.

Teaching particular topics

There are some topics in teaching science that necessarily depend to a large degree on transmission. For instance, the popular topics of dinosaurs and the Solar system are difficult to teach without books, pictures, models and perhaps a visit to a museum. However, this is not to suggest that the teaching of the topic can proceed only through these means. There are activities that you could construct which involve the children actively. For instance, in the case of dinosaurs, an activity could involve children observing living dinosaur relatives, such as lizards and birds. Electricity is another challenging area to teach to young children, and a case study of a teacher developing her own subject knowledge and using it in her teaching has suggested a set of electricity concepts that can be taught effectively (see Chapter 7).

Providing a shared base of knowledge at the start of a topic

Before children undertake investigations, provide them with a knowledge base from which they can draw to make sense of their findings. Two key concepts are night and day, and seasonal change. Examples of building a shared knowledge base follow.

Teaching ideas – night and day

In a transmission approach for science learning about Earth and Space, some everyday activities are helpful for drawing attention to thinking about night and day. The following activities can support drawing attention to the science in everyday life and finding or creating teachable moments about night and day. Some of these ideas include having resources on hand for supporting your teaching:

- tracing shadows at different times of the day
- installing a sun-dial and shadow clocks in the playground
- sequencing events that occur in everyday life associated with day and night, such as animal movements (birds at dawn and dusk), plants (opening and closing), humans (rising in the morning and going to bed at night)
- mapping nocturnal and diurnal plants in the classroom
- feeding nocturnal animals, such as possums, or looking for evidence of their activity from the night before
- having a felt board or magnet set of the soar system available for play and teaching
- setting up a library of books on night and day and the Solar system
- posters about the Solar system available for instruction.

Teaching ideas – seasonal change

Teaching ideas about seasonal change can include demonstrations such as the following:

- creating a relational model of the Earth, Sun and Moon (this could be a globe and light source or a commercial kit – as we saw at the beginning of the chapter)
- using a strong light source and a tray of soil with different heat sensors, position the light at different angles in relation to the tray of soil and note the differences in temperature.

Transmission approach in early childhood

Helping children make connections in their understanding

A teacher who is monitoring children's learning encounters in many situations where his or her intervention is justified to explain or to make connections between new knowledge and a child's existing knowledge.

In planning a science topic, a teacher might decide that a transmission element is appropriate to follow another approach, such as a discovery approach. In the example of teaching at the opening of this chapter, the class group was asked a series of questions while the teacher demonstrated a model of the spinning Earth. This situation followed from the children's observations of their own shadows and other activities exploring the phenomena of night and day. The teacher's exposition drew together a number of children's discoveries.

> *Day*
> - *The Sun is made from gases and fire.*
> - *When it's day time here in Australia, it's night time over there.*
> - *The Sun is out.*
> - *Lots of animals are awake.*
> - *The Moon is gone.*
> - *The world turns around and we are back to the Sun.*

Figure 3.6 Making connections – group discussion about night and day (Year 2).

Digital technologies supporting learning

Interactive white boards can act as a useful demonstration tool for teachers. Information on shadows can be plotted and analysed as a group, as shown in Figure 3.7, or it can be used to transmit images of the night sky, planets and other relevant material for children to observe and discuss with the teacher.

Figure 3.7 Using an interactive white board to support group thinking about night and day.

Chandler (2013) has written that in the use of interactive white boards or IWBs the word 'interactive' is in the title … the central issue is 'who is using the technology', because if it's a tool for the teacher to use, then the technology is probably not advancing the 'collaborative' cause very much. If students are using the board – or working together to help the teacher use the board – then collaboration is much more likely (p. 257).

Developing the use of scientific language

Any approach to the teaching of science will involve the use of scientific terminology, but a transmission approach will tend to give more attention to this than others. We discuss in Chapter 2 that it is important to support children so that they move on from a reliance on their use of everyday and commonsense language when dealing with the world of science. This is not simply a matter of providing them with scientific language and new definitions to add to their stock of knowledge. We need to consider how the language of science can be used sensitively and productively in learning environments. It is a form of border-crossing (see Chapter 2), as children become part of the cultural practices associated with engaging with and using Western science.

It is important (particularly with older primary children) for teachers to present the language of science as a human product and to encourage the interpretive voice of children. Teachers should regard language as a 'medium for conversation about ideas', not just for receiving 'the truth'. We must not ignore children's existing use of language, which may be different or unrefined from a scientific point of view; there is a need to build bridges between their use of words and more scientific usage.

The reading of books to the children provides the opportunity to introduce new terms in a learning context in which children will readily understand its meaning. You should be wary of introducing scientific terms simply for their own sake; you need to consider both the value of learning to use new terms and how they might be incorporated to enhance the learning process.

Children transmitting their knowledge to other children

In transmission, knowledge is usually passed through a teacher to children, but it is also in operation when a child reports to other children on his or her findings or conclusions after some science activity. Such transmission is likely to have the positive feature of being couched in language understood by other children. It is also a learning experience for the children who have had to prepare the presentation and explanation.

There are compelling reasons for incorporating transmission into the teaching of science. If it is planned carefully and based on the type of principles discussed previously, transmission strategies can be an effective way of helping children to learn in science.

Figure 3.8 Rachel shares her understandings of night and day (preschool).

Classroom management in a transmission approach

A transmission approach may be attractive because of the apparent central role of the teacher in managing the communication process. In a traditional setting, the teacher transmits knowledge and dominates the questioning, while the children put a lot of effort into answering teacher questions. A more effective approach will ensure that the children are more active, by engaging with hands-on activities, using the internet and other resources, working in groups, asking questions and applying new knowledge. In that respect, management of the class will require the teacher to carefully plan sequences of varied activities and to monitor the children's activities continuously. We are therefore suggesting that the management of an effective transmission approach may be as demanding as that of other approaches. If it is not, then we might suspect that the children's learning is relatively passive and ineffective.

Assessment in a transmission approach

Assessment in a transmission approach may appear to be deceptively straight-forward, with acquired knowledge readily tested in pen-and-paper exercises (having children name parts of a flower on a stencil is one such common example from the past). However, effective teaching through transmission involves much more than the accumulation of new facts. It includes children's growth in terms of conceptual understanding and the development of attitudes. If assessment is to have an educational function, we need to provide the children with the opportunity to use their knowledge and demonstrate their understanding. For instance, rather than require children to recite new knowledge about the Sun and its relationship to the Earth, we might ask individuals or groups to consider the hypothetical question, 'What would happen if the Sun stopped shining for six months?'. Assessment tasks in a transmission approach require as much creative and careful planning as in other approaches.

Why can't we see the Sun at night?

We can't see the Sun at night because it's on the other side of the world. When we have night, the other people in a different country have day.

Figure 3.9 Checking for understanding – group discussion about night and day (Year 2).

Planning for learning

REFLECTIONS 3.5: PLANNING FOR LEARNING

Select a small topic to teach to children. (Look at the Australian Curriculum – Science for suggestions.) Ensure that the topic has a focal point and can be taught in one or two lessons.

Adopting a transmission approach, develop a draft overall plan of how you will teach the topic to a group of children (specify the year level). Include in your plan the learning outcomes, the content to be taught and the teaching strategies you plan to use. State how you will assess the children's learning.

Share your plan with another student and ask for critical feedback within the framework of an effective transmission approach.

In a transmission approach it is important that the teacher has good understandings of the concepts she or he is seeking to transmit to the children. The teacher in the case study needed to research the science understandings detailed in the Australian Curriculum – Australia for Earth and Space science. She also needed to identify the central concepts for Earth and Space science.

The Australian Curriculum – Science

Under the strand of Earth and Space Science, the curriculum specifies that:

The Earth and space sciences sub-strand is concerned with Earth's dynamic structure and its place in the cosmos. The key concepts developed within this sub-strand are that: Earth is part of a solar system that is part of a larger universe; and Earth is subject to change within and on its surface, over a range of timescales as a result of natural processes and human use of resources. Through this sub-strand, students view Earth as part of a solar system, which is part of a galaxy, which is one of many in the universe and explore the immense scales associated with space. They explore how changes on Earth, such as day and night and the seasons relate to Earth's rotation and its orbit around the sun. Students investigate the processes that result in change to Earth's surface, recognising that Earth has evolved over 4.5 billion years and that the effect of some of these processes is only evident when viewed over extremely long timescales. They explore the ways in which humans use resources from the Earth and appreciate the influence of human activity on the surface of the Earth and the atmosphere (ACARA 2014, p. 7).

In studying the curriculum, what is evident is that in each year of the child's schooling, science content on Earth and Space is continually being built. This is shown in Table 3.1.

Table 3.1 Curriculum content for Earth and Space science

	Foundation	**Year 1**	**Year 2**	**Year 3**	**Year 4**	**Year 5**	**Year 6**
Earth and Space sciences.	Daily and seasonal changes in our environment, including the weather, affect everyday life.	Observable changes occur in the sky and landscape.	Earth's resources, including water, are used in a variety of ways.	Earth's rotation on its axis causes regular changes, including night and day.	Earth's surface changes over time as a result of natural processes and human activity.	The Earth is part of a system of planets orbiting around a star (the Sun).	Sudden geological changes or extreme weather conditions can affect Earth's surface.

Source: ACARA | The Australian Curriculum | Version 6.0 dated Tuesday, 18 February 2014.

Science content knowledge

As a teacher of science, you will be interested in gaining background information on the science content of Earth and Space science. In Figure 3.10 is a conceptual map of the concepts associated with Earth and Space that are in the Australian Curriculum – Science. This figure gives a relational understanding for the flow of concepts detailed in Table 3.1, where the progression of content for Earth and Space is presented across year levels.

In researching the topic of Earth and Space, some key concepts are presented in more detail to help you with planning. More information can be found in Chapter 8.

Year 7, Module 3, Unit 7–9

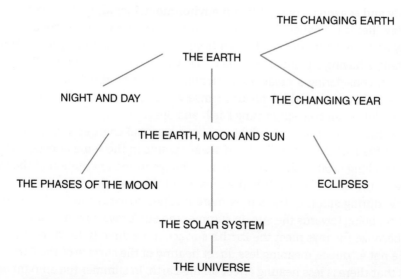

Figure 3.10 Concept map of the concepts associated with Earth and Space.

Earth's rotation on its axis causes regular changes, including night and day: Every 24 hours the Earth turns on its axis once. This is what causes day and night. At any one time half of the Earth's sphere is in sunlight (day) and half of it is in darkness (night).

The Earth is part of a system of planets orbiting around a star (the Sun): The Sun is at the center of the Solar system. The Earth, Moon and Sun are part of that Solar system. The Earth orbits the Sun, taking one year to complete one orbit. The Moon is a natural satellite for the Earth. It takes one lunar month to complete one obit of the Earth. Understanding the spatial relationship the Earth, Sun and Moon is important for children to know before they attempt modeling the whole Solar system.

The Sun is a star that is as the centre of our Solar system. The Sun is the only body in our Solar system which gives out light. The Sun is the main heat source for our planet. Planets orbit the Sun. Some of the planets in our Solar system have natural satellites called moons.

The Universe is a term used to name everything that exists. The Universe is made up of galaxies. Galaxies are a collection of millions of stars. Our Solar system is part of a galaxy. This galaxy is called the Milky Way.

Observable changes occur in the sky and landscape: The Sun lights up half of the Moon's surface. The phases of the Moon occur because of the part of the Moon we can see in the sky from where we are on the Earth, in relation to the illuminated part of the Moon. That is, the part of the illuminated side of the Moon that is visible to us. The phases make up a regular monthly pattern.

An eclipse is caused when an astronomical body casts a shadow over, or obscures from sight, another astronomical body. Knowing about the spatial relations between the Earth, Sun and Moon is needed to understand an eclipse.

Daily and seasonal changes in our environment, including the weather, affect everyday life: It is challenging for children to learn about the seasons, length of the day and the inclination of the Sun from an astronomical perspective. What is important is having a point of reference – i.e. where the child is on the Earth's surface when considering a model of a scientific view of he tilted Earth orbiting the Sun. The child can then think about themselves in the model, rather than outside of the model, when conceptualising Earth and Space.

In preparation for teaching children about seasonal changes, it is important to note that the Earth's axis is tilted and always points in the same direction. During the Earth's long orbit of the Sun, there is a change in the orientation of the Earth, relative to the Sun. The result is the seasons of the year that we experience. For instance, during summer the Sun is more inclined towards the Earth due to the Earth's tilt being towards the Sun. In summer the Sun's rays have a greater heating effect because the rays meet the Earth's surface more directly. In winter the Sun's rays are not as direct, meaning less direct heating of the surface of the Earth. This means that there is less heating effect on the Earth. In summer the amount of the Earth's surface in sunlight (in a particular latitude) is greater than that which is in darkness, so a place on that latitude has longer daylight than in winter.

Why do we need the Sun?

We need the Sun to help the plants ripen.

We need the Sun to be healthy.

We need the Sun to help the animals grow.

We need the Sun to help us grow.

Figure 3.11 A shared base of science in the classroom (Year 2).

Summary

A transmission approach to teaching science can be attractive for its apparent ease, efficiency and level of teacher control to those who do not recognise the potential problems of using the approach. The assumptions in transmission about the nature of science and about learning in science can result in ineffective teaching. However, a transmission approach to the teaching of science can be an effective strategy, depending on the teacher's degree of care and creativity. In some contexts, transmission can play a useful role in initiating scientific investigations or in helping children bring together learning that might have occurred through other activities. The approach might be justified when it is difficult to teach a topic in science in which hands-on and direct experience of materials or processes is not possible. The effectiveness of a transmission approach depends on the extent to which the knowledge to be taught:

- is carefully selected and sequenced
- is couched in language that is easily understood by the children
- introduces the language of science in appropriate learning contexts
- uses strategies that will capture children's interest.

The approach also depends on encouraging feedback from children to check their scientific understandings and providing them with the opportunity to practise using their new scientific understandings.

References

Australian Curriculum, Assessment and Reporting Authority 2014, Australian Curriculum – Science. Available at http://www.australiancurriculum.edu.au/Science/Curriculum/F-6. (Accessed September 2014.)

Australian Government Department of Education, Employment and Workplace Relations 2009, *Belonging, Being and Becoming. The Early Years Learning Framework for Australia*, Canberra: Commonwealth of Australia.

Chandler, PD 2013, 'The collaborative science classroom: ICT-based approaches' in C Redman ed, *Successful Science Education Practices. Exploring What, Why and How they Worked*, New York: Nova Science, pp. 245–63.

Regan, E 2013, 'The role of demonstrations in successful science practices: The promotion of chemistry in school projects' in C Redman ed, *Successful Science Education Practices: Exploring What, Why and How they Worked*, New York: Nova Science, pp. 129–50.

Acknowledgement

Special thanks to my colleague Dr Gloria Quinones for providing the infant photo in this chapter.

CHAPTER 4

A discovery-based approach to learning science

Introduction

In the previous chapter we examined a transmission approach to teaching science. A transmission approach has a long history, and many people have experienced this approach as learners of science at one stage in their schooling. In this chapter we examine another approach that also has a long history in schools – a discovery-based approach to learning science. A discovery-based approach to learning science still holds a strong place in schools and in many early childhood settings.

In Figures 4.1 and 4.2 are presented snapshots of children's activities centred on the *Science Understanding* of Physical Sciences – Sound. In the Australian Curriculum – Science it states that children should learn that *light and sound are produced by a range of sources that can be sensed* (ACARA 2014). In this chapter we take a look at how the concept of sound can be learned through a discovery-based approach to learning science. Through looking at a case example, we examine this approach, detailing its strengths and limitations, and the ways in which it can successfully be used in classrooms and centres.

HAVE YOU EVER WONDERED ABOUT ... ?
CONTEXTS OF SCIENCE

Have you ever wondered why a whip makes such a loud sound when someone cracks it? Did you know that the whip breaks the speed of sound? But how does that happen?

CAMBRIDGE
DYNAMIC
SCIENCE

Year 9,
Module 4,
Unit 9

Figure 4.1 Exploring human sounds using a balloon: sounds can be heard by the human ear when the sound reaches the ear.

Have you also wondered what causes the thundering sound during a storm? Did you know that the heated air around the lightning expands faster than the speed of sound? What might be the relationship between when you hear the thunder and when you see the lightning? You may be thinking, how does sound travel? Vibration is the key concept for understanding sound.

Looking inside the classroom

REFLECTIONS 4.1: WHAT DID YOU DISCOVER?

Examine the following scenario and consider how the children have been organised for learning. What do you notice about the children's thinking in science? What is the role of the teacher?

Discovery workstations in classrooms

A Year 4 group of children is clustered into small groups of four to five children. The children move from one discovery workstation to the next. At each workstation is a particular activity related to the concept of sound. The teacher moves between the workstations, clarifying requirements, assisting with resources, reading work cards located at each station, or asking children what they are discovering as they work with the materials. The instructions for most of these activities are detailed in Appendix 4.1.

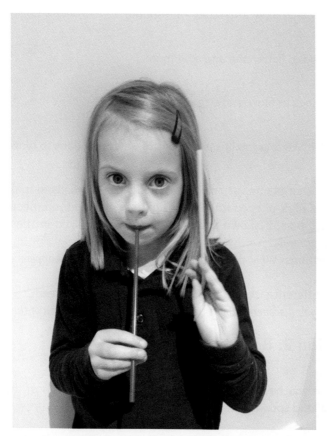

Figure 4.2 Sound – drinking straws can make interesting sounds when they are cut; the higher the frequency, the higher the sound (pitch).

Workstation 1: Making a reed from a drinking straw

Allyson: Look, straws! I wouldn't mind a nice cold drink now.

Mark: What do we have to do here?

Simon: (Reading card.) Flatten the end of a drinking straw with your fingers. Cut the end to make a point. Look, here is a picture of it!

Allyson: That's easy. Give me the scissors. (Cuts end of drinking straw to form a point.)

Mark: Now what do we have to do?

Simon: (Reading card.) Hold the cut end of the straw between your lips. Now flatten the end gently near your mouth. Blow gently.

Allyson attempts to blow into straw – no sound.

Mark: You need to flatten the end a bit more.

Allyson continues to blow into straw – still no sound.

Melissa: I will make one too. (Cuts end of straw and proceeds to blow into it.)

After several attempts by various children, Allyson succeeds in making her straw reed produce a high-pitched sound. The children cheer simultaneously. The focus questions on the card (shown in Figure 4.8) are overlooked in the excitement of using the straw reeds.

Focus questions: *What do you hear? What do you think is happening? What makes the noise?*

Now add different-sized straws to the end of your straw reed.

What have you discovered about the effect of changing the length of the straw?

Workstation 2: Bottle blowing

Andrea: What you have to do is blow across the top of each of the bottles. We should hear a loud sound.

Each child takes a bottle and attempts blowing across the top. Some children are more successful than others.

Jackie: Wow, what a good sound!

Helen: It says here that we must put different amounts of water into the bottles to see what happens to the sound.

Jackie: That's what I did at home.

Children proceed to put water into the bottles. Some discussion is forthcoming about the differing amounts of water.

Jackie: It will make a lower sound or a higher sound depending on how much water you put in.

Children discuss this idea and play around with a range of musical tunes.

Teacher: What have you discovered here?

Helen: If you put water in the bottles the sound that the bottle makes changes.

Teacher: How does it change?

Jackie: The bottles which have lots of water make a high sound and the others make a deep sound.

Teacher: So what can you say about that? What pattern have you observed?

Jackie: The more water you put in, the higher will be the sound that you can make.

Teacher: Good thinking. Now write up your findings.

Figure 4.3 Sound – what do we learn about children's scientific thinking when we observe children experimenting with bottle blowing?

The other workstations available to the Year 4 children included investigations with tapping suspended metal tubes (tubular bells), stretched elastic bands, vibrating a hacksaw blade and a ruler, travelling sound through solids, liquids and gases, whirling a flexible plastic pipe and playing with human sounds (whistling, humming, talking and simulating vocal cords with a balloon). In addition, the teacher provided a tuning fork for the children. Using a tuning fork in some of the discovery activities allows the children to make the connection between sound and vibration – they can tap a tuning fork and hear the note – then touch it against their ear lobe and feel the vibrations or put the vibrating tips in a dish of water and note the splash. Furthermore, it can be touched against a suspended ping-pong ball or touched against the skin of a drum that has rice seed scattered on it.

Were there positive aspects to the teaching? Were there negative aspects to the teaching? Clearly there is a great deal of hands-on activity occurring, with children's full engagement. However, what level of scientific learning do you think is taking place? For example, what are the children learning about how sound travels? Do they think about vibrations?

Figure 4.4 Sound – using elastic bands and coat hangers.

Digital technologies supporting learning

Digital white boards can provide an interesting context for sound and movement explorations. Many technologies available to adults now have interfaces suitable for young children. The technologies can also give new and interesting contexts for thinking about how sound travels. Using a coat hanger as shown in Figure 4.4 is one way, but using voice activated systems, such as Siri can lead to interesting questions being asked, such as 'How does Siri actually work?'. How might you deal with this? How might this give a context for science learning? What might children discover?

Approaches to discovery learning

Guided discovery: A number of contexts for discovery learning can be found in the formal education system today. The first is guided discovery, which has been described here through the use of boxes of equipment and cards, or learning stations. In this learning context the investigation or problem is owned by the teacher and introduced to the children. The teacher suggests or, as described in this chapter, provides the equipment needed in order for the children to work through the problems detailed on cards. By providing cards for the children to follow, the teacher recommends the steps that the children need to take in order to solve the problem.

Teachers who use guided discovery learning as their main science pedagogy are able to guide the children's observations by asking questions (either orally or on card) that highlight the pertinent observations; for example, 'What happens when … ?' Similarly, the teacher guides the children's inferences when he or she asks 'What can you say? What did you think? Why did … ?' The teacher also guides the children's hypothesising by asking questions such as 'If you did … what would happen? Why?' Finally, the teacher guides further investigation. This can be seen when the teacher asks 'What other … ?'

Elastic Band Sounds

Investigate how the length or width of elastic bands affects the sounds they make.

- *Place an elastic band around a jar, tin or box. Place a pencil under the band, across the top of a jar, and pluck sections on each side of the pencil.*
    - *How does the <u>width</u> of a band affect the sound?*
    - *How does the <u>length</u> of a band affect the sound?*
    - *How does the length of the vibrating section of the band affect the sound?*
    - *What do you discover?*

Figure 4.5 Guided instructions to help children with their scientific thinking.

Discovery boxes and science table: The second type of discovery learning involves placing materials in the children's environment and allowing the children to use the materials as they wish. This is generally associated with the nature table or science table. Discovery learning in early childhood settings tends to follow this approach. We often see a science table in these settings. The science table usually features natural objects, such as a bird's nest, shells and leaves. Sometimes the table contains processed materials, such as magnets, and both attracting and non-attracting materials, such as nails, bottle tops and plastic straws. Teachers often provide tools, such as magnifying glasses or insect boxes, to assist children in their observations. In this type of discovery learning the teacher provides the learning context, but leaves the children to decide which problem they wish to investigate. Often, children play with the materials, developing a strong experiential base. Children do not always set problems for themselves. Teachers might ask children questions about what they are discovering as they manipulate the materials. For example, 'What do you know about sound travelling through solids and liquids?', where children will discover that the material vibrates, allowing the sound wave to be transmitted. Similarly, the teacher might initiate activities or arrange situations that give opportunities for children to ask questions.

Modified discovery learning: The third type of teaching pedagogy used by teachers is known as 'modified discovery learning'. In this approach, the teacher sets the problem but allows the children to suggest how they might go about solving it. Often, the teacher provides a range of equipment but does not restrict the children to using only that equipment. Children are usually encouraged to work in groups to solve the problem. The teacher circulates among the groups, assisting as required. The teacher acts as a resource person, guide or someone who poses questions. The timing of the teacher's questions is of great importance in the success of this approach.

What assumptions underpin a discovery-based approach?

All three learning environments draw on common principles of discovery learning.

Discovery learning, which grew out of the curriculum development movement in the 1960s, was a deliberate move away from the philosophy that children are the passive recipients of knowledge through traditional styles of teaching, such as the transmission approach discussed in Chapter 3. Discovery learning has changed the role of the teacher from that of delivering facts to organising learning so that children are empowered to retrieve knowledge and skills from a range of resources. In this approach, the teacher is often viewed as a:

- classroom resource
- counsellor and friend, or
- neutral person.

In science, children used to be encouraged to be the discoverers of the nature of things. The role of teacher as demonstrator in science was de-emphasised. The Nuffield Science program, supported by the Nuffield Foundation, strongly influenced the direction of science teaching around the English-speaking world. The approach encouraged children to engage in 'real' experimentation and 'real' discovery. The children, in collaboration with the teacher, were to act in a scientific manner, emulating the role of 'real' scientists. This inductive approach to learning relies on children gradually increasing their familiarity with new concepts through the exploration of materials provided by the teacher. Rather than being presented with the teacher's definition of the concept at the beginning of the topic, the children construct their own understandings as a result of exposure to a whole range of activities and experiences with materials. Science is viewed as a subject that explores the laws of nature that are out there ready to be discovered by children.

Historically, discovery learning was embraced as an innovative and desirable teaching approach, particularly in science. Until its introduction, children were not directly involved in the learning process; they were passive recipients of science facts.

REFLECTIONS 4.2: YOUR EXPERIENCES WITH DISCOVERY LEARNING

Think back to your school days. *Do you recall the teaching of science following a discovery approach?*

If yes, record an example of a lesson you were involved in. If no, then draw upon the case study presented at the beginning of this chapter. Think about what you might have learned from the experience. From the vantage point of hindsight, consider what the teacher might have been trying to achieve. Now examine the science content knowledge about sound over the page. *Did you discover all those concepts? What were the limitations and what were the strengths of the discovery approach?*

Consider the following questions for this approach.

1   How did I learn in this approach?
2   What was the role of the teacher in this approach?
3   How do I feel about this approach to teaching and learning in science?
4   In this approach, what assumptions are being made about:
    • children's learning
    • the nature of science?

Preparation and planning

When planning for a discovery-based approach to teaching science, it is important to know the concepts that you want the children to discover through the experiences you provide. This knowledge helps you as a teacher to select the right materials and to make available the right resources, including the preparation of useful guiding questions. The key ideas for understanding the concept of sound are presented here as a quick overview to get you started.

Science content knowledge – sound

Vibration is the key concept for understanding sound. All sounds are produced by vibrations, such as strings or drums. A vibrating string is easy to recognise. However, how we hear the human voice from a distance is less obvious. That is, we don't see any evidence of the vibrations.

Sounds can be heard by the human ear when the sound reaches the ear. The eardrum vibrates when the sounds reaches the ear. The vibrating eardrum causes other parts in the ear to vibrate, allowing sensory information to be transmitted to the brain, where the sound is translated into words or a recognised sound.

Sound travels through materials: this material can be a gas, such as air, a solid such as a door, or a liquid such as water in a swimming pool. The material vibrates, allowing the sound wave to be transmitted.

Sound takes time to travel: sound travels at different rates through different kinds of material, such as water, air or a solid wooden door. Sound travels slower than light.

Sound can be reflected, absorbed or transmitted: when sound reaches a surface it does three different things – it can be transmitted, absorbed or reflected. This is a difficult concept to understand. In order to fully understand this, children need to know the particulate nature of matter. For young children, understanding that sounds can be muffled allows them to gain an appreciation of this idea. Similarly, the reflection of sound producing an echo can help children to think about this concept. Sound is absorbed through soft materials, such as fabric, and reflected from hard surfaces, such as walls.

Sound has three characteristics: these are loudness, pitch and quality or timbre (i.e. what is making the sound). Understanding these characteristics requires being able to differentiate between amplitude (loudness) and speed of vibration (pitch).

1 *Loudness* – sound is measured in decibels. Loudness of sound is dependent on how large the vibration is from its source (amplitude). The smaller the amplitude, the quieter the sound; the larger the amplitude, the louder the sound will be.
2 *Pitch* – how fast the source (e.g. elastic or metal) is vibrating (frequency). A high frequency has more vibrations per second. The higher the frequency, the higher the sound (pitch). A low pitch means a slower vibration. *Exploring the source material by changing the vibration can help with this idea.* For instance, when we think about a string vibrating, we have to consider the frequency of the vibration and the length. The thickness of the string matters, but also how tightly strung

the string is too. A shorter string will have a higher frequency, and therefore a higher pitch. You can also experiment with the thickness of the string and how tightly it is strung to alter the pitch. What is important here is the frequency of the vibration in the source material.

3 *Sound waves*: vibrations create sound waves that travel through any source material nearby (solid, liquid or gas).

Energy transfer: when sound travels, it transfers energy. Sound can be converted into electrical oscillations. It can also be transmitted as current over long distances and converted into sound waves again – for example, a telephone wire.

A critique of a discovery-based approach to learning

In this section we examine student teachers' perspectives and experiences of a discovery-based approach to learning science.

Providing a rich 'hands-on' environment

Lara: Um, I just think it's a good approach because it would make the children interested in learning how something works. Because they've sort of had fun with it and then later on they can start thinking about how it actually works. Consequently, it makes it more relevant if they play with the materials and think through how it actually works. Later they can work out the theories or the scientific principles behind it.

Lecturer: So you think it gives them the practical knowledge before they get into the next stage, which is to analyse what's happened?

Lara: Yes.

Getting off track

The student teachers also believed that careful management of the children was vital for the approach to be successful. They felt that children could easily be distracted from the assigned task – simply playing with the materials and not seeing any patterns.

Tim: I found that the instructions guided the students through the activities, but I initially thought that with some kids they might go off the track a bit, and go a bit overboard and some of the activities would have a high interest level, but then kids could quite easily start throwing things around the room and not stay on task.

If you used this approach to teaching science, what might you do to minimise this problem that Tim has identified?

Discovering what it does, but not finding out why

Of greatest concern to the student teachers was the emphasis on discovering what the materials actually did and not focusing on why. They felt that the materials themselves, and even the questions on cards, may not provide a framework in which children would learn sophisticated scientific principles. Student teachers felt children would gain a lot of experiential knowledge about what they could do with the materials, but were not really stimulated into thinking about why the materials were behaving in the manner presented.

Jenny: We thought that the children didn't think about the scientific things behind it at all really.

Tanya: Um, looking back now we can see that the children didn't really get into the scientific principles behind the differences in sound in regards to speed and length of the source material.

Tim: It was more about having fun and doing the activity.

Shelley: Mm, discovering what it does rather than why.

Lecturer: That's quite an interesting point.

Tanya: Or just 'cause with the activities, um, the ones that the children liked doing were really enjoyable so they just kept doing things. They didn't really think about the scientific questions.

High teacher–child ratio

One student teacher was anxious about the teacher–child ratio that would be required for the discovery approach to be successful.

Tim: You need a higher teacher–child ratio sort of thing because with things like the balloons the children did not read the instructions, like, everyone knows that when you get a balloon you blow it up and let it go!

Teacher–child interaction: more guidance

A number of student teachers felt that for the approach to successfully engage children conceptually, where they are motivated to find out why and able to see relationships and patterns, a great deal of adult assistance would be needed.

Kylie: The children didn't really think about the scientific principle, you know why, 'cause we as teachers hadn't actually given the children any direction saying 'Well, when you're doing these, think about such and such'. So the children read the instructions, did what it said on there and that was that.

Rose: Yeah, they didn't find the questions very helpful either 'cause it just said, 'What have you discovered?', so we wrote down what we discovered.

Kylie: The children discovered things but they didn't think about it.

Gabrielle: But if the questions had been more directional or focused the children would've had to think about it a lot more and they might have come up with something else.

Kylie: And if we as teachers had said at the beginning 'Well, why are you doing it?', then the children would have had to think about why or the scientific processes involved. As teachers we didn't give the children any direction so they just did what it said.

Angela: But they had fun!

Lecturer: So you just said to the children: 'Go and discover'.

Kylie and Angela: Yeah.

Rose: And then they did discover and what they discovered was, not really scientific – well it wasn't deeply, I don't think.

Lecturer: But it could have been had you been directed a bit?

Rose: Yes!

Using previous knowledge to understand the sound activities

The science content knowledge that student teachers already possessed was drawn on to help them make sense of planning their science lessons. The student teachers also found that children with greater science knowledge were in a better position to be able to lead a discussion in their group. As a result, the thinking about the activities related most closely to what the most able children understood in each group.

Michelle: One of the children I was teaching said she remembered hearing noises when she was under the water in the swimming pool and things like that.

Felicity: This one [card] actually says, 'Why is this so?' This started the children in the group thinking. This was useful when the children moved to the station on rubber bands, where they were still thinking of why. They said it was because of the vibrations and things like that. But this card doesn't – when I looked at it, it doesn't say anything about why, but this one did. So it's probably the only reason why the children started to think in a scientific way.

Infants, toddlers and preschoolers working and playing scientifically – discovery learning in early childhood

Discovery learning in science is possibly the most common approach adopted by early childhood teachers. After considering discovery learning generically, the student teachers decided to critique the approach in relation to very young children. A number of important factors were immediately evident to the student teachers.

Tanya: Small children in preschool and early childhood wouldn't be able to read these instructions to start with, so you'd have to set up the experiments. You could have most of activities, but you just wouldn't have cards with instructions with the materials, the children would just play …

Shelley: To experience them.

Tanya: … and experience them, but if you were going to use the discovery approach on its own you're not going to get a scientific outcome, you're not going to get the children discovering what happens with sound. We thought it could be a …

Shelley: … an introductory lesson.

Tanya: … initiator to something else or at the end after you've talked about concepts of sound and travel but that would be less interesting to talk about the concepts on their own and then play with things than to use it as an initiator and then say, well …

Shelley: … 'What do we relate to those experiences?'

Tanya: … what you know and then asking questions, you know they could say, 'Well, why did this happen?', or they might come up with things like that.

Shelley: Children will learn about what it does – it makes sounds and the sounds change. But will the children ask why? I mean why would you, you know, go into why it happens? I mean some kids would want to know that and they come and run up and ask you why it happens but they're not going to suddenly work it out by themselves without a little bit of …

Tanya: … guidance.

Shelley: … guidance of some sort. I mean it doesn't have to be very structured guidance but, how to work out experiments, how to work out just how to do an experiment to find out what they want.

The student teachers have identified some constraints of the discovery approach to teaching science, yet there are also advantages. Clearly, it is important to know what the strengths and limitations of this approach are if we are to develop our own approaches to teaching science.

Following is a discussion of the assumptions inherent in using the discovery approach to teaching science. As you read, make notes about how you react to the material. You might like to draw parallels with the critique provided above by the student teachers.

Discovery of what?

Discovery learning in science implies that children can easily find out the scientific principles or understandings by interacting with materials. Clearly, there are many scientific ideas, such as electricity, which are not directly observable. In addition, there are other concepts, such as force, that have taken scientists many centuries

Figure 4.6 Priyom explores a sound game with Mahbub. What can he discover? The role of the adult is really important for developing children's understandings of scientific concepts.

to fully understand. For example, when children observe a ball being thrown, the only force acting on this ball, in their view, is the thrower. Children do not intuitively consider the air resistance and the gravitational force acting on the ball. Similarly, many children believe that the ball contains the force. This Aristotelian perspective (rather than the current Newtonian view, as labelled by science researchers) is a commonly held alternative view that has been formed by children's experiences with balls. It might then be asked, how can children discover such a sophisticated idea if scholars took centuries to arrive at this perspective? The resources themselves do not always provide the answers that scientists have agreed on as the best possible explanation at the time.

No such thing as neutral direction by the teacher

In discovery learning, the role of the teacher is de-emphasised because the teacher acts more as a facilitator and an organiser of resources. Consequently, teachers refrain from direct teaching by following a policy in which the children themselves are required to generate ideas and to learn by direct experience.

During interactions between children and the teacher, the children may take their lead from the teacher or from other children. In addition, children are still strongly influenced by the non-verbal cues that teachers present. As a result, the children's real task becomes one of guessing what the teacher wants them to do or 'discover'.

The teacher's dilemma is that he or she must foster scientific understanding while apparently eliciting it. In science, children need to be given a framework within which to examine the materials they are manipulating. The teacher's role is crucial to children's understandings, and hence his or her role should not be of following, but, rather, of leading conceptual development – particularly where the science principles are not directly observable, or where the ideas are counterintuitive.

Owning the learning

Science learning, when introduced to children via a discovery approach, is often organised so that the problem to be discovered is introduced by the teacher. The children might take some part in deciding how they will use the materials provided (or what materials they need), but will often not be involved in setting the problem. As a result, the adult questions posed might not always relate to the children's real interests. In Chapters 5 to 7 you will consider the role of the teacher and the questions they pose versus children's questions in more detail. In those chapters, you will see that the children's questions are far more sophisticated, more true to life and much more empowering than those of the teacher.

REFLECTIONS 4.3: ASSUMPTIONS ABOUT THE NATURE OF SCIENCE

Now look back to the student teachers' comments and see how these ideas correlate.

The student teachers made many comments about the unhelpfulness of the cards. They felt that the children had learned a great deal about how the materials worked, but very little about the science principles of sound.

OVERCOMING THE PROBLEMS

If you were the teacher introducing the concept of sound via the learning stations, how would you get around the problems mentioned by the students?

Classroom and early childhood setting management in a discovery-based approach to learning science

Managing children's learning using a discovery learning approach relies on you, the teacher, to:

- Select materials that children can manipulate and that will easily lead them to discovering the scientific concept(s) under study.
- Decide whether the whole group will do the same thing or whether small groups will be formed.

- Organise enough materials for all the children to have the opportunity to use the materials and to effectively participate in each activity at the station (e.g. having enough straws for everyone in the class or centre to play with it at one time).
- Think through the safety and cleaning issues before you start, so that you have all the necessary materials available and in an accessible place (e.g. sponges and cloths ready for mopping up water spills when children experiment with sound travelling under water).
- Allow enough time for children to mess about with the materials and fully engage in the experience (this always takes longer than you expect).
- Organise the children into groups – and have the room set up to support this – before you set the scene or give the instructions.
- Allow recording and sharing time immediately after the hands-on activity.
- Think through how you will deal with some groups finishing before others (What role will the early-finishers take?).
- Allow enough time to clean up after the activity – so that you are not left with all the work at the end of a busy teaching day!

Assessment in a discovery-learning approach

In this approach to teaching and learning, children's physical participation in the experience is very important. The approach cannot occur unless the children are given opportunities to investigate a range of materials. When this approach was developed, the learning of scientific concepts (as opposed to just inquiry skills,

Figure 4.7 Assessing children's learning through analysing work samples.

see Chapters 5 to 6) was deemed important – the belief being that by interacting with the materials children would acquire scientific understandings. As such, assessment for this approach tends to rely on ticking off the activities that children have investigated or been involved in. Children's participation in the activity often means that teachers assume that the children discover the science ideas behind the hands-on experience. In Figures 4.7 and 4.8 are examples of children's records of what they have done and noticed. These are helpful for making assessment of children's learning in science using a discovery-based approach.

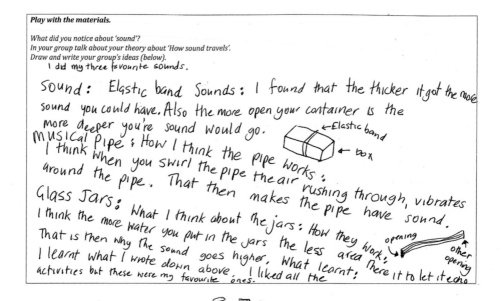

Play with the materials.

What did you notice about 'sound'?
In your group talk about your theory about 'How sound travels'.
Draw and write your group's ideas (below).

I did my three favourite sounds.

Sound: Elastic band Sounds: I found that the thicker it got the more sound you could have. Also the more open your container is the more deeper you're sound would go. ← Elastic band box

MUSICal pipe: How I think the pipe works: I think when you swirl the pipe the air rushing through, vibrates around the pipe. That then makes the pipe have sound.

Glass Jars: What I think about the jars: How they work: opening other opening I think the more water you put in the jars the less area there it to let it echo That is then why the sound goes higher. What I learnt: I learnt what I wrote down above. I liked all the activities but these were my favourite ones.

Figure 4.8 Natalie's theory – how does it actually work?

Leading change in science education

Shukla Sikder is researching what infants and toddlers learn about science through their day-to-day interactions at home with family and friends. Very little is known about this age group, yet this early period of a child's life is most informative and lays important foundations for learning, including learning science. In her work, Shukla Sikder has found that infants and toddlers build understandings through day-to-day interactions with their social and material world that often goes unnoticed. She has called this *small science*. This idea is closely linked with guided discovery learning. But like the critique of a discovery-based approach, Shukla Sikder has found the role of the adult is critical for helping children think scientifically about their everyday experiences.

Figure 4.9 Shukla Sikder has found that there is very little research into infants' and toddlers' experiences of learning science at home.

Discovery learning for infants and toddlers

Four categories of small science have been observed in everyday life, they are:

- multiple possibilities for science
- discrete science
- embedded science
- counter-intuitive science.

Multiple possibilities for science means that one moment of a day-to-day inter-action can lead to a range of small science concepts being formed. For example, water play can lead to understandings of density, force and gravity.

Discrete science means that one moment of a day-to-day interaction can lead to a specific science concept being developed. For example, playing with a prism in a toy can lead to the understanding in time of the refraction of light.

Embedded science means that one regular day-to-day interaction can, over time, lead to the development of scientific concepts, but they may not be noticed ini-tially, and it is difficult to determine when the concept was finally formed for the child. For example, bedtime routines of turning on and off the light at night can lead to the understanding of darkness being the absence of light. But this will take time to establish, requiring many experiences over time, with a sensitive adult who draws attention to this idea.

Counter-intuitive science means that a child's day-to-day observations of, for example the sky, makes it difficult for that child to understand that the Earth moves around the Sun (rather than the other way around, as would be suggested by the child's observations of the sky during the day).

The pedagogical research of Shukla Sikder is important for better understanding the role of early childhood educators in infant and toddler learning of science, and for primary teachers to gain insights into the continuum of learning in science from birth to 12 years and beyond. Working and playing with science concepts is foregrounded in the curriculum of EYLF (2009), and through focusing on science in the early years, understandings can build over the birth to 12-year period. In guided discovery we can conceptualise the range of ways that small science forms (multiple possibilities for science, discrete science, embedded science and counter-intuitive science) (Sikder and Fleer 2014).

Summary

In this chapter we have reviewed the discovery approach to learning science. Research into student teachers' thinking has shown that the idea of discovering science knowledge and skills within an activity is problematic. As teachers, we can never be sure what children are discovering. It was also shown that for children to feel ownership over their learning, they need to be engaged with the materials in a personal way – that is, being driven by their own research questions. In the next set of chapters (Part 3) we take up this idea further as we examine a range of ways of promoting inquiry learning and teaching.

References

Australian Curriculum, Assessment and Reporting Authority 2014, Australian Curriculum – Science. Available at http://www.australiancurriculum.edu.au/Science/Curriculum/F-6 (Accessed September 2014.)

Australian Government Department of Education, Employment and Workplace Relations 2009, *Belonging, Being and Becoming. The Early Years Learning Framework for Australia*, Canberra: Commonwealth of Australia.

Sikder, S, Fleer, M 2014, 'Small science: Infants and toddlers experiencing science in everyday family play', *Research in Science Education*. (DOI 10.1007/s11165-014-9431-0.)

Appendix

Stretched string

Attach a nylon line to a length of wood. Secure a load (e.g. a bucket filled with water) to the end of the line and add a wooden support (see Figure 4.10). Pluck the nylon line.

Listen to the sound. Change the load (e.g. empty half of the load from the bucket). Pluck the line again. Keep the position of the wooden support the same.

What did you notice about the sound? Why do you think this happens?

Now move the support, keeping the weight in the bucket constant. Pluck the line again.

What have you found? Why does this happen?

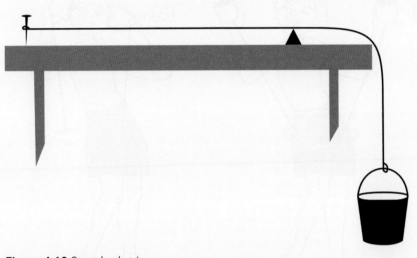

Figure 4.10 Stretched string.

Elastic band sounds

Investigate how the length or width of elastic bands affects the sound they make. Place an elastic band around a jar, tin or box. Place a pencil under the band across the top of the jar, and pluck sections on each side of the pencil.

How does the width of a band affect the sound? (Choose bands of the same length for comparison.)

How does the length of the band affect the sound?

How does the length of the vibrating section of the band affect the sound?

What do you discover?

Tapping bottles

Many instruments played by tapping have a fixed pitch, for example bells (although if struck too hard or in the wrong place they will be out of tune).

Line up five empty glass bottles and tap them with a wooden rod. Now put some water in the bottles and tap them again. What happens? Repeat this, but have different amounts of water in each bottle. Try tapping one bottle continuously as water is poured into it.

What have you found? How do you explain this?

Hanger sounds

You need a partner for this activity. Attach two paper cups to a coat hanger with a string, as shown in the diagram. Hold the paper cups up, with the metal hanger hanging freely, as shown. Have your partner tap the hanger. Listen to the sound. Now repeat the process, but this time put the cups over your ears. Try altering the shape of the hanger and hit it with different things.

Figure 4.11 Hanger sounds.

Vibrating ruler

Hold one end of a ruler onto a firm surface – clamp it to the desk if necessary. Now lift the free end and set it vibrating. Attach different sized bullnose clips to the free end.

What have you discovered? How does this relate to stringed instruments?
You might have noticed that deeper notes are produced form thicker strings.
Can you explain why?

Sound absorption

Put a wind-up toy, clock or radio into a shoe box. Vary the lining of the box (e.g. foil, newspaper, carpet and other materials).

What have you found? How can some materials absorb sound better than others?

Travelling sound

How does sound travel through solids and liquids?

Put an ear against the surface of a bench. Ask a friend to tap the other end of the bench at intervals as he or she gradually moves closer to you.

What have you found? Can you explain this?

Ask a friend to gently tap two sticks or stones together inside an empty plastic tank.

Place your ear against the tank wall and listen to the sound made. Fill the tank with water and repeat the exercise.

What have you found? Can you explain this?

Flexible pipe

Obtain a length of flexible pipe (of thin corrugated plastic, available at science centres). Hold the flexible pipe at arm's length and whirl it through the air. By varying the speed, try to make up to five different sounds.

What have you found? How does whirling the pipe around create the sounds? What has happened?

Acknowledgement

Nina Sharpe's children, Heidi and Alice Sharpe, kindly field tested the discovery learning approach. The children are pictured in this chapter.

PART 3

Inquiry-based Approaches

In this section of the book are three chapters that are all pedagogically related. They each showcase inquiry-based approaches to teaching and learning, but the focus of each chapter is slightly different.

The chapters are: Chapter 5: Inquiry-based approach to teaching science, Chapter 6: Inquiry-based approach to learning science and Chapter 7: Teaching for conceptual change: constructivism.

What is common across these chapters is:

- inquiries
- inquiry skills development
- constructivism

However, what is different is who leads the inquiry. As you read these three chapters, please plot on the following chart where you would locate the particular approach in terms of if the inquiry is *student-led* or *teacher-led*.

As you read both chapters there are **key things to look for.** You will notice that sometimes there are several starting points for inquiries. Sometimes the initial inquiry is very broad, and the subsequent inquiry is much more focused. Think about what conditions were created by the teacher at each point and why. Also look closely at the types of questions asked by children, and what the teacher might need to do to make the inquiries doable – reflect on what is presented, as well as what you imagine might have happened in each classroom. Chapter 6 shows some examples of science learning through work samples, leaving it to you to try to determine what happened to bring about the rich work from the children. Finally, analyse the types of investigations that took place as the children followed their inquiries and found the answers to their scientific questions.

Things to think about are: What were the differences in what happened and what was learned when the inquiry was child-led and when it was teacher-led?

We begin the first chapter (Chapter 5) with a focus on the biological sciences. The content is oriented towards Year 5 and 6 children, with the latter part of the chapter showing content for science from birth to the Foundation year. The second chapter (Chapter 6) takes up the same content, but is more geared towards the middle years of primary school – children's interests and learning achievements. Together, these two chapters provide examples of thinking scientifically from birth to 12 years in the biological sciences following the Australian Curriculum – Science.

In the third and final chapter, you will examine the physical sciences. We take up the challenge of mapping children's conceptual thinking about light and electricity from preschool to the end of primary school. You can find the other areas of sound, force and materials and their properties in other chapters. In this third chapter, we deliberately focus on the physical sciences so that you can see how inquiry-based approaches can be used for all the content areas of the curriculum. This chapter draws upon the knowledge of inquiry-based approaches gained from reading the first two chapters in the set. In the third chapter (Chapter 7) we specifically examine the foundational idea of teaching for conceptual change, and the theory that supports this way of framing science inquiries – constructivism.

CHAPTER 5

Inquiry-based approach to teaching science

Introduction

In this chapter we take a look at one of the most internationally prevalent approaches to teaching science – an inquiry-based teaching approach (Alake-Tuenter, Biemans, Tobi and Mulder 2013). Inquiry-based teaching has been conceptualised and implemented differently in a range of countries. For instance, how it looks in Singapore may be slightly different from how it happens in the UK or in New Zealand. In this chapter we specifically take a close look at an inquiry-based teaching approach as originally conceptualised in *Primary Connections* where the 5Es model of teaching and learning is elaborated (Hackling and Prain 2008). This is one relevant example for better understanding of how children and teachers can take an active role in learning science, following a step-by-step approach for engaging, exploring, explaining, elaborating, evaluating and assessing science learning for primary school children.

We begin this chapter by following a group of student teachers as they learn about micro-organisms. The students experienced an inquiry-based teaching approach where they made different kinds of bread. The focus was on Year 6 science content of biological science and science inquiry skills but, as you might expect, the university students engaged and researched bread making and micro-organisms at their own level. However, many of the questions asked and investigations undertaken mirror those found in Year 6 classrooms (see Australian Academy of Science 2005).

In the second half of the chapter we continue with biological science and science inquiry skills, but with a focus on the Birth to Preschool period where children studied living things, and the Foundation to Year 2 band where children investigated organisms found in the compost bin. Here we seek to show how both

Singapore: www.youtube.com/watch?v=CWnsxkfoQHo **UK:** www.youtube.com/watch?v=vC2PFKxWTpU **New Zealand:** http://scienceonline.tki.org.nz/Nature-of-science

Early Years Learning Framework: https://docs. education. gov.au/ node/2632 **Australian Curriculum:** www. australian curriculum. edu.au

biological sciences and science inquiry skills can develop from birth to 12 years, across school and preschool contexts. For the Birth to Preschool period the Early Years Framework (Australian Government 2009) is drawn upon to make relevant curriculum connections to an inquiry-based teaching approach. For the Foundation to Year 2 the Australian Curriculum: Science – science is used (ACARA 2014). Here the three interrelated strands of science as a human endeavour, science understanding and science inquiry skills are showcased.

Figure 5.1 There are many different types of bread and a correspondingly large number of techniques for making bread: 'How have people from different cultures used sustainable and local products for bread making?'

REFLECTIONS 5.1: WHAT IS THE SCIENCE IN BREAD MAKING?

Strolling down the street past bakeries or restaurants, you can often smell food baking or cooking. When you think about the smell of moon cakes cooking, damper and bread baking or roti cooking what comes to mind?

What kind of science might be involved in the making of moon cakes and damper, cooking roti or baking bread? In Figure 5.2 is a mind map where you are invited to talk about what you know about bread making. List here all the ways that science learning can be promoted if you were to introduce a cooking experience of bread or roti making to Year 6 students.

Idea 1: ....

Idea 2: ....

Idea 3: ....

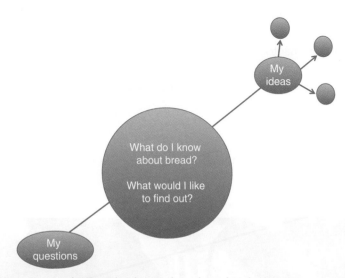

Figure 5.2 Mind map of 'What do I know about bread making?'

Science involves making and testing predictions, gathering data and using evidence

There are so many different kinds of bread from all around the world. There is even a diversity of bread from within one country. During the process of making bread, students talked to each other about the different kinds of bread they make daily, or buy at the local shops, or actively seek out so as to have more naturally produced and less processed forms of bread to eat. For instance, one student said:

I am from Poland originally. We have about 300 recipes for bread. Having said that, I first made bread about two months ago – stressed out making assignments, I started growing my own sourdough culture. After my pet died, I thought I would get another one – a small one!!! [Referring to the idea of a microbe being his living pet.]

Biodiversity in the bread adds to the taste, and perhaps adds to the health benefits of the bread.

Another student from Nepal said:

We have a bread that looks like roti, but it is a bit thicker. What my mum does, is that she puts baking powder and yeast, and it rises. It is really soft and it is really nice. It is very simple. She puts it on a flat pan and covers it, and in five minutes it is done. It is really nice, and I have not tasted such good bread! We call it Palais.

Grace from China said:

The Chinese bun (mantou) 馒头 – the reason why I chose this is because I always make this with pumpkin inside, with flour, and I put yeast in too, and leave it to rest for maybe one hour, then I put it into a big pot and steam it for 15 minutes.

Angela from Australia said:

I know that the damper does not need yeast. We have made damper bread many times when out bush!

Figure 5.3 Making bread together creates the opportunity to share cultural and family-specific ways of preparing or eating bread.

Making bread together creates the opportunity to share cultural and family-specific ways of preparing food. It also opens up many questions about how bread is made and what is the role of yeast or absence of it in the process of preparing and cooking bread. Some of the questions the students asked were:

- How does yeast make bread rise?
- Does it matter if we don't use yeast? What happens?
- Why do we need salt? What is its role in bread making? Does it matter when we put it into the mixture?
- What makes the holes in the bread?
- Why do we have to use warm water to activate the yeast? What happens if we use cold water?
- Do we have to be accurate when we add all the ingredients or can we just throw them in?
- Why does the dough have to rest?
- Why do we put a cloth or cling wrap over the kneaded dough?
- What is the role of kneading?
- Is there a difference if we make bread by hand or if we use a bread maker?

For a quick overview of bread making and the importance of yeast see www.finecooking.com/articles/yeast-role-bread-baking.aspx

REFLECTIONS 5.2: WHAT DO YOU KNOW ABOUT MICRO-ORGANISMS?

You probably studied micro-organisms at school. What insights did you gain? How might these ideas help you with planning a unit of work following an inquiry-based approach to teaching science? How much science understandings do you think you need to have?

Idea 1 (science understanding): ....

Idea 2 (science understanding): ....

Idea 3 (science understanding):

....

For general information on micro-organisms see www.bbc.co.uk/education/clips/zbbygk7

What are microbes or micro-organisms?

CAMBRIDGE DYNAMIC SCIENCE

Year 8, Module 1, Unit 1

- Microbes have an everyday understanding and a scientific understanding.
- Microbes in the everyday sense are a cluster of a diverse group of organisms – viruses, bacteria, fungi, single-celled animals and plants. The only characteristic that is common is their invisibility to the naked eye.
- There is no consensus about whether all fungi can be classified as microbes.
- Microbes are variable in size, for instance, microscopic to long fungi.

- Viruses are different from other microbes because they can be crystallised. Viruses appear to be non-living when isolated. That is, viruses appear to have the living characteristic of life because when they go into living cells they hijack the metabolism of the host cells.
- Microbes are in the air, soil, water, food and in organisms' bodies.
- The majority of microbes are beneficial for:
    - disposing of dead organisms
    - contributing to recycling
    - controlling of microbes for beneficial effect – medical techniques in antibiotics, immunisation, agricultural practices for encouraging bacterial action in the soil, for food preservation.
- Examples of useful microbes:
    - yeast: bread, alcohol, marmite
    - bacteria: yoghurt, sauerkraut, salami, olives, coffee
    - fungi: mushrooms, truffles, soy sauce, quorn (also for developing penicillin).

How might knowing about microbes in food matter in everyday life for you or the children you will be teaching?

Looking inside the classroom

A case example of using the 5Es model from *Primary Connections*

An inquiry-based teaching approach when used by teachers in the teaching of science gives a structure to how science can be taught to children in primary schools and preschool settings. The inquiry-based approach detailed in *Primary Connections* follows the following five phases:

Primary Connections: https:// primary connections. org.au

- Engage
- Explore
- Explain
- Elaborate
- Evaluate.

We discuss each of these phases through sharing examples of what the students did during the process of making bread, when asking questions about bread making, as they were setting up experiments to answer their questions, during their presentation of their findings, and finally when reflecting on their own learning. The 5Es is just one way of representing an inquiry-based approach to teaching science. Other ways of conceptualising inquiry-based teaching follow in Chapters 6 and 7. There is no 'right way', but, rather, there is a range of ways of doing inquiry-based teaching. We illustrate some of the common approaches used by teachers.

Table 5.1 Overview of bread making unit

Phases	Summary of activities
Engage	Investigating different types of bread and related products (e.g. roti, chapatti, buns, moon cakes). Eating different bread. Talking about their experiences of bread making. Mind map of understandings.
Explore	Making bread following a common recipe.
Explain	Explaining observations during bread making using science concepts.
Elaborate	Student-planned investigations. Preparing a scientific report.
Evaluate	Represent understandings through the Arts (but could also be media, literacy-based report).

Engage

Making bread in the classroom is an example of how students can be actively engaged in science. Bread making can generate interest, stimulate curiosity and give a space in which questions can be raised in conversation. Here the students can share with each other their existing knowledge of bread making (and micro-organisms). In the example of bread making, the students smelt the bread as they walked into the science lab (bread was cooking in the oven in the science lab), and explored all the different types of bread that were provided for them to eat with a hot beverage. The students were encouraged to sit together and talk about what they knew about bread making and to prepare mind maps of what they knew (see Figure 5.2).

In the *engage phase*, the teacher has the opportunity to listen for any alternative views held by the students. Learning about and understanding yeast micro-organisms is complex. The longstanding literature on students' thinking in this area is quite comprehensive, and gives some guidance about what to expect (e.g. Bandiera 2007). For instance, Bandiera (2007) asked, 'What deep-rooted conceptions exist regarding the presence and action of micro-organisms?' and 'What are students' non-school information sources?' (p. 214). These are important questions for teachers to have in their mind during the engage phase.

Research into children's thinking about bread making

Children will have heard about the word 'yeast' and will potentially know that it is used in baking and brewing, but not know that different types of yeast are used. The literature suggests that children tend to think of yeast as an ingredient rather than a microbial agent. The literature suggests that children do not know about the beneficial effects and uses of microbes.

The topic of micro-organisms goes beyond the yeast organism used in bread making. Some of the alternative views that may be held by children about micro-organisms extend to the area of composting and 'food going bad' (food spoilage). In everyday life children have direct experiences of these, and as such they form views about what happens when 'food goes off' or is said to be 'bad'. Decay and the conservation of matter are important processes that take place in our environment.

Decay is understood as:

- Micro-organisms through their feeding break down the material they are consuming, such as sewage, compost and dead organisms. This breakdown is known as decay. Materials that can be broken down in this way are called biodegradable.

Conservation in this process is understood as:

- When something has completely decayed the material is still there. However, it has changed into gases and dissolved substances.
- The process of decay allows for the re-use of biological material. That is, through the decaying process, the material that is decaying is turned into a raw material that is then available for other organisms to use.

Some of the alternative views held by children in relation to decay and the conservation of matter include:

- When children look into compost or see something that has died (plant or animal), they think that dead organisms and waste products just disappear. Most children do not realise that the size of material changes during decay. It is only later, with familiarity, that they begin to think differently. Here they begin to attribute rotting to a natural process, but they think that it is somehow inherent in the material itself. They believe that the passage of time and conditions such as dampness contribute to the process.
- Children notice physical properties, such as bruised fruit, and attribute this to the onset of decay.
- Children think that other animals, such as birds, mice, worms and insects are responsible for eating the already rotting material. Older children may believe that 'germs' (everyday understanding) feed on rotting material, or somehow cause decay but do not know how. Sometimes children will use the word decompose in relation to bacterial and fungal activity.
- Young children do not have a concept of conservation of matter. In their thinking, when something is dead, it simply disappears, leaving no products. Older children have a partial conception of the conservation of matter. These children may say that rotting material somehow enrich or fertilise soil. Some children think that waste products increase the size of the earth. They believe that decay returns minerals to the soil. However, very few children think about the gases that are produced through decay or consider how gases are a product of decay.

In the engage phase the teacher should also keep in mind the relevant science understandings for the topic being investigated. In the example of bread making, the following science understandings were deemed important for students to learn.

Scientific understandings relevant to bread making

- Yeast is a living micro-organism.
- Yeast requires sugar and warm water to activate and takes time.
- Bubbles of gas are produced when yeast is activated (carbon dioxide).
- Yeast activity changes when you alter the substances.
- Yeast works better with warm water than boiling or cold water.

REFLECTIONS 5.3: WHAT DO YOU NOW KNOW ABOUT THE SCIENCE OF BREAD MAKING?

Go back to Reflection 5.1 and compare what you wrote with what is described here about science understandings relevant to bread making.

Figure 5.4 The engage phase: engaging students in microbes through making bread in small groups.

Key idea: microbes act as agents of change.

It is possible to control the activities of microbes as well as what they produce. Biotechnology is making use of microbes to help humankind. Biotechnology as a human endeavor is evident through what already exists in our communities, such as bakeries, breweries and dairy-product factories. Knowing about microbes helps us to make informed decisions about the products we buy, as well as supporting our health and wellbeing.

The Australian Curriculum – Science

Contained in the Australian Curriculum – Science is information that explicitly links with learning science through bread making (Table 5.2).

Table 5.2 The Australian Curriculum – Science: Year 6

Strands	Elaborations as examples of what this could mean
Science understanding: biological sciences	
The growth and survival of living things are affected by the physical conditions of their environment (ACSSU094).	• Observing the growth of fungi such as yeast and bread mould in different conditions. • Investigating how changing the physical conditions for plants impacts on their growth and survival such as salt water, use of fertilizers and soil types. • Researching organisms that live in extreme environments such as Antarctica or desert. • Considering the effects of physical conditions causing migration and hibernation.
Science inquiry skills: questioning and predicting	
With guidance, pose questions to clarify practical problems or inform a scientific investigation, and predict what the findings of an investigation might be (ACSIS232).	• Refining questions to enable scientific investigation. • Asking questions to understand the scope or nature of a problem. • Applying experience from previous investigations to predict the outcomes of investigations in new contexts.
Science as a human endeavour	
Important contributions to the advancement of science have been made by people from a range of cultures (ACSHE099).	• Investigating how people from different cultures have used sustainable and local products for bread making. • Learning how Aboriginal and Torres Strait Islander knowledge, such as the medicinal and nutritional properties of Australian plants, is being used as part of the evidence base for scientific advances. • Investigating the development of biotechnology around the world where microbes have been used.

Primary Connections suggests in the *engage phase* that students should experience three activities or learning experiences in order to fully engage them with the topic of bread making and microbes. They are:

Activity 1: Exploring bread.

Activity 2: Examining the bread making process.

Activity 3: Learning about microscopes through finding out about the work of Anton van Leeuwenhoek or how penicillin was discovered and used in society in different countries.

In the example presented in this chapter, the students were involved in the engage phase of the inquiry approach to teaching science, where they explored the bread that was provided. The other experiences suggested by *Primary Connections* arose in the *explore* and *elaborate* phases.

Anton van Leeuwenhoek: www.history-of-the-microscope. org/anton-van-leeuwenhoek-microscope-history.php
Penicillin discovery: http://australia. gov.au/about-australia/ australian-story/ howard-florey

Explore

In the *exploration phase* the students are given opportunities for hands-on experiences in order to invite more questioning, and to begin to think about a range of ways in which they can answer their questions. The idea is that all the students have a common experience to talk about – the students were asked to make their own bread in small groups. The same recipe was provided to all the students. However, the conversations in each group were very different. Different experiences of making bread emerged and distinct sets of questions arose.

In the bread making activity, the students gathered the materials they needed, following the recipe as given, but then had to make decisions about accurate (or not) measurement of ingredients, and when to add the ingredients. In this context, many questions arose about timing, about why particular ingredients were added, such as the salt, and also about the specific techniques being used, particularly in relation to kneading. The questions that arose during bread making were later drawn upon by the students to frame their inquiries.

Some key questions that can be drawn out as the students are engaged in making bread can include knowing about the importance for determining the best temperature to activate the yeast in the dough. What might be the best temperature to make gas bubbles in the bread?

In Figure 5.5 are the details of the instructions and points of observation given to the students for making their own bread. The instructions were put inside a rigid plastic recipe stand. One stand per group was given. This was done to encourage the students to collectively work out how to make the bread. Due to the nature of bread making taking some time, with periods of waiting (i.e. resting time of the dough), the questions embedded in the instructions helped focus the students' attention on points of interest for science learning. The students documented their observations, thinking and questions in a 'thinking book' (see the *Science for Children* website for examples).

Examples of a 'thinking book': www. cambridge. edu.au/ academic/ science

Making bread – sponge and dough method

Step 1: Activation of yeast

Ingredients

220 g flour (can be ordinary plain flour or strong bread flour)

220 ml water (tepid)

10 g compressed yeast (or 20 g dry)

Instructions

Combine the ingredients to form a sponge. Once mixed well, set aside in a warm place and allow to double in volume. Once it starts to collapse it is ready. Once you have mixed everything together – observe what happens.

Questions

Go to the website in the margin box and then answer the following questions.

1   What do you notice?
2   What is happening to the mixture here?
3   What do you think is the role of yeast?

Step 2: Dough

Ingredients

10 g compressed yeast

730 g baker's flour (strong high-protein bread flour)

90 g semolina flour, or just normal plain flour

500 ml water (tepid)

10–20 g salt

Instructions

Dissolve yeast in warm water. Warm the flour slightly first if possible. Place the sponge from Step 1 and the water together with the baker's flour and semolina (or plain flour) and knead gently until all the ingredients are combined. Add the salt and knead for at least 15 minutes, until the gluten has formed and we have a smooth dough (you can take off a piece and smooth it out like a balloon when it is ready). Set aside in a warm place to rise and double in size (about one hour).

Questions

1   What is happening when we knead the dough?
2   Did you know that you are using 'high-protein flour'. Why do you think this matters?
3   What is the role of yeast in this process?

Instructions

Divide and shape (stretch and tuck the dough under to create a smooth tight top to trap the gas and help the bred rise), and place in loaf tin.

What do you notice? How strong and smooth is the gluten? When does it become elastic-like?

Gluten window test: break off a piece and stretch it out to make it thin. Then, hold it up the light. Can you see light through it?

Leave to prove (about 20 minutes).

Question

1 Why do you think this is needed?

Instructions

Bake in a preheated oven, 250 degrees, with tray of water for steam.

Role of yeast in bread baking: www. finecooking. com/articles/ yeast-role-bread-baking. aspx

Figure 5.5 Collectively making bread: instructions and points of interest (front and back of recipe stand).

Figure 5.5 can be found on the *Science for Children* website and can be downloaded and used as a resource.

Figure 5.5: www. cambridge. edu.au/ academic/ science

Primary Connections and many other resources that use bread making for supporting science learning suggest that in the *explore phase* the students should experience three activities or learning experiences in order to have a shared experience of bread making and microbes. *Primary Connections* suggests the following activities:

Inquiry 1: *Using yeast in bread making:* have a shared experience of the yeast micro-organism (what happens when yeast is mixed with other substances, such as sugar and water; setting up a fair test).

Inquiry 2: *Activating yeast:* having a shared experience of yeast micro-organism by testing out the best temperature to activate yeast and make a gas (carbon dioxide).

Inquiry 3: *Using a bread machine and kneading the dough and using an oven:* exploring a range of ways of kneading and preparing the dough and observing the outcomes.

(NB: It was through the process of making bread that the students became curious about not just the process of making bread, but also about the reasons for activating yeast, the need for salt, and many other questions that they later followed up by setting up their own investigations.)

The *exploration phase* is important as it allows all the students to have a common experience on which they can draw later when they discuss their explanations – in the subsequent phases of teaching and learning following an inquiry-based approach.

Primary Connections specifically suggests the experiences shown in column 1 of Tables 5.3–5.5. The tables summarise possible experiences for helping students to think more deeply about microbes during the process of bread making.

Figure 5.7 shows drawings made by students detailing the production of yeast cells, and the stages of formation of gluten visible under a powerful microscope,

Table 5.3 Inquiry 1 to support the achievement standards in the Australian Curriculum – Science: Year 6

Activity 1	Key ideas to draw children's attention to	The science of bread making – science content knowledge
Activating yeast in bread making: have a shared experience of the yeast micro-organism (what happens when yeast is mixed with other substances, such as sugar and water; setting up a fair test).	Set up a set of bottles with a small balloon attached to the top (as shown in Figure 5.6). In each of the three bottles will be the same quantity of yeast. Discuss with the children the need for a fair test. In each of the three bottles include a different substance to mix into the yeast. Label as follows and use warm water, immediately attaching the balloon to seal the bottles: • water and yeast • water, yeast and sugar • yeast and sugar • sugar and water. Swirl the bottles gently and then observe what happens after one hour and again the next day (if possible).	Yeast is used in bread making. As a living micro-organism it needs food and the right temperature to grow. Yeast can be activated by milk or water. Yeast breaks down the sugars for energy, producing carbon dioxide and alcohol as waste products. To break down the starches found in flour, yeast uses an enzyme to turn carbohydrates into sugar. Sugar does not need to be added to the mixture, but if added it can make the activation process faster. When the micro-organism produces waste products (carbon dioxide and alcohol), the carbon dioxide becomes trapped in the dough. During cooking the gas expands, making large spaces in the bread, causing the bread to rise. The alcohol evaporates or is burnt off during cooking.

Table 5.4 Inquiry 2 to support the achievement standards in the Australian Curriculum – Science: Year 6

Activity 2	Key ideas to draw children's attention to	The science of bread making – science content knowledge
Having a shared experience of yeast micro-organism by testing out the best temperature to activate yeast and make a gas (carbon dioxide).	Devise an experiment using bottles, balloons and yeast to test out the effect of the water temperatures on the yeast.	Yeast as a micro-organism grows best at 32 degrees Celsius. This is why the dough is put into a warm place. Hot water is not used, as this kills the micro-organisms. The heat during the cooking process kills the yeast.

Figure 5.6 Rowan's (aged 12) report on what happened. Recording the results of our fair test.

Table 5.5 Inquiry 3 to support the achievement standards in the Australian Curriculum – Science: Year 6

Activity 3: What does the yeast do?	Key ideas or questions to pose	The science of bread making – science content knowledge
Using a bread machine, kneading the dough, and using an oven: exploring a range of ways of kneading and preparing the dough and observing the outcomes.	How could you investigate the role of yeast? Could we make a loaf of bread using yeast and one that does not use yeast? What might be the difference if we use a bread maker or if we prepare the dough by hand? Why might it take three hours for a machine to make a loaf of bread? How does the carbon dioxide (gas) that the yeast makes become trapped in the dough/bread? After making different kinds of bread (with and without yeast) slice the bread and examine the slices. What do you notice?	Leavened bread uses yeast. When yeast and water are combined and flour and salt are added, the enzymes from the yeast begin to break down the carbohydrates in the flour. This process forms sugar and these sugars are used by the micro-organisms as a source of food. Carbon dioxide (and alcohol) is produced as the micro-organisms feed on the sugars. Kneading the dough helps the wheat proteins (glutens) in the dough to join and form long stretchy fibres. These fibres give strength and elasticity to the bread dough. The elasticity of the dough captures the bubbles of carbon dioxide. When this happens the dough is said to 'rise'. Make sure that unbleached flour is used, as this is the only type of flour that can form long fibres and give strength to the dough.

where it was possible to see two proteins of wheat four, glutenin and gliadin. They join together when flour is mixed with water.

James (2013) has argued that much of science has to be imagined rather than seen – as we see in this case example. She suggests that when children draw their understandings it helps them to make sense of the concepts they are exploring. In the research of James (2013), she found that the use of dots in drawings had an important pedagogical role, stating that:

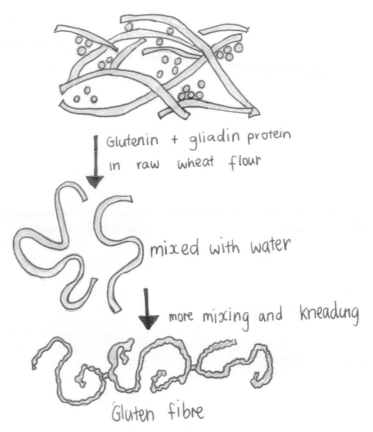

Glutenin + gliadin protein in raw wheat flour

mixed with water

more mixing and kneading

Gluten fibre

Figure 5.7 Freya (aged 12) records what happens: kneading the dough helps the wheat proteins (glutens) in the dough to join and form long stretchy fibres.

The dot is a very powerful visualization tool used in the construction of scientific ideas and theories (p. 209).

Dot drawing enables us to think about the signs stored in the material dimensions and their meaning, by forcing us to attend to the material appearance of the world as the product of the self as creator, the re-constructor of the end products form their constituent materials. Such re-creation is a type of hypothesis making. This is important for science education (p. 205).

In analysing textbooks and other science-related resources, James (2013) notes that the dot supports the reader to visualise what is being presented in the text. It has been used in astronomy to illustrate maps of the night sky, in biology to illustrate cells and other structures, as we also see in Figure 5.8, and in geology for showing composite materials in rocks. James (2013) suggests that dots can also be used as an animation technique. The dots can be used in model making where the dots are animated. For instance, James taught primary aged children how to use a series of sheets of paper, with dots on them that were flicked rapidly to create a sense of dot motion. This technique gave the appearance of a model in motion to illustrate specific concepts that the children were exploring.

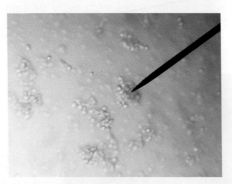

Figure 5.8 Stages in the formation of gluten. Here the Year 6 teacher helps the children to prepare the slide and to set up the microscope.

James has also used this technique to illustrate the beginning, middle and end of a scientific story. For example, in telling the story of pollution, dots were used to represent particles of pollution. James (2013) says, 'Such drawing makes visible that which we often choose to ignore, pollution. Invisible means we can't see it. It does not mean it is not there' (p. 221).

Explain

In the *explain phase* of an inquiry-based approach to teaching science, the teacher supports the children to summarise, represent and explain their observations. The *explain phase* focuses on children discussing their experiences and their observations. Key here is identifying patterns and relationships evident in the observations made. Children use science concepts for explaining the science phenomenon.

It is through both oral and written explanations that teachers can find out about children's thinking, and how they are using science concepts to explain the science phenomenon being explored. However, it is important to keep in mind that children can talk about their ideas better than they can write about their understandings. Giving opportunities to develop both is important for building scientific thinking, and learning how to represent their learning in a scientific manner.

In the 5Es approach for micro-organisms, the explain phase also includes presenting observations and understandings to others orally and in some literary form. If the 5Es approach is used, then the teacher has the opportunity to find out about how students think the yeast micro-organism develops. During the process of explaining their observations a lot can be learned about children's thinking. The children should review their original mind map of what they knew about bread making, and consider their current understandings – has their understanding changed? What new observations and understandings can they add to their mind map or thinking books? Can they give a scientific explanation of bread making?

Some students made *Thinking Books*, pictorially presenting their findings, as shown in Figure 5.9. These formed the foundational knowledge for the role-play.

Figure 5.9 Using *Thinking Books*.

In the example of the student teachers, the students were invited to share what they had learned in a range of ways. Later, the students used their thinking books to present a scientific report of: 'What I now know as a result of studying bread making and yeast micro-organisms', and also to give a creative response, drawing upon the Arts to share imaginative and insightful ways of communicating their findings. Some examples are shown in the photographs throughout this chapter.

Questions that the teacher may ask students in a whole-group session that support the *explain phase* include:

1 What have you observed during the process of bread making/activating yeast/ when using different bread making techniques?
2 What was your observation/investigation about?
3 What do you now understand when you think about yeast as a micro-organism?
4 How does yeast become activated? How do you know?
5 How does yeast grow? How do you know?
6 What do you now know about the gas carbon dioxide and its role in bread making?

It is important for students to initially share their thinking orally. This helps them to focus on what was key to giving them new scientific understandings. As a teacher, you can support students while they are observing, and also after they have made their bread, by drawing out what is key for them to share about their ideas, and then support them to summarise their findings. You could ask them:

1 What is it you now know about yeast that we didn't know before?
2 What is the role of yeast in bread making?
3 What are the steps (procedure) for making bread?

Elaborate

In the *elaborate phase* students plan and implement an investigation that builds upon the new scientific understandings they have acquired through the previous phases of the inquiry-based teaching approach. The reports prepared by students provide opportunities to assess students' learning. In the *elaborate phase* it is possible to further support both the science understandings and the science inquiry skills. In Table 5.6 are summarised all the science inquiry skills that are in the Australian Curriculum – Science, alongside what the teacher may do to develop those particular science inquiry skills.

This phase can also be used for summative assessment to investigate the learning outcomes of the students.

Table 5.6 The Australian Curriculum – Science: Year 6: Science Inquiry Skills

Strands	What the teacher does
Questioning and predicting	
With guidance, pose questions to clarify practical problems or inform a scientific investigation, and predict what the findings of an investigation might be (ACSIS232).	In the elaborate phase the teacher helps the students to refine their questions so that a scientific investigation can be set up. Because the students have already learned a lot in previous phases, then it is becomes important to apply this experience from the previous investigations to predict the outcomes of the investigations in new contexts.
Planning and conducting	
With guidance, plan appropriate investigation methods to answer questions or solve problems (ACSIS103).	The teacher encourages the students to draw upon learning about a fair test, for designing and following a procedure for answering a new question. The teacher discusses with the students what might be the best methods for solving the problem posed or particular question asked.
Decide which variable should be changed and measured in fair tests and accurately observe, measure and record data, using digital technologies as appropriate (ACSIS104).	In the previous phases, the students learned about keeping the amount of yeast constant, in order to undertake a fair test. To develop the students inquiry skills further, the teacher uses familiar units such as grams, seconds and metres and introduces where appropriate the use of standard multipliers such as kilometres and millimetres. The teacher also introduces the idea of an independent variable (even though this terminology is not specifically used) as something that is being investigated by changing it and measuring the effect of this change. Where possible, the teacher also uses digital technologies to make accurate measurements and to record data.
Use equipment and materials safely, identifying potential risks (ACSIS105).	In all instances, the teacher always discusses any potential hazards involved in conducting investigations, so risks can be reduced.
Processing and analysing data and Information	
Construct and use a range of representations, including tables and graphs, to represent and describe observations, patterns or relationships in data using digital technologies as appropriate (ACSIS107).	One of the important processes undertaken with children is the documenting of data gathered from experiments. Here the teacher helps the children to consider a range of ways of representing data. This is important for showing different aspects of a relationship, different processes or new trends or patterns. Digital technologies are useful for showing data and assisting children to analyse the data. Digital technologies are also useful for representing findings and making them interactive.

Strands	What the teacher does
Compare data with predictions and use as evidence in developing explanations (ACSIS221).	When students predict the outcomes of their investigations, the teacher should encourage them to document these predications. Students should be encouraged to share their ideas with others, and to examine if their observations match their predictions. The teacher plays a key role here in discussing the possible reasons for the predictions being incorrect. The teacher should also discuss with the students the difference between data and evidence, and should encourage students to refer to evidence when explaining their outcomes of their investigation.

Figure 5.10 Explaining bread making with new science concepts.

When the students bring their learning together they do so in the form of a scientific report. Some examples are provided in the margin box.

Concept cartoons: http://conceptcartoons.com/what-is-a-concept-cartoon-.html

Scientific report comic strips: http://mrshallfabulousinfourth.blogspot.com.au/2012/10/scientific-method-comic-strips.html

A free template for creating comic strip scientific reports can be found at http://www.teacherspayteachers.com/Product/Comic-Strip-Template-Pages-for-Creative-Assignments-149469

Evaluate

In this final phase of an inquiry-based teaching approach children reflect on their own learning. This is known as the *evaluate phase*. In *Primary Connections*, the children create a literacy-based product as a way of representing their own conceptual learning gained through the *elaborate phase*, where they produced a scientific report.

It is important to ensure that the outcomes of the inquiries relate to the learn-ers' everyday lives in order to encourage engagement in science learning. Working with the students' questions supports this focus – that is, the questions they are answering are meaningful to them, as they wish to know the answers to their ques-tions. In the example of the student teachers, the students shared many cultural home practices that related to the use of microbes through bread making. The idea of having the option of using local and natural products for bread making gave the students new ways of thinking about 'buying bead'. It was through examining closely 'what is in bread' – and what might be the processes that take place during the manufacturing of bread making, such as how bread is kept artificially fresh – that their everyday experiences of buying bread changed. This allows for other questions and ideas to emerge, such as mapping the general health of a commu-nity based on the difference between home-produced and commercially manufac-tured food. Considering these bigger societal issues is important in the evaluation phase. In presenting their ideas and findings, the teacher has the opportunity to support the students to evaluate their own work.

In the Australian Curriculum – Science, students are specifically encouraged to think about a range of approaches for presenting their findings. This is spe-cifically mentioned under *Communication* in the *Science Inquiry Skills* strand. The students are also encouraged to evaluate the methods used, and to reflect on their learning in the strand *Science Inquiry Skills* under *Evaluating*. Table 5.7 sum-marises these.

Table 5.7 The Australian Curriculum – Science: Year 6: Science Inquiry Skills

Evaluating	The role of the teacher
Suggest improvements to the methods used to investigate a question or solve a problem.	At the end of all science inquiries, the teacher should encourage the students to discuss possible improvements to the methods used. Here the focus should be on discussing how these improved methods would increase the quality of the data obtained.
Communicating	
Communicate ideas, explanations and processes in a variety of ways, including multi-modal texts.	The teacher discusses with the students the best way to communicate their science ideas. In particular, the teacher works with the students in thinking through a plan for their text, and what might be the possible modes for effectively communicating their results. For instance, they could prepare reports, explanations, arguments, debates and procedural accounts to communicate science ideas. The teacher should also help children to label diagrams, including cross-sectional representations, in order to communicate ideas and processes within multi-modal texts.

The evaluation phase represents a summative assessment of the students' con-ceptual outcomes. Role-play is one way by which scientific understandings can be demonstrated. For example, one group of student teachers created a story of

Figure 5.11 Using a scripted *role-play* to show the conceptual outcomes.

visiting a bakery, and made cards of the bread making process. Using the cards, they acted out being the micro-organisms. Figure 5.11 shows a group of students role-playing, wanting to make high quality bread rather than buying bread. They presented the question of 'What is in bread' in their role-play. They explored some of the social and health issues associated with wide-scale bread production.

REFLECTIONS 5.4: REFLECT ON AN INQUIRY-BASED APPROACH TO TEACHING SCIENCE

The student teachers who participated in the bread making, and who are illustrated in this chapter, were invited to reflect on their own learning. They were asked:

- How did I learn in this approach?
- What was the role of the teacher?
- How do I feel about this approach to teaching and learning science?
- In this approach, what assumptions are being made about:
  – students' learning
  – the nature of science?

HOW I LEARNED THROUGH THIS APPROACH

- Learning was hands-on and involved actively finding out information for myself.
- Researched my own questions on an interest basis.

- Identified what I already knew.
- Controlled my pathway of learning and tested my own ideas.
- Broke down the topic and focused on a small part in detail.
- Used a wide variety of resources.
- Learning from our peers was very important.
- When resources were used, they were used for a specific purpose.
- Safe environment encouraged us to take risks in our learning.
- Encouraged to reflect on the learning we had achieved.
  Developed a sense of achievement as we learned.

THE ROLE OF THE TEACHER (IN THIS CASE A LECTURER IN THE WORKSHOPS)

- The teacher affirmed students' contributions and accepted their ideas.
- The teacher was a co-learner, who acknowledged the limits to his or her own understandings of the topic.
- The teacher reflected ideas and clarified students' understandings.
- Sometimes the teacher answered students' questions with other questions.
- The teacher added information at appropriate times; that is, it was given in a context of specific learning.
- The teacher selected and provided resources that helped with setting up experiments for answering students' inquiries.
- The teacher was a guide, a non-dominating facilitator.
  Support for students' learning was really important.

What assumptions underpin an inquiry-based approach to teaching science?

The nature of science

This approach to teaching claims that it more effectively reflects the reality of how scientists work than the other approaches. That is, it allows for, and encourages, a diversity of strategies when investigating the world (particularly the elaborate phase). Inquiry-based teaching reflects the multifaceted nature of science and emphasises science as a human endeavour. This approach focuses on the importance of developing science concepts and using the processes of science. It also portrays science as accessible to everybody; we all construct meanings in science, and do this not only in special settings such as laboratories, but throughout our daily lives.

Teaching

This approach has been developed out of the research that has led to a view of learning as constructivist. Inquiry-based teaching in the *engage phase* assumes that children will come to class with understandings of their world and meanings for many words used in science teaching.

It should be noted that constructivist views on how children learn most effectively are not without their critics. There are longstanding concerns about the extent to which constructivism has become undeservedly influential in science education research circles, where it is argued that constuctivism fails to recognise its own epistemological and pedagogical limitations.

Notwithstanding the constructivist roots of the inquiry-based approach and the associated concerns, an inquiry-based approach to teaching science, as exemplified through the 5Es model (Hackling and Prain, 2005), has been positively reviewed (Ergul, Simsekli, Sevgül Calis, Özdilek, Gocmenceleb and Meral Sanli 2011). It was noted by Hackling and Prain (2005) that the science units produced as exemplars of the 5Es model were found to:

- provide a progressive development of science understandings
- allow for the integration of science with literacy learning
- change teacher practices in classrooms so that science was taught in a more practical way
- support more diagnostic assessment of the understandings students brought with them into the classroom
- increase the amount of cooperative work taking place in the classroom when teaching science
- support student development of a wide range of ways of documenting science knowledge, such as drawing, diagrams, graphs, tables and text
- increase the use of digital technologies for data gathering in the classroom during investigations
- increase teacher confidence to teach science
- increase the amount of science being taught
- change teachers' focus from activities and strategies when teaching to student learning.

Children's learning

The construction of knowledge is not typically a solitary activity; the child in the classroom is in a social situation, and ideas are usually negotiated with the teacher and with other students. There is a critical and complex role for the teacher. The intervention of the teacher in the learning process has been on the grounds that meaningful learning occurs when the student meets new knowledge that connects with what they already know. Teacher support is needed, as students may not necessarily make the connections on their own. The 5Es actively support teacher engagement in children's learning. You will remember that this is a criticism of some discovery learning situations (see Chapter 4).

Allowing children to have significant control over the learning process is critical for an inquiry approach to teaching science. Although most of the phases of the 5Es model are organised around what the teacher has planned, the elaborate phase does allow children to generate their own questions based on what they have learned to that point in the sequence of science lessons. However, formulating a question is challenging for learners. This ability of children to ask helpful questions will be discussed further in the next chapter (Chapter 6), where one teacher developed the topic of ants. The children asked many questions, including: 'Why do ants bump into each other?', 'Are ants insects?', 'Why do ants run so quickly?', 'Do ants talk?', 'How many types of ants are there?', 'What do ants eat?'. Our experience, and that of many teachers using the inquiry-based approach, is that the assumption about young children's capability to take control over their learning is well justified. There is research evidence that, when children have that opportunity in science, they prefer learning from their own questions and value learning about other children's questions, as this often challenges them to think about aspects of a topic they have not considered.

An inquiry-based approach to teaching assumes it is important that children have knowledge of their own understanding and learning processes, and that they should be taught to recognise these. Inquiry-based teaching, then, incorporates a metacognitive element where students comment on their own learning. This is especially notable at the beginning and ending of the sequence of phases – that is, 'Before views (engage)' and 'Reflections at the end (evaluate)'. However, the other phases also incorporate levels of metacognition. For instance, exploratory activities also allow more questions and comments to be made (explore); sharing their findings with each other (explain); and elaborations of what they know through further investigations which builds upon their learning (elaborate). In the evaluation of the 5Es model in for teaching science *Primary Connections*, it was found that the students:

- believed they had learned more science
- enjoyed science using this approach
- responded positively to the approach and the activities that had been designed
- had increased their science understandings.

Teacher reports on the level of student outcomes in science showed that more science learning had featured (quantity).

Classroom/centre management in an inquiry-based approach

Teachers who have implemented an inquiry-based approach usually observe high levels of children's interest and commitment when they are allowed to have substantial control over the learning process (see Smith 2013). In the *elaborate phase*, the approach allows for individuality, catering for a wide range of abilities, background experience, prior knowledge and interest – maybe more so than most of the other approaches. Inquiry-based teaching explicitly incorporates these characteristics of children into its planning. It can cater for children regarded as gifted and talented, those with different racial and ethnic backgrounds, and children whose experiences and interests have been influenced by their gender. If the classroom is developed as an authentic community of discourse (Smith 2013), different contributions can be drawn on and celebrated. Sensitive grouping of children will be an important consideration to ensure that all participate effectively in their investigations. If it is considered desirable, some children might work alone for part of their investigation.

It is important to help children in this approach and to introduce them to each phase. Such staging can also help the teacher to develop confidence in the ability to manage the approach (Fittell 2010). Children need to understand and agree to clear ground rules about responsibility for their own learning and to support their peers in this open learning environment.

It is important that the teacher watches out for possible frustration when children are unable to make the progress they desire in constructing answers to their questions. Given the diversity of the work pursued by the children, monitoring of the activities and being available when needed can often place heavy demands on the teacher. Some teachers therefore have older primary students or parents to work with groups and individuals. If you do this, it is essential that you brief those assisting you adequately, so that they appreciate the philosophy behind an inquiry-based approach to teaching and so they have some knowledge base about the topic being investigated. Assistant teachers and parent volunteers should then be able to interact sensitively with the children and support them in their construction of new understandings. Preparing cards with key information on them for the volunteers can help, such as:

- Your role in the *engage phase* is to be with the children to hear about their comments and questions, documenting these for later discussion with the teacher/other children. This is a diagnostic opportunity.
- Your role in the *explore phase* is to help create the hands-on experience for the children, supporting them to undertake the investigation that has been planned by the teacher.
- Your role in the *explain phase* is to help the children to orally share what they have found out, and then to support them with documenting their observations. You can help them to express their understandings scientifically.

- Your role in the *elaborate phase* is to support the children to build upon what they know and to help them form useful questions to investigate. Guide them to make connections from what they now know to a new context. Your role is to help them plan out their investigation. This is a student-planned investigation phase. At this time the students will prepare a scientific report of their student-planned investigation. This is an opportunity for the teacher to find out what they have learned about the topic. Document what they may leave out of their reports, but which you feel they are able to express orally, and share this with the teacher.
- Your role in the *evaluate phase* is to help the children to reflect upon their own learning. It is useful to ask the children to look at what they originally wrote they knew about the topic (or that you documented for them) and compare this with what they now know as a result of their student-planned investigation and the classroom activities planned by the teacher. Be encouraging and praise their reflections on their own learning.

Assessment in an inquiry-based approach

In this approach, assessment needs to be focused on the changes in children's conceptions as an outcome of their learning experiences. This, of course, requires you to assess their preconceptions as well as their later ideas about a topic. The children will also have learned new facts, and possibly enriched their understanding of science as a human endeavour. Children would also have constructed new questions and developed interests in new areas of investigation (especially during the *elaborate phase*). Authentic assessment would examine all of these areas of development and would require an approach that is diverse in its methods. These could include the use of mind maps, word associations, anecdotal records, individual group reports of investigations, and discussions with groups about the learning processes involved. Students are taught to access their own understandings and to analyse the ways in which they are learning, and so self-assessment should be built into the process. It is clear that assessment in inquiry-based teaching is not something simply added on: it is integral to the teaching–learning process itself. The *engage* and *evaluate* phases ensure that the process of assessment is built into an inquiry-based teaching approach.

Table 5.8 Assessment in inquiry-based learning

Phase	Focus	Assessment approach
Engage	By engaging the students in the topic, the children are more likely to express their thinking and ideas.	Diagnostic assessment.
Explore	Hands-on experiences are provided through a teacher-planned activity. Here the children will be working with the materials in groups, talking about what they are doing and what they are noticing. This is a good opportunity to listen in and find out how their thinking is going about the topic.	Formative assessment.
Explain	The children are given time and space to share what they have observed. Here the children are encouraged to explain what they are observing or may have learned scientifically.	Formative assessment.
Elaborate	Students are asked to extend what they have learned to another context, making connections between what they learned and what they want to know more about. Here the students plan their own investigations and try to design useful investigations for answering their questions. They also prepare a scientific report, which is very useful for summative assessment.	Summative assessment of the investigating outcome.
Evaluate	The students represent their understandings in another type of format (e.g. literacy – role-play; digital media project). This gives another way of assessing what they know, as some formats give better possibilities for some children in sharing their conceptual understandings. At this stage the students are also invited to reflect upon their own learning, collecting evidence about achievement of conceptual outcomes.	Summative assessment of conceptual outcomes.

Concerns about the inquiry-based approach

While you might find a number of aspects of the approach attractive, you could also recognise some risks in implementing it. These might include concerns about:

- classroom management
- keeping a focus when activities cannot be planned ahead in complete detail
- knowing when and how to intervene during children's activities
- the time taken to teach a topic using this framework
- the depth and extent of the knowledge needed to guide the children, and
- the approach being challenging to implement in Birth to Preschool period.

These concerns are valid and quite common (Tytler 2007), even among experienced teachers who use an inquiry-based approach (Hackling and Prain 2008). We take up the latter point by illustrating some possibilities in the next section. Touhill (2012) has suggested that child-initiated inquiries are often unpredictable because there is no certainty for the educator about where they might lead, but he argues that this is also part of their success.

Inquiry-based teaching across year levels: Birth to Preschool

REFLECTIONS 5.5

Do you think it is possible to use an inquiry-based approach to teaching in early childhood?
　　What do you think might be the barriers? Record three ideas:
　　Idea 1: ....
　　Idea 2: ....
　　Idea 3: ....

Touhill (2012) clarifies the differences between inquiry-based learning in the context of an early childhood project, and one that is thematic-based project, arguing for the former for supporting science learning. For instance, the inquiry-based project 'involves children investigating a question or problem over a period of time. While a project often starts off with a particular question or area of interest, how it develops is affected by children's changing ideas and responses'(p. 4). However, the theme-based approach is really only 'a central question or idea [which] provides the stimulus for a collection of pre-planned activities or experiences' (p. 4).

Enablers

An inquiry-based approach to teaching science as described in this chapter is more challenging for the Birth to Preschool group, than when used in the Year 3–6 Band. However, some important enablers have been noted.

Responsive teaching: Inquiry-based projects generally develop in relation to things that emerge in the preschool, and which engage the children. Touhill (2012) says that although 'educators plan with experiences and outcomes in mind, the essence of a project is that it is responsive, flexible and open-ended, able to move with the children's ideas and questions as they arise' (p. 4). As in primary school, inquiry-based approaches in early childhood also take on many different forms. For instance, back in 2003 Worth and Grollman developed an inquiry model specifically for teaching science to very young children. The inquiry model captures the following features:

- notice, wonder and explore (this leads to sharing ideas)
- take action, extend questions
- focus observations, raise questions, clarify questions
- engage in more focused explorations:
  - plan, explore, observe investigate
  - collect and record experiences and data
  - think about and organise experiences; look for patterns and relationships
  - try new investigations
- bring together data/ideas and formulate patterns and relationships
- share ideas (this leads back to engaging in more focused explorations).

In their model they advocate for the development of inquiry skills, stating that these skills are fundamental to any science program in early childhood settings. They argue that science learning is enabled through inquiry when teachers:

- help children to notice things in their environment and encourage them to **ask questions** about the objects and events around them
- support young learners to act on their environment in some way by **actively exploring** (Explore) objects, organisms and events using all their senses
- help children to make observations (Explain)
- invite children to compare, to sort, to classify and to **make statements about** the observable characteristics of things (Explain)
- engage (Engage) children in **simple investigations** (Elaborate)
- together with children **document ideas** in a range of ways (Evaluate).

A curriculum that supports science in early childhood: The Early Years Learning Framework also promotes science learning when it states that 'Active involvement in learning builds children's understandings of concepts and the creative thinking and inquiry processes that are necessary for lifelong learning' (DEWR 2009, p. 32). According to Touhill (2012), inquiry-based learning is supported when:

> **Educators see themselves as co-learners, working with children as they learn.**
> When this happens educators feel less focused on transmitting knowledge and are more likely to support and extend children's own attempts at understanding.
> **Children have the time, space and resources to become deeply involved in their investigations.**
> Learning is richer and more effective when it develops over time and when there are opportunities for planning and reflection throughout the experience.
> **The physical environment contains materials and spaces that encourage curiosity, investigation and wonder.**
> Interesting and engaging materials or resources can provide the stimulus for children's questions and investigations. It is also important to ensure that children can access the materials and resources that they need easily and quickly. When this happens, they are able to resource their own learning and to follow their own investigations in whichever direction they lead (p. 4).

What is undersold in the 5Es is the 'connections' between what children do in the Engage, Explore, Explain and Elaborate phases. Rather, the conceptual connections are less pronounced in the model, and could be left to chance.

Barriers

In a review of *Primary Connections* by a national panel of early childhood experts to see if it could be modified to make it suitable for the early childhood period (see Fleer and March 2008). It was noted that educators needed to actively consider adjusting the pedagogy.

It was found that there were five barriers to implementing an inquiry-based approach to teaching science following the 5Es model. They were:

- personal barriers
- interpersonal barriers
- systematic barriers
- design-related barriers
- research-oriented barriers.

Personal barriers: There is evidence that there is a lack of confidence and knowledge about teaching science evident in the early childhood sector. As in other approaches to teaching science, an inquiry-based teaching approach demands a reasonable amount of knowledge of science to support student-generated inquiries in the *elaborate phase*. Even if little science knowledge is known, then it is important for the teachers to feel confident about where they can find the information they need as a background for supporting the young learners.

Interpersonal barriers: It was acknowledged that while very young children may ask many questions generally, it was more challenging to support children to formulate their questions into scientific investigations. That is, the review suggested that a general lack of ability to extend or capitalise on the children's science thinking may need to be considered. In addition, young learners need more active support in developing scientific thinking during hands-on activities. Careful consideration would need to be given to how to move from the exploration phase to the elaborate phase because each child needs a great deal of adult help.

Systematic barriers: There is not a tradition of teaching a lot of science in early childhood settings. A more holistic approach has tended to feature, rather than a discipline-based approach for supporting children's development. Since the review was undertaken, the professional association – Early Childhood Australia – has actively supported environmental and sustainability education. This has resulted in more attention being paid to studying the environment, with more resources available to support early childhood teachers. However, these resources generally discuss the provision of hands-on experiences, and the reasons why it is important to study the environment, but these resources do not necessarily follow an inquiry-based approach to teaching science.

Some interesting examples can be found at:

- Environmental Education in Early Childhood http://www.eeec.org.au
- Education & Communities Sustainability Resources http://www. dec.nsw.gov.au/what-we-offer/regulation-and-accreditation/early-childhood-education-care/useful-links-and-resources/sustainability-resources
- Australian Association for Environmental Education http://www.aaee.org.au/members/special-interest-group-1/

Design-related barriers: The review found that the terminology of *Primary Connections* would be difficult for unqualified educators in the sector. Many educators in early childhood settings have certificates rather than degree qualifications. However, there is a lot of team teaching in early childhood setting, which augers well for working together in creating science programs. With good pedagogical leadership from an experienced educator, better conditions are created for supporting less qualified staff in the teaching of science.

Research-oriented barriers: There is a general lack of research into early childhood science, but particularly for the Birth to three-year-olds. Play-based settings are very different environments from schools. Research undertaken in schools may not necessarily translate into effective pedagogical approaches for using an inquiry-based approach to learning science within a play-based setting.

Focusing on science concepts: Touhill (2012) highlights specifically the importance of deep learning by advocating for an 'Extended learning – more than a one-off' approach in early childhood:

> Learning can be shallow or deep. It can skim the surface of many things or it can engage deeply with a few ideas. Inquiry-based approaches aim to encourage deep learning – learning where children are absorbed and fascinated; learning where children are active and involved; and learning where children make connections and develop significant understandings (p. 2).

A case example follows in the next section.

Infants, toddlers and preschoolers working and playing scientifically: looking inside an early childhood setting

Inquiry-based teaching across year levels: studying living things, a case example of the Birth to Preschool period

Educators from a childcare centre collectively brainstormed how they could prepare a unit of work on living things for the babies' room and also the toddler and preschool room. For the babies the focus was on pets and for the preschoolers it was on the preparation of an environmental impact statement to present to the outdoor playground designers. The content for each of the age periods is shown below in relation to the particular inquiry phase. In Table 5.9 the unit of work for each of the rooms of the childcare centre was in keeping with the National Quality Standard (NQS) (ACECQA 2011), which supports inquiry learning in the following areas:

Quality Area 1: educational program and practice:

Each child's current knowledge, ideas, culture, abilities and interests are the foundation of the program (1.1.2).

Each child's agency is promoted, enabling them to make choices and decisions and influence events and their world (1.1.6).

Educators respond to children's ideas and play and use intentional teaching to scaffold and extend each child's learning (1.2.2).

Organisational structures that will help educators with implementing an inquiry-based approach to teaching science in preschool settings include:

- Create 'wonder charts' (laminated which educators and children add to).
- Predict and report wall charts (make these and model how to use them with children).
- Daily messages (what we are studying; what we found out today).

Conversation starters to support science learning during inquiries:

- Tell me about what you are doing.
- What are you trying to find out?
- What do you think might happen when/if?
- Can you say a bit more about that?
- Do you have a question that you are trying to answer?
- What did you find out?

In Table 5.9 the inquiry program is summarised for infants, toddlers and preschoolers. The programs are framed using the 5Es or phases: engage, explore, explain, elaborate and evaluate.

The questions that the preschool children asked about their pets for their special child-planned investigation were:

- What does it eat?
- Where does it sleep?
- Does it have nap time?
- Does it like to listen to music?
- Where does it go when it is not living here with us?
- Does it have a mummy?
- Does it have a friend?
- What does it like to do?

Table 5.9 Inquiry-based program for supporting infants and toddlers learn about living things

	Infants	Toddlers and preschoolers: children prepare an environmental impact statement
Engage	A family pet is introduced into the infants' room in the childcare centre and the infants observe, feel, smell, and listen to the pet (e.g. dog). The family pet is put into a playpen and the infants are introduced to the pet in a range of ways.	Announcing to the children that the outdoor area is going to be re-developed by playground designers, and the children need to find the living things in the environment so they are not harmed. What might they find? What is living and what is not? How do you know?
Explore	The infants' families bring in pets or other animals from home over a period of time suitable for infant handling or observations (e.g. cat or chicken). The infants with help from the educator take digital photos of the animals, they gather samples of hair/feathers etc., and put them into bags, they help feed and groom the animals. The educator invites the infants to observe how the animals move.	Using magnifying glasses to investigate the outdoor area – using clip boards to document finds. Using digital devices, such as iPads, to take close-up photos of the smallest creatures. Printing the images and studying them.
Explain	The photographs are printed and laminated as the basis of their report. The infants select a photograph, sample of the hair/feather, and photo of the food, and other care products for that animal, and they are put together as a book (report). The adult narrates each page, and the infant points.	Creating a floor map of the outdoor area. On this map the children place cut-outs of the living things they have documented and printed on the iPad. Children explain the finds and the location using the floor map.
Elaborate	The infants experiment with what toys the animals like to play with. Their findings (i.e. the toy being played with) are photographed, printed, laminated and added to their animal report.	Children with the help of the teacher prepare an 'environmental report' for the playground designers. Children prepare questions for the playground designers. Children elaborate on their floor map in relation to a special creature they would like to study. In this study, the children focus on their own questions. Parent support is enlisted, as some reports are prepared with the help of the family at home.

Table 5.9 (*cont.*)

	Infants	Toddlers and preschoolers: children prepare an environmental impact statement
Evaluate	The educator uses the book for storytelling and role-play. The children pretend to be the animal in the book, acting out care and play of the animal – all being narrated by the educator, as the infants move and act out being pets (i.e. mimicking their movements).	The children design costumes and role-play the creatures in their environment. The children act out the characters based on what they have learned from and prepared in their environmental report. The children present their role-play to the families.

Figure 5.12 Silvana smells the flowers and wonders why they smell different to the lavender at her house.

In the next section we examine the topic of living things for the early years of primary school.

Inquiry-based teaching across year levels: studying the organisms in the compost bin, Foundation – Year 2

The children from a local primary school decide to set up a compost bin. All the children contribute to the compost bin by disposing of their lunch and fruit scraps into the compost bin.

The compost bin engages the children in the topic of living things, and a number of questions are asked by the children. They are:

- So what are all those wiggly things? Are they dangerous?
- Why does it smell so much?
- Where did my sandwich go?
- What do the worms do?
- We keep putting things in, but it never gets full. Why?

The children make observations of the compost bin, including taking digital photographs of the inside of the compost bin. The children prepare a scientific report of the life inside the compost bin. The children find YouTube clips on composting. The children elaborate on their understanding by setting up their own child-planned investigations. For instance:

What do I want to know about worms?

- Do worms kiss on the mouth?
- How do worms run?
- Do worms run?
- Are worms babies?
- How do worms cross the street?
- Do mother worms feed their babies?
- How do worms play?
- Do worms fight?
- How do worms talk?

What we learned about worms by observing them.

- Worms feel tickly and soft. They don't bite.
- They look really big when you look at them through the magnifying glass. They get bigger and smaller.
- Worms like to crawl under things like paper and leaves.
- Sometimes when worms get broken, one piece keeps moving.

Table 5.10 Inquiry-based program for supporting children in the early years of school to learn about living things

	Inquiry skills: Foundation	Inquiry skills: Year 1 and 2	Activities
Engage	Questioning and predicting: respond to questions about familiar objects and events.	Questioning and predicting: respond to and pose questions, and make predications about familiar objects and events.	Building a class compost bin. Collecting food scraps from lunch boxes to put into the compost bin.
Explore	Planning and conducting: explore and make observations by using the senses.	Planning and conducting: participate in different types of guided investigations to explore and answer questions. Use informal measurement in the collection and recording of observation, with assistance of digital technologies as appropriate.	Observing the changes to the food scraps put into the compost bin. Gathering samples and putting them under a powerful microscope.
Explain	Processing and analysing data and information: engage in discussions about observations and use methods such as drawing to represent ideas.	Processing and analysing data and information: use a range of methods to sort information, including drawings and provided tables. Through discussion, compare observations with predictions.	Daily drawing and writing about the contents of the compost bin. Drawing the organisms shown under the microscope.
Elaborate	N/A	Evaluating: compare observations with those of others.	Identifying questions (e.g. How do worms move?). Setting up and undertaking investigations to answer questions. Preparing a scientific report to show findings to questions investigated.
Evaluate	Communicating: share observations and ideas.	Communicating: represent and communicate observations and ideas in a variety of ways such as oral and written language drawing, electronic book or role play.	Re-present observations and findings as an electronic book or as a scripted role-play.

My worm report

How do worms move?

They move by stretching. When they stretch they get really long. You can use a stick to measure the worm by checking to see if the worm is as long as the stick.

Links to the National Curriculum – Science: living things have needs, including food and water.

You may have noticed that what was missing from the early childhood inquiries, was 'child planned investigations'. Examples are shown in the next chapter – An inquiry-based approach to *learning*.

REFLECTIONS 5.6: WHAT DO I NOW KNOW ABOUT AN INQUIRY-BASED APPROACH TO TEACHING SCIENCE?

Take a moment to think about all the case examples shared in this chapter and analyse how an inquiry-based approach to teaching science might be useful to you as a teacher of science. Record five key ideas about inquiry-based teaching. You can do this for early childhood or primary contexts.

Idea 1: ....

Idea 2: ....

Idea 3: ....

Idea 4: ....

Idea 5: ....

Summary

Teaching within the framework of inquiry-based approach emphasises the importance of exploring and engaging with children's initial understandings, encouraging them to assume a high level of responsibility for their own learning. Inquiry-based teaching presents many challenges in the early years. It gives a framework for primary teachers to teach science more effectively and generates many positive outcomes for both the children and the teacher. Importantly, inquiry teaching is motivating and can result in deep learning of science concepts and inquiry skills.

References

Alake-Tuenter, E, Biemans, HJA, Tobi, T Mulder, M 2013, 'Inquiry-based science teaching competence of primary school teachers: A Delphi study', *Teaching and Teacher Education*, vol. 35, pp. 13–24.

Australian Academy of Science 2005, *Primary Connections: Linking Science with Literacy. Marvellous micro-organisms. Stage 3. Life and Living.* Canberra: Australian Government.

Australian Children's Education and Care Quality Authority (ACECQA) 2011, *Guide to the National Quality Standard*, Sydney: ACECQA.

Australian Curriculum, Assessment and Reporting Authority 2014, Australian Curriculum – Science. Available at http://www.australiancurriculum.edu.au/Science/Curriculum/F-6. (Accessed September 2014.)

Australian Government Department of Education, Employment and Workplace Relations 2009, *Belonging, Being and Becoming, The Early Years Learning Framework for Australia*, Canberra: Commonwealth Government.

Bandiera, M 2007, 'Micro-organisms: Everyday knowledge predates and contrasts with school knowledge' in R Pinto and D Couso eds, *Contributions from Science Education Research*, Derdrecht: Springer, pp. 213–24.

Ergul, R, Simsekli, Y, Sevgül Calis, S, Özdilek, Z, Gocmenceleb, S, Meral Sanli, M 2011, *Bulgarian Journal of Science and Education Policy (BJSEP)*, vol. 5, no. 1, pp. 48–68.

Fleer, M, March, S 2008, 'An investigation of the feasibility of extending the *Primary Connections* programme to preschool settings', unpublished report to Department of Education, Science and Technology, Canberra.

Fittell, D 2010, 'Inquiry-based science in a primary classroom: Professional development impacting practice', PhD thesis, Queensland University of Technology, Brisbane.

Hackling, M, Prain, V 2008, *Impact of Primary Connections on Students' Science Processes, Literacies of Science and Attitudes Towards Science.* Canberra: Australian Academy of Science.

James, C 2013, 'Dot drawing in science education: Making learning visible' in C Redman ed, *Successful Science Education Practices: Exploring what, why and how they worked*, New York: Nova Science, pp. 203–55.

Smith, P 2013, 'Improving classroom discourse in inquiry-based primary science education', PhD thesis, Edith Cowan University, Perth.

Touhill, L 2012, 'Inquiry-based learning', *National Quality Framework Newsletter*, no. 42, pp. 1–4. http://www.earlychildhoodaustralia.org.au/nqsplp/wp-content/uploads/2012/10/NQS_PLP_E-Newsletter_No45.pdf

Tytler, R 2007, *Review. Re-imagining Science Education. Engaging Students in Science for Australia's Future.* Australian Education Review, Australian Council for Educational Research. Camberwell, Victoria.

Worth, K, Grollman, S 2003, *Worms, Shadows, and Whirlpools: Science in the Early Childhood Classroom*, Portsmouth, NH: Heinemann

Acknowledgement

Special thanks to my colleague Dr Gloria Quinones for providing the infant photo in this chapter.

CHAPTER 6

Inquiry-based approach to learning science

Introduction

In the previous chapter we examined an inquiry-based approach to *teaching science*. However, in this chapter we introduce an inquiry-based approach to *learning in science*. While both chapters focus on inquiries, this chapter moves the focus of attention from mostly teacher-led inquiries where child-initiated inquiries follow (Chapter 5), to a focus on child-led investigations only (this chapter), where the investigable questions are posed about a topic by children as the starting point for learning science. In this latter inquiry approach, the learning is centred directly on the children's questions. The child-designed investigations are used to answer the children's own questions.

Although there are many views about how an inquiry-based approach to learning science may be conceptualised (see Haug and Odegaar 2014), in this chapter it is argued that an inquiry-based approach to learning science captures a common set of principles that:

- position children as active agents in their own learning processes
- ensure that children participate in meaningful, hands-on activities and excursions or field trips
- encourage collaborative learning
- develop child-focused investigations
- utilise the local surroundings and resources in the investigations
- help children to learn how to identify, plan and structure an inquiry.

In this chapter examples of inquiry learning are illustrated initially through the topic of ants, followed by other examples (worms, zoo in my garden) that fall broadly under the popular topic of mini beasts. The Australian Curriculum – Science is featured to show the links between children-led inquiries for learning the science content strand of biological science and the strand science inquiry skills. We have chosen to deliberately feature biological sciences in both Chapters 5 and 6, so that a more nuanced understanding of the relations between inquiry teaching and inquiry learning can be made.

In the next chapter the science content of the physical sciences found in the Australian Curriculum – Science is examined in detail in relation to teaching for conceptual change. As was mentioned in the previous chapter, the three chapters of inquiry teaching (Chapter 5), inquiry learning (Chapter 6) and teaching for conceptual change (Chapter 7) are presented together so that a better critique of the role of the teacher in developing inquiry skills can be undertaken.

Looking inside a classroom

Inquiry context: exploring ants

A multi-age group of children aged 9–11 years are investigating ants. Children are seated around small tables, on the floor or are working at specifically organised workstations. Resources are scattered across an expansive learning space and children are moving between or are located in learning areas (e.g. reading area, green room, theatre space, etc.) (see Figure 6.1). Three teachers and a parent volunteer are working across all the groups of children who are busy with their learning inquiries.

Figure 6.1 Inquiry-based approach to learning science in action.

In one small area of the learning space can be found a display area where examples of children's inquiries at different stages of investigation can be found. Seated around a small table is a group of three children, Jenny, Akrum and Nari. They are discussing what they know about ants. The teacher has positioned herself at eye level with the children and is listening to their discussion. She finds a moment in the discussion, where she will not interrupt their thinking, and asks:

Teacher: So what question are you investigating?

The children who have documented their prior ideas, say 'We think that ants like eating jam and sugar, but we don't know why?'

Teacher: Umm. What makes you think that?

Akrum: Well, this is what we see ants do.

Nari: My mum goes crazy when she sees a line of ants along the wall in the kitchen.

Teacher: Umm. What have you noticed when this happens?

Nari: The ants steal food from the kitchen. I once found an ant in our honey pot.

Children: Oooooooouuuuu, Yuk!!!!

Teacher: What else do you know about ants?

Akrum: We know they bite!

Jenny: I remember an ant bit my foot once.

Teacher: Was that the same kind of ant that you think likes jam and sugar?

Jenny: I don't know.

Akrum: No, I don't think so.

Teacher: What do you think Nari?

Nari: I wrote down on my ant poster 'What do ants eat?'

Teacher: That's a really interesting question, isn't it? That will help you decide if ants really do like jam and sugar, or are attracted to honey.

Jenny: There might be different kinds of ants too?

Teacher: Yes, and they may eat different things.

Jenny: I wonder how many ants there are in the world?

Teacher: That's also an interesting question. Do you think it is related to your first question?

Nari: Yes, we have to find out about the different kinds of ants too. Then we can say what ants like to eat?

Jenny: I think all ants eat jam and sugar. I have seen them doing it.

Nari: No they don't?

Jenny: Yes they do!

Teacher: So Jenny thinks that all ants eat jam and sugar? But Nari doesn't agree. How might you find out for sure?

Jenny: I can follow the ants and see what they do with the sugar that they carry.

Teacher: Umm. That is one important way. What is another way you might find out the answer to your question?

Jenny: We could give them different kinds of food and see which food they will eat.

The children begin discussing how they will go about their investigations, and brainstorm a number of ideas, including using the internet, going to the library and ringing up a scientist from CSIRO (www.csiro.au). The teacher then draws their attention back to Jenny's observations at home, and asks them about if they think there might also be ants in their playground to observe?

Teacher: Earlier, Jenny made some suggestions about carrying out an experiment to find out what ants eat.

Nari: I know, let's put different types of food out to see what they like.

Teacher: What kind of food do you think you could put out for them?

Akrum: Honey.

Nari: Lollies.

Akrum: But also we can find some bread and make some crumbs for them.

Teacher: Can you think of a way of conducting a fair test so you feel confident you know which food they really like?

The children and the teacher discuss their ideas further in the context of a fair test. The children turn their attentions to their ant posters and write down their questions on the ant poster (see Figure 6.2), and continue discussing how they might answer their questions.

The teacher wrote in her evaluation at the end of the unit on ants the following:

One of the groups of children had accumulated 'food' to see what the ants would eat. These were cake crumbs, honey, jam, bread, biscuit crumbs, lollies and fruit. The children took the goodies outside and placed them strategically around the nests, and then waited and watched. They returned disappointed that the ants had appeared uninterested in the introduced food. One girl said, 'The only thing they liked was my shoe'. This set the group to discussing exactly what ants ate, and how they could find this information.

Figure 6.2 Our ant inquiries – What do ants like to eat?

REFLECTIONS 6.1: AN INQUIRY-BASED APPROACH FOR LEARNING ABOUT THE TOPIC OF 'ANTS'

Consider what happened in this group.

Record what you think was being done in this situation by:

- the teacher, and
- the children.

What were the positive aspects of the teaching and learning?

What were the negative aspects of the teaching and learning?

In this inquiry-based approach to learning about ants there is a great deal of discussion among the children about their questions. The children generate a lot of ideas that they could explore. With the support of the teacher, they tease out and record their inquiry question. They also discuss how they might answer their inquiry question. In examining this extract, we gain a sense that the interactions between the children are dynamic and we do not always know where things might move to next. There is an important discussion among the group of children attempting to clarify what ants might eat and if all ants eat the same food – although it is the teacher who guides them in this direction. This discussion is important for the children when later reflecting on why their initial assumption proved to be unhelpful – that is, their initial belief that all ants will eat jam and sugar – which they found did not hold true for the ants they were investigating. The children were drawing upon existing observations of ants they had watched in their homes.

The teacher plays an important role in guiding the children in several ways – supporting the development of their ideas, raising new questions, and suggesting ways they might explore initial answers and develop new questions. Siry (2013) has argued that 'pedagogical approaches can position children as experts on their experiences so that we can facilitate children's sense of ownership in the process of learning science' (p. 4).

Your own reflections on what the teacher said and did might cause you to think that the teacher is not providing enough guidance. Should the teacher have told them the answer or tried harder to unpack the assumptions they held about ants? It is argued in an inquiry-based approach to learning science that it is the children's question that builds the inquiry. Siry (2013) has argued that in primary schools and in early childhood settings teachers need to value the 'science knowledges and questions that the children bring to their school science investigations' (p. 16). In this example, the children were able to re-think their assumptions about ants in a really meaningful way to them, and this gave the possibility for them to genuinely move forward in their thinking. That is, the children eventually asked new scientific questions that led to a deeper knowledge of ants. Samarapungavan, Patrick and Mantzicopoulos (2011) in their review of the expansive literature on inquiry approaches noted that 'adopting more authentic inquiry-based pedagogies will lead to deeper conceptual understanding as well as a greater awareness of the nature of science and of the processes of scientific inquiry among students' (p. 416).

An experience of an inquiry-based approach to learning

The challenge in Reflections 6.2 has been provided so that you can experience, as a learner, an inquiry-based approach to learning. The focus is on ants, but if you think it is going to be difficult for you to collect live specimens, then other small animals (e.g. earthworms, slaters [woodlouse] or snails) could substitute for the topic. These all fall under the broader common and popular topic of mini beasts (see a range of work samples from children in the latter part of this chapter).

REFLECTIONS 6.2: INQUIRY-BASED APPROACH TO LEARNING

CREATING THE INQUIRY CONTEXT: ANTS

We are going to explore those amazing creatures called ants. Undertake the following activity and gather data on your own experiences of this activity or the experiences you have doing this activity with a group of children.

Before we begin, record what you already know about ants. Draw a concept map, with the word 'ants' in the middle, and then link it to your ideas and knowledge about ants, feelings you have about ants and incidents you have had with ants. Think freely and laterally; any thoughts that come into your head that have a connection to ants should go onto your concept map. Now draw an ant, labelling any parts you know. No looking in books or at the real thing yet!

Through these activities you should have found that you already know quite a bit about ants and that they feature in your life to some extent (maybe quite a lot). There might also be areas in which you are not too sure, and that is fine at this stage, because we are going to learn more about these interesting insects.

Now collect three or four live ants (if you can) of the same type. Place them in a glass or plastic jar with clear walls so that you have a good view of them. A magnifying glass might also be helpful.

1   Observe what the ants do as individuals and as a group.
2   Introduce some food and a small container of water and see what happens.
3   Put some sandy soil (say 2–3 cm) into the container and leave it for a while, then observe the ants.
4   Observe them discreetly at night after you have left them in the dark for a few hours.

After doing these activities, and from all that you already know about ants, you probably have quite a few questions. *What would you like to know about ants?* Write out a list of questions you have about ants and for which you would like the answers.

If possible, share your questions with another person who has carried out these activities. Then aim to agree on three or four questions for further investigation from your lists that you will work on together. Try to ensure that your questions are the kind that you can readily investigate. Rule out questions that require elaborate equipment or that would be very time-consuming. Focus on your questions, either by yourself or, preferably, with a partner. Consider how you might find answers to your questions.

Develop a range of strategies and write them down. Attempt to ensure that, for the investigations you have chosen, you use several different strategies.

For instance, do not depend on books or the internet to answer all of your questions, and ensure that at least one of your investigations involves working with the ants you have collected. (There may be some interesting possibilities if the ants you and your partner have collected are different types.)

Plan your investigations together (or by yourself if you are not working with a partner). While you might decide to divide the work, make sure that a good proportion of it is done together – especially the direct work with the ants.

Before you begin each investigation it is helpful to record your initial ideas about a possible answer(s). Record what you do to find answers. Your record should be fairly comprehensive and clearly structured. The following is a useful recording format to try out. (It is a format used successfully by children in schools.)

AN INQUIRY ABOUT ANTS

My question is …

I think the answer might be …

In order to find the answer I …

What I found out was …

I do not fully understand …

Questions that I now have are …

Repeat the planning and recording process for each of your questions. You might find that different formats are a good idea for different investigations. Attempt to use some creative means of reporting. If possible, report on your investigations to a group of interested others.

The final task is to return to your original concept map and drawing of an ant. You should add to your concept map (in a different colour) the ideas you now have about ants. Consider also your original drawing: draw alongside it your picture of an ant and label it with what you now know about an ant's features. *How do the two pictures differ?* Think about how much you have learned about ants through these activities. Consider how you learned what you now know about ants. *Have you new questions you would like to pursue?*

When you have completed your investigations and reporting, return the ants to where you found them, as we should not disturb the environment unnecessarily – this is acting responsibly as we work scientifically.

Personally experiencing an inquiry-based approach is important for knowing how it feels to be a learner of science where you investigate things that matter to you. You may not have had an opportunity to learn in this way previously. It also gives you an experiential base from which to evaluate the approach, and to make comparisons with the other approaches that are detailed in this book.

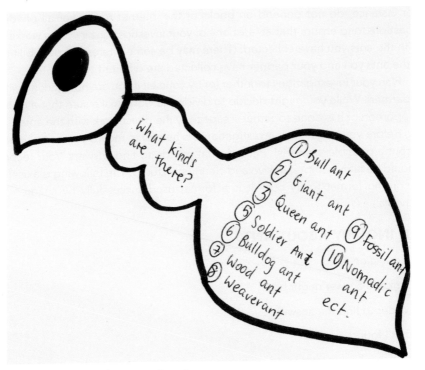

Figure 6.3 What kinds of ants are there?

REFLECTIONS 6.3: AN INQUIRY-BASED APPROACH TO LEARNING

CAMBRIDGE
DYNAMIC
SCIENCE

Year 7,
Module 1,
Unit 1–5

Now that you have experience of an inquiry-based approach to learning or have recorded observations of your own lessons about ants (or other mini beast topics) with a group of children, consider the following questions.

1   *How did I learn in this approach?*
2   *What was the role of the teacher (in this case, the authors of the book)?*
3   *How do I feel about this approach to teaching and learning in science?*
4   *In this approach, what assumptions are being made about:*

- *Children's learning?*
- *The nature of science?*

Discuss and compare your analysis with others who have completed this experience.

Note that while the example of an inquiry-based approach to learning considered so far in this chapter focused on the strand of Biological Sciences, the approach can be used for all the content strands in the Australian Curriculum – Science. For instance, some student teachers have developed and taught very effective programs with 'bicycles' as the theme. Everyday technology was used as the context for investigations in science of such concepts as energy, materials, forces and motion. Other examples of an inquiry-based approach to learning across the content strands of the curriculum can also be found in the next chapter, Chapter 7: Teaching and learning for conceptual change.

So what have I learned?

- *That it is very important for science activities to be student centred.*
- *Children have a great deal of prior knowledge.*
- *Use the children's prior knowledge to build your lessons.*
- *Children love to investigate and explore.*
- *Learning occurs when children are actively engaged with an activity.*
- *Children learn well when there is a visual stimulus.*

Figure 6.4 What I learned about an inquiry-based approach to learning: student–teacher reflections.

Samarapungavan, Patrick and Mantzicopoulos (2011) have argued that an inquiry-based approach to learning science increases children's learning and interest in a broad range of topics in science. In particular they note that children 'enjoy science and feel efficacious about engaging with the content and processes of doing science' (p. 417). However, what is significant to the success of inquiry-based approaches is the role the teacher takes when interacting with and talking to children (Haug and Odegaard 2014).

Haug and Odegaard (2014) followed two teachers as they used an inquiry-based approach to learning and noted that learning of science was deepened when children were given the possibility to talk about their ideas, and when the teacher actively used children's prior ideas and questions to support conceptual learning in science. They state:

> Our results suggest that conceptual learning occurs when students are required to apply key concepts in their talk throughout all phases of the inquiry, with the teacher closely scaffolding the students' use of language. In contrast, conceptual understanding is not promoted when teachers do the talking, rephrase students responses into the correct answer, or fail to address students' everyday perceptions of scientific phenomena (p. 797).

We can learn a lot about how to organise an inquiry-based approach when we examine the research literature. However, it should be kept in mind that there are many different interpretations of what is an inquiry-based approach.

REFLECTIONS 6.4: CRITIQUING THE DIVERSITY OF THINKING ABOUT INQUIRY-BASED LEARNING OF SCIENCE

Below are a number of ways of conceptualising an inquiry-based approach to learning science. They are provided to give you a sense of the diversity, and to give you the opportunity to critique the range. Examine two examples and reflect upon:

1   How are the children positioned? Are they active agents in their own learning processes?
2   Is the children's participation meaningful? Does it include hands-on activities? Are there possibilities for working outside and for going on field trips or excursions?
3   Are the children encouraged to collaborate with others in learning the topics?
4   Do the experiences genuinely develop child-focused investigations?
5   Have the children been encouraged to draw upon the local surroundings as resources for their investigations?
6   Do the children learn how to identify, plan and structure their own inquiries?

Example 1: In line with the introduction to this chapter and the previous one, there are many conceptions of inquiry-based approaches. Bianchi and Colburn (2000) argued that inquiry-based approaches to learning could be conceptualised as:

For further details and types of inquiries see http://www.ubclts.com/docs/Inquiry_Primer.pdf

- structured inquiry
- guided inquiry
- open inquiry.

These three categories can be summarised as follows:

Structured inquiry: In a structured approach to inquiry learning it is the teacher who sets up a common inquiry for the children. The children are given hands-on experiences by the teacher, and it is for the children to determine the relationship between variables and to make sense of the data.

Guided inquiry: In this inquiry approach to learning, the teacher sets up the problem that the children investigate. The teacher also provides the resources. It is the children who devise the procedure for their inquiry.

Open inquiry: An open inquiry approach to learning science is child-centred and driven. In an open inquiry approach it is the children who formulate the problems. An example of an open inquiry is a science fair.

Which of these fits best with an inquiry-based approach to learning as described in this chapter? Why?

My response:

_____

Example 2: 'Concepts to classroom' is presented by Thirteen Ed Online. They ask what do inquiry-based lesson plans look like. Do they fit with an inquiry-based approach to learning as described in this chapter? Why/Why not?

My response:

_____

Example 3: Project Butterfly WINGS is a comprehensive STEM program designed for preschool aged children. Does this program fit with an inquiry-based approach to learning as described in this chapter? Why/Why not?

My response:

_____

Example 4: On this website by Annenberg learner, teacher resources and professional development that features learning across the curriculum are given. Do these resources fit with an inquiry-based approach to learning as described in this chapter? Why/Why not?

My response:

_____

Share your findings with another person or your group. Discuss what was central to an inquiry-based approach. Samarapungavan, Patrick and Mantzicopoulos (2011) state that in an inquiry-based approach 'children ask meaningful questions, make predications about outcomes, observe and record evidence, revise and represent their knowledge and communicate their findings' (p. 417). Did this come through in the examples your critiqued?

Concepts to classroom: http://www.thirteen.org/edonline/concept2class/inquiry/demo_sub1.html

Project Butterfly WINGS: https://www.flmnh.ufl.edu/wings/Doc/WINGS_scientific_inquiry.pdf

Annenberg learner: http://www.learner.org/workshops/inquiry/resources/faq.html

More about what I've learnt

- *It is important to try and make the topic relevant – for example pick up on popular culture, such as Harry Potter or Nemo (even if they are no longer showing in cinemas, children are still viewing DVDs).*
- *Listen to the children – they love to share their knowledge. Listening makes us better educators.*

Figure 6.5 Student–teacher reflections: critiquing the diversity of thinking about inquiry-based learning of science.

A final thought ...

Children's thinking seemed to depend on their prior knowledge, their experience and their surroundings. It was from these facts that they drew their conclusions. Children's thinking also depends on other ideas and knowledge because generally it is a conversation that really gets their minds working!

Figure 6.6 What children already know is foundational for planning for their learning.

These final reflections shown in Figure 6.6 by a student teacher on children's thinking have also been noted in research by Siry (2013) into preschool and primary aged children. She stated that in her research 'Children revealed their ways of knowing as individual and collective. I suggest that science as culture emerged from this dialectic relationship, as children engaged with their own investigations and created new ones with others through dialogue and exchange' (p. 19). Do you agree with this statement by Siry? Why/why not?

After critiquing the examples of existing resources or conceptualisations of an inquiry-based approach to learning, you will be in a good position to think about preparing your own lesson plans or full program for a unit of work using an inquiry-based approach to learning. In Planning Section 6.1 is an example of planning for two lesson for an inquiry-based approach to learning. A quick overview is given. In Planning Section 6.2 we return to the original example introduced at the beginning of this chapter. This is a more detailed example of the planning and thinking done for a whole group when using an inquiry-based approach to learning. As you read, reflect on the different pedagogical strategies used between 6.1 Planning and 6.2 Planning.

6.1 Planning two lessons: an overview of an inquiry-based approach to learning with a small group of children

Below is a framework to support you with planning for facilitating children's investigations of ants over two lessons. It follows the same format as we introduced you to at the beginning of this chapter.

Preparation: Select the topic and find background information for your own use.
Before views: The children record what they already know about ants.
Draw a concept map with ants in the middle.
The children draw an ant, labelling the parts they know about.

Exploratory activities: The children (with the teacher) collect three or four live ants of the same type.

Put the ants in a glass or plastic jar.

Provide some food and water and see what happens. Magnifying glass can be used.

Put some sandy soil into the container and observe what happens.

Children's questions: The children write a list of questions they have about ants and for which they would like the answers. The children choose three or four main questions that they would like to investigate. Have them consider how they might find answers to their questions. Different members of the group can focus on specific questions, or all can focus on a question they agree upon.

Investigations: Before they begin their investigation, the children record initial ideas about possible answers. A format example is shown on page 155 (an inquiry about ants).

The children report on their investigations to the rest of the group.

After views: Return to the original concept map and drawing of an ant. The children can add their new ideas in a different colour.

Reflection: The children can think about how they have learned about ants through these activities.

Do the children have any new questions they would like to pursue?

6.2 Planning a sequence of lessons – an inquiry-based approach to learning with the whole class

Teacher diary

Authentic context for building an inquiry-based approach to learning about ants

Ants as a topic for a science investigation came about by chance. We were sitting in the library on the carpet looking at books, when a commotion arose, as one ant had found its way onto one of the children's legs. The child jumped up and down, calling out to the other children that he was 'being attacked by an ant!'

To restore order, the ant was removed (via a piece of paper) and put outside into the school garden. Then it began … question after question. Seizing the moment, the questions were recorded on the library interactive white board. The whole group discussed what they knew about ants. The children's knowledge of where ants could be found in the school grounds was astonishing – this led to a walk around the school grounds, as the children showed me the ant nests. This constituted lesson one – a genuine inquiry for learning science had begun. As a group we agreed that it was important to study ants, and that this would be the very next lesson!

What came to mind from the Australian Curriculum – Science was **Questioning and predicting:** 'With guidance, identify questions in familiar contexts that can be investigated scientifically and predict what might happen based on prior knowledge'. The Year 4 children were right in this zone. However, I wanted to also make sure that the Year 5 and 6 children were also stretched further, so that I needed to help the Year 5 children to 'pose questions to clarify practical problems' and the Year 6 children to 'predict what the findings of an investigation might be'.

These latter points are detailed in content strand of the biological science for Year 5s and Year 6s.

Before views

What we know about ants:

- they bite
- they are small
- they have more than two legs – some think they have six, others think they have eight
- an ant is an insect
- they live outside in the ground, but we can see them walking around
- they make holes
- they like to eat jam and sugar.

Exploratory activities

The children were full of enthusiasm for investigating ants – lesson two. The children guided me around the school grounds again to six different ant nests, one of which appeared to be deserted. We spent the whole lesson observing the ants, following them as they moved to and fro. We looked closely at the cone of sand that was made at the entrance to their nests.

One group of children rushed back to the classroom and collected pencils and clip boards and began to map all the nests within the school grounds. Another group of children went to the library and began searching for books on ants. A third group headed to the digital tablets and began documenting the ant activities in photo form and video form. A fourth group decided to make a digital animation for their 'ants project'.

As the children worked in their small groups, I found I needed to draw out specific inquiry skills. For instance, with the Year 4 children I helped the them to 'suggest ways to plan and conduct investigations to find answers to questions', with the Year 5 and 6 children I supported them to think about how to 'plan appropriate investigation methods to answer questions or solve problems'. These came directly from the Australian Curriculum – Science.

Children's questions

The children worked in groups (library group, interactive white board group, the observers of the ant nests, the mapping group, the digital recording group, etc.) and discussed what they specifically wanted to investigate. The inquiries developed as the children and teachers continued to discuss what they knew and what they wanted to know more about.

The children also discussed how they might present their inquiries to the rest of the school. One of the children drew a picture of an ant, and this image was made into a basic proforma for documenting the children's work. Figure 6.2 and Figure 6.3 show an example of the proforma of an ant that was populated with the children's inquiry questions and a summary of their findings. A further example of other questions and findings is shown in Figure 6.8 as a standard report.

Question: Do ants communicate?

My report: They communicate by rubbing their feelers together.

Figure 6.7 Our questions (and what we found out about ants).

What the children wanted to investigate about ants:

- How do ants communicate?
- Do ants kill their queen?
- How fast can ants travel?
- Do ants sleep?
- How many rooms are there in an ant nest?
- How long do ants live?
- How many ants live in the world?
- How many eggs does a queen bee lay at one time?
- Do ants have a brain?
- What do ant eggs look like?
- Why do ants bite?
- Do ants have teeth?
- Why can't ants swim?
- Do ants have enemies?
- How long does it take to build an ant nest?
- Are ants social insects?

Investigations

One group made a model – an ant nest, the different types of ants (queen bee, worker bee, drone) and the eggs.

Another group created a digital portfolio of the ant activities they had observed. This was turned into a YouTube video and shared with the families.

The third group prepared a display of their map of the school grounds, and explained the features of the yard, the directions the ants were travelling and showed how the ant nests changed.

A fourth group prepared a tunnel of the ants nests. They used the completed ant proformas to display the inquiry questions and findings.

The fifth group prepared a cut out of an ant colony and created an animation on the digital devices we had in the school.

During the children's investigations I focused on supporting them in two distinct ways in order to help them develop inquiry-based skills as outlined in the Australian Curriculum – Science. First, I focused on 'safety' as they worked, and second I concentrated on supporting them to represent their findings in a range of ways.

Specifically for the Year 4 children I considered how to encourage them to: 'Safely use appropriate materials, tools or equipment to make and record observations, using formal measurements and digital technologies as appropriate'; for the Year 5 children to also use the equipment safely, but to especially pay attention to 'identifying potential risks' in advance of using the equipment. This was important for the group working on model making, as they used a range of equipment, such as hot glue guns and Stanley knives. I assumed the Year 6 children could already do this, but kept an eye on their use of equipment.

Processing and analysing data and information: Here I specifically focused the Year 4 children's attention on using 'a range of methods including tables and simple column graphs to represent data and to identify patterns and trends'. I also asked them to make and then compare their 'results with predictions, suggesting possible reasons for findings'. This was important for the children who were seeking to find out if the ants ate sugar and jam. Because some Year 5 children were working with the Year 4 children, I had to also make sure I stretched some of the Year 5 children as they worked in their groups. For instance, I invited them to take a lead in considering the range of ways they could construct and make 'representations, including tables and graphs, to represent and describe observations, patterns or relationships in data using digital technologies'. In this context I also invited the Year 5 children along with the others to compare 'data with predictions' but I specifically drew out the skill of 'using this as evidence in developing their explanations' Of course, the Year 6 children were asked 'to represent and describe observations, patterns or relationships in data using digital technologies'. In this way the inquiry skills were being developed across the year levels as presented in the Australian Curriculum – Science, but in ways that drew out specific characteristics for Year 4, 5 and 6 children who made up my multiage class.

After views

The children found:

- ants like to eat plants, other insects, dead insects, and mould
- ants have teeth-like bumps on their jaws
- ants live all over the world and there are many types
- worker ants live two to four years but some ants live 18 years
- ant eggs are oval in shape and white
- ants are social insects, they live in big groups and share jobs
- don't stomp on an ant hole as it is the top of an ant nest, it's their door, and they won't be able to get out
- ants can communicate with each other.

The children created a book on 'What we found out about ants'.

Ants feel things with their feelers and smell with their feelers. Ants also use their feelers to communicate. An ant will often stroke the face of another ant with its feelers and legs. That is the way an ant says 'Give me some of your food'. Then the other ant will give it a drop of food. Sometimes an ant finds a piece of food that is too big to carry. Then the ant gets excited and runs back to its nest. On the way, it stops many times. It presses its body against the ground and leaves some smelly stuff. When the ant gets back to its nest, the other ants follow the smelly trail and find the food.

Figure 6.8 What we found out about ants.

Evaluating and communicating: In reflecting on what the children were to present, I worked closely with them to support them in evaluating and communicating – as detailed in the Australian Curriculum – Science. Specifically, I invited the Year 4 children to 'Reflect on the investigation, including whether a test was fair or not'. This proved to be quite challenging, as the children (and I) were captivated by the insects, and had to keep reminding ourselves to gather evidence in a systematic way. The group who examined if ants eat jam and sugar had to refine their method significantly if they were to investigate their question robustly. This was important for the Year 5 and 6 children who develop their inquiry skills so that they can 'Suggest improvements to the methods used to investigate a question or solve a problem', as is outlined in the Australian Curriculum – Science.

Communicating

According to the Australian Curriculum – Science, the Year 4 children need to 'Represent and communicate ideas and findings in a variety of ways such as diagrams, physical representations and simple reports'. The reports produced by the children (see example in Figure 6.8) were simple and brief, but in future report writing I would focus more on engaging with more detail and might show a range of formats for the children to consider. Most successful were the children's detailed diagrams and models of the ant colony. Here the children spent considerable time accurately representing their learning, using labelling techniques effectively. The Year 5 and 6 students did produce more developed reports, as would be expected, but they specifically communicated their results 'through a range of multi-modal texts' where the digital devices gave different possibilities for making physical models. The digital animations and the video documentary proved to be engaging ways of reporting their investigations.

As part of researching the details of the content knowledge for this inquiry-based approach to learning biological sciences for this unit on ants, the following was researched (see Table 6.1).

Please note: The information represented in Table 6.1 is not what is taught to children; rather, the content is important background scientific information for supporting the teacher. Knowing key concepts about the biological sciences that frame what is discussed for Year 4, 5 and 6 helps when planning and interacting with children during investigations, but also when shaping up findings for presentation in reports, displays, electronic portfolios and other multi-modal forms. Research has consistently shown that having access to or knowing about the concepts is important for teachers when using an inquiry-based approach to learning science (or other approaches) (see Alake-Tuenter, Biemans, Tobi and Mulder 2013).

Table 6.1 Important background content knowledge for the teacher

Year 4	Year 5	Year 6
Science understanding: Biological Sciences (Australian Curriculum – Science)		
Living things have life cycles. Living things, including plants and animals, depend on each other and the environment to survive.	Living things have structural features and adaptations that help them to survive in their environment.	The growth and survival of living things are affected by the physical conditions of their environment.
Children's everyday concepts (sometimes called alternative views or children's science)		
Living and non-living		
Young children associate living with movement. If it moves, it is alive. For example, clouds, fire and a bicycle are thought to be living because they move.	Older children think that if something moves by itself it must be living. Some children use just the criterion of breathing as evidence that something is alive.	Much older children do not tend to think about plants as living. They also have difficulties with conceptualising seeds and eggs as living. Similarly, dormant trees and plants are though to be non-living.

Year 4	Year 5	Year 6
Diversity and classification		
Very young children do not think about animals and plants as broad categories for systematically organising living things. Mostly children draw upon one visible characteristic at a time, such as it has hair, or it is green. Children do not think of themselves as animals.	Young children generally do not use terms such as insects, fish, mammals, birds, amphibians, moss or fungi as scientific terms. They tend to think of these as alternatives to the term 'plants' or 'animals'. They do not necessarily think of them as sub-sets of animals or plants.	
Cells		
Older children generally confuse the terms cell and molecules. They tend to think that a cell represents the smallest unit in the body.		
Adaptation		
Children mostly relate the form and function of the biological structure of an organism to themselves (egocentrism), sometimes even giving human characteristics to other animals (anthropocentrism). They will also look at form and function in relation to aesthetic values, such as a how pretty a flower looks, or consider it in relation to personal function, such as meat is a food for eating, or a tree gives you shade or is used to build a house.	Adaptation is usually personalised to an individual organism and not generally thought about in terms of a whole species.	Children do not think about the genetic basis for the categorisation of species. Children do not think about time as an important dimension in the adaptation of species. Some understandings of evolution are understood, but not usually the time scale involved.
Scientific concepts (also known as Western science)		
Living and non-living		
Living things is a term used to cluster together organisms that perform the basic life processes, such as respiration, excretion, nutrition, movement, sensitivity, growth and reproduction.	Non-living may appear similar to living things, but do not perform all the basic life processes.	Living things are composed of cells.
Cells		
Living things have tissues and organs, such as blood, bone, heart, leaves, wood, etc.	Living things are made up of many cells. But some organisms are made up of only one cell (e.g single amoeba). A cell is the basic unit of life. It performs all the life processes. Life processes depend upon the chemical interaction that takes place in the substances of the living cell.	The cells in living things are mostly not alike. The cells carry out different functions. Cells that are similar are grouped together to form a tissue. The tissue has a particular function. Tissues are grouped together to form an organ. An organ works together as a system in the organism. Cells contain genetic material. All cells come from pre-existing cells.

Table 6.1 (cont.)

Year 4	Year 5	Year 6
Diversity and classification All living things are classified. In Western science, two sets are evident – plants and animals.	Living things can be grouped together in different ways for different purposes, such as their relationship. The term animal is used to classify living things which consume other animals or plants. The word plant is used to classify all living things which contain chlorophyll and which make their own food.	Some of the smaller sets of living things do not fit this classification, such as microbes (see Chapter 5). Humans are animals.
Adaptation Animals respond quickly to their environment. Most animals can move about (e.g. sea sponges are animals and mostly cannot move). Plants are slow to respond. They are mostly rooted in the ground. Growth is a form of plant movement.	*Adaptation can mean the structure is suited to perform its function*, such as how particular beak shapes are suited well for cracking particular seeds and nuts by birds. Adaptation can also feature the whole organism or the survival of a species in its environment. *Adaptation can also mean the process of change.* This is where the whole species or individual becomes adapted to the new conditions. This can be temporary or permanent. An example of temporary change is when some characteristic is not passed on to the next generation, such as when humans who live in high-altitude conditions have increased red blood cell counts. Another example is the development of large, thin leaves by a tree, as a result of growing in the shade.	Adaptation to an environment is when a species is well suited to its surroundings. Natural selection – this usually means that the species' variety of genetic variation is suited to dealing with changes in the conditions of the environment. Those that survive will reproduce more offspring, resulting in more of the species with the new characteristics. In time, the species with the new characteristics will then dominate and survive. Changes in species over generations, occurs as a result of natural selection. Changes to the Earth have taken place over thousands of millions of years and in this context species have evolved. Extinction occurs when a particular species is unable to survive in a new environment.

REFLECTIONS 6.5: PLANNING AN INQUIRY-BASED LESSON

In reflecting on the different pedagogical strategies used between 6.1 Planning and 6.2 Planning what did you notice? Record your ideas:

Pedagogical approaches that are the same.
Pedagogical approaches that are different.

Working with multi-age groups: drawing on the Australian Curriculum – Science

Table 6.2 shows the progression of content that the teacher who set up the inquiry on ants needed to consider when working with her multi-age group of children. As a teacher, you are likely to have more than one age group in your class at some stage in your career. Table 6.2 shows the broad range of concepts that a teacher may have to work with in his or her classroom.

Table 6.2 The Australian Curriculum – Science: Year 6

Year 6	Year 5	Year 4
Science understanding: Biological Sciences		
The growth and survival of living things are affected by the physical conditions of their environment).	Living things have structural features and adaptations that help them to survive in their environment.	Living things have life cycles. Living things, including plants and animals, depend on each other and the environment to survive.
Science inquiry skills		
Questioning and predicting:	**Questioning and predicting:**	**Questioning and predicting:**
• With guidance, pose questions to clarify practical problems or inform a scientific investigation, and predict what the findings of an investigation might be.	• With guidance, pose questions to clarify practical problems or inform a scientific investigation, and predict what the findings of an investigation might be.	• With guidance, identify questions in familiar contexts that can be investigated scientifically and predict what might happen based on prior knowledge.

Table 6.2 (*cont.*)

Year 6	Year 5	Year 4
Processing and analysing data and information:	**Processing and analysing data and information:**	• Suggest ways to plan and conduct investigations to find answers to questions.
• With guidance, plan appropriate investigation methods to answer questions or solve problems.	• With guidance, plan appropriate investigation methods to answer questions or solve problems.	• Safely use appropriate materials, tools or equipment to make and record observations, using formal measurements and digital technologies as appropriate.
• Decide which variable should be changed and measured in fair tests and accurately observe, measure and record data, using digital technologies as appropriate.	• Decide which variable should be changed and measured in fair tests and accurately observe, measure and record data, using digital technologies as appropriate.	**Processing and analysing data and information:**
• Construct and use a range of representations, including tables and graphs, to represent and describe observations, patterns or relationships in data using digital technologies as appropriate.	• Use equipment and materials safely, identifying potential risks.	• Use a range of methods including tables and simple column graphs to represent data and to identify patterns and trends.
• Compare data with predictions and use as evidence in developing explanations.	• Construct and use a range of representations, including tables and graphs, to represent and describe observations, patterns or relationships in data using digital technologies as appropriate.	• Compare results with predictions, suggesting possible reasons for findings.
Evaluating:		**Evaluating:**
• Suggest improvements to the methods used to investigate a question or solve a problem.	• Compare data with predictions and use as evidence in developing explanations.	• Reflect on the investigation, including whether a test was fair or not.
Communicating:	**Evaluating:**	**Communicating:**
• Communicate ideas, explanations and processes in a variety of ways, including multi-modal texts.	• Suggest improvements to the methods used to investigate a question or solve a problem.	• Represent and communicate ideas and findings in a variety of ways such as diagrams, physical representations and simple reports.
	Communicating:	
	• Communicate ideas, explanations and processes in a variety of ways, including multi-modal texts.	
Science as a Human Endeavour		
Science involves testing predictions by gathering data and using evidence to develop explanations of events and phenomena.	Science involves testing predictions by gathering data and using evidence to develop explanations of events and phenomena.	Science involves making predictions and describing patterns and relationships.

Digital technologies supporting learning

Digital technologies provide a valuable tool for children to document their scientific understandings and through this a useful resource for the teacher when making judgements about children's learning. Making physical models helps children to put their ideas into a form that they can play with. Similarly, using digital tools allows for the creation of a virtual representation of their thinking. As with physical models, children can play with their ideas. Physical models (see Chittleborough 2013) and digital models support and extend other forms of representation, such as the 'ant thinking books' shown previously in Figures 6.2 and 6.3.

In the next section, a brief overview of three different inquiry-based learning projects is given to illustrate understandings in the biological sciences for children from Foundation to Year 3.

Year 3 children explain their inquiry: an inquiry-based approach to learning about the zoo in my garden

Before views

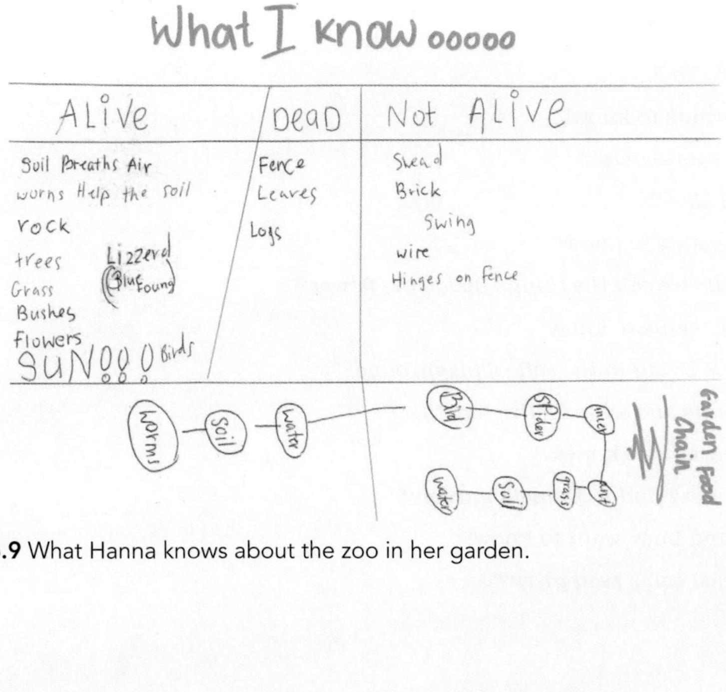

Figure 6.9 What Hanna knows about the zoo in her garden.

Exploratory activities

> *A report on Danils Garden*
>
> *What I notes about Danils garden*
>
> *There lots of Bugs*
>
> *Theres lots of liken on the*
>
> *fence*
>
> *theres lots of moss on the Bricks*
>
> *Th eres lots of liken on the rockes*
>
> *Witch was rough*
>
> *There is not many flowers*
>
> *There is brown grass and green grass.*
>
> *the rose bush is starting to blum there*
>
> *is lots of thornes*
>
> *The likens is Roght*
>
> *There are little buds*
>
> *There are cases on the rocks and in the garden*

Figure 6.10 Exploring Daniel's garden: what he noticed.

Children's questions

> Lucy wants to know:
>
> 'What eats slaters?'
>
> 'Is soil alive?'
>
> Carey wants to know:
>
> 'What do we call the things inside the flower?'
>
> Sharon wants to know:
>
> 'What is living in the school playground?'
>
> 'Do plants and animals live together?'
>
> Kathy wants to know:
>
> 'What can I find in Daniel's garden?'
>
> Colin and Lucy want to know:
>
> 'How fast can a seed grow?'

Investigations

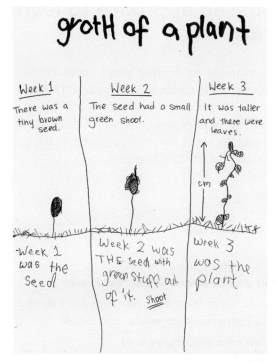

Figure 6.11 Carey's investigation

After views

What I learnt

1   Gardens grow diffent to other gardens. All the time.
2   All trees are plants need to be respected.
3   Plants have bodys kind of like people body.
4   Plants grow everywhere. Some times plan grow over house grage carport. Cuby house and more.
5   I learnt that worms can be different colour then brown and black or grey and pink.
6   I leant that plan can have peoples names like the sweet willam.
7   Ants can hurt. Bit. Crull and drown by getting in water mud and can not get out.

Figure 6.12 What Lucy learned about the zoo in her garden.

Year 1 children explain their inquiry: an inquiry-based approach to learning about worms

In this section we examine an inquiry-based approach to learning, following how it was experienced by the children. This topic is the same as that detailed in Chapter 5.

Compare how the unit was experienced by the children with how an inquiry-based approach to teaching about worms is presented in the previous chapter – An inquiry based approach to teaching (Chapter 5).

What is the same?

What is different?

Exploratory activities

> **Worms and other garden creatures – My field notes**
>
> This session was started by the teacher reading a story about a worm. After the story the children shared their knowledge and beliefs:
>
> They eat leaves and roots from the ground.
>
> They grow another head if they break.
>
> They eat soil and it comes out on the other end.

Figure 6.13 *Worm* inquiries.

Before views

> **Worms**
>
> Worms live in dirt thay eat things under the gond thcy are wet and Frindly.

Figure 6.14 Nathan explains what he knows about worms.

Children's questions

> **Questions**
>
> 1 How do worms move?
> 2 How can you tell if a worm is pregnet?
> 3 How do worms eat and drink?

Figure 6.15 Karen's questions about worms.

Investigations

The children set up their own investigations to answer their questions. They acted as both biologists and soil conservationists, observing that:

- Worms are important for breaking up the soil.
- Worms let air and water into the soil.
- Worms have an important role in mixing up the soil, especially for compost and other dead matter.
- Worms pass out the soil they eat as waste. The waste is good for plants (e.g. nitrogen).
- Earthworms mix up humus with other materials in the soil.
- Our worms love to be in wet soil.
- The body of a worm is made up of many small segments. The hairs in each segment help the worm to move. But we cannot see the hairs very well.
- Worms have lots of muscles but no skeleton.
- Worms have a mouth, a small brain but no eyes or a nose.
- Worms feel vibrations and sense light.

After views

As with the approaches examined in previous chapters, using an inquiry-based approach to learning science means we are making certain assumptions about science and science teaching and learning. These assumptions will now be discussed.

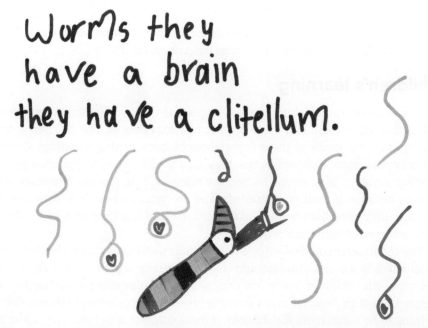

Figure 6.16 Cecilia's report on worms.

What assumptions underpin an inquiry-based approach to learning science?

The nature of science

An inquiry-based approach to learning science changes the relationship the child has with science. Rather than science being viewed as a body of knowledge that is created by scientists that children learn, an inquiry-based approach to learning science positions children as knowers and constructors of knowledge. Siry (2013) argues in her research that 'children can, if given the space to do so, begin their own deconstructing of notions of "science" at their own level' (p. 19). She says that there are 'normative discourses that position children as mere recipients of knowledge' which her research challenges (p. 20). 'Instead children are knowledge workers in their own right' (p. 20).

Teaching

The focus of an inquiry-based approach to learning science is on achieving change in the ways children make sense of their world. It is closely related to the 'conceptual change teaching approach'. This approach has been developed out of the research that has led to a view of learning as constructivist. An inquiry-based approach to learning science assumes that children will come to class with understandings of their world and meanings for many words used in science teaching. These are likely to be noticeably different from the ideas of scientists. If children's ideas are ignored in teaching it is likely that they will remain unchanged, or changed in unexpected ways – reinforcing, for instance, incorrect ideas (Samarapungavan, Patrick and Mantzicopulos 2011). There is solid longstanding research evidence for these assumptions, and these are discussed in detail in Chapter 7 (Teaching for conceptual change).

Children's learning

A key assumption about children's learning is that there is interaction between the initial ideas of children and those in their new experiences. The children actively attempt to make sense of these experiences by constructing meanings. Children not only assimilate new concepts – they also modify, develop and change their existing concepts. In science, children are more likely to process information differently because of their prior scientific and everyday real-world experiences and the ideas they bring than because of how old they are (see Chapter 8 for a cultural–historical view of learning science).

The construction of knowledge is not typically a solitary activity; the child in the classroom is in a social situation, and ideas are usually negotiated with the teacher and with other children. There is a critical and complex role for the teacher. The intervention of the teacher in the learning process has consistently shown that for learning to be meaningful for children, it must connect with their prior ideas (see Haug and Odegaard 2014). Children will make the conceptual connections when their experiences of everyday life and the everyday concepts they form, become more meaningful as a result of the new ideas they are introduced to through the carefully planned experiences of the teacher (see also Chapter 8 Cultural–historical approach to learning science Vygotsky, 1987). You will remember that this is a criticism of some discovery learning situations (see Chapter 4).

Allowing children to have significant control over the learning process is critical. Generating their own questions, and being encouraged to investigate them assumes that, with teacher guidance in a supportive learning environment, children can ask relevant questions. However, as argued in Chapter 5 (Inquiry-based approach to teaching science), creating the conditions for children to ask scientific questions can be challenging. A further challenge is how to find out children's prior ideas. That is, what are the best pedagogical strategies for creating the conditions that encourage children to talk about what they know?

REFLECTIONS 6.6: THE TEACHER'S ROLE

Re-read the transcript at the beginning of this chapter about the group of children who were investigating their question on the topic 'ants'. Focus particularly on what the teacher is saying and doing.

Are there indications that an inquiry-based approach to learning science *is a complex process? Did the teacher create a community of discourse? Can you suggest how the teacher might have further increased the effectiveness of the learning?*

Classroom/early childhood setting management in an inquiry-based approach to learning science

Managing children in a classroom or early childhood setting when using an inquiry-based approach to learning science is perceived to be the hardest thing to do. However, it is very easy when the process is conceptualised following the principles of an inquiry-based approach to learning. First, the actual structure of an inquiry-based approach to learning already suggests what has to take place – that is, what to focus on:

1 Preparation.
2 Gaining children's before views.
3 Arranging some exploratory activities.
4 Supporting children to ask investigable questions.
5 Supporting children in conceptualising and implementing their investigations.
6 Inviting the children to present their new understandings as a report and oral presentation of some kind (after views).
7 Reflecting with the children on their learning, where it may transpire that follow-up questions and investigations are necessary (as we saw in the example of the ant project).

What is central throughout these seven phases of an inquiry-based approach to learning and what makes this approach different to an inquiry-based approach to teaching is how the child is positioned in the whole experience. Siry (2013) has argued that in inquiry-based approaches to learning 'Power over the investigative process in this classroom became distributed as the children began the investigations and the teachers observed and mediated by asking open-ended questions' (p. 19). As has been argued throughout this chapter, it is the children's questions that are key here, and that should drive the whole science experience. Through focusing on children as active agents in their own learning, it becomes possible to see that 'Participatory structures that combine open-ended investigations, high-levels of student interaction, and a focus on teacher/student facilitation can support this, especially when adopting critical theoretical stances to empower children and those who work with them' (Siry 2013, p. 20). In Table 6.3, we examine how the child can be actively positioned throughout the entire inquiry approach to learning.

Table 6.3 Managing the inquiry-based approach to learning science – focusing on the child's perspective

Management principles	The child's perspective	Management strategies
Position children as active agents in their own learning processes.	Children should have opportunities in which they can feel free to share their reactions to events around them, and make links to things they have experienced in the past – as a point for further exploration.	*The teacher looks for opportunities where something interests many of the children –* such as the ant crawling upon a child's leg.
Ensure that children participate in meaningful, hands-on activities and field trips.	The inquiry should be owned by the children. That is, they should feel engaged in the experience and genuinely wish to find out the answer to the question they are investigating.	*Inviting the children to suggest ways of setting up an investigation* is important for children learning how to set up experiments. An active role for the child ensures that all the senses are engaged in learning science.
Encourage collaborative learning.	Children should at all times work together with others, talking, sharing, showing, making, etc.	*Children talking about their ideas is important for learning.* Learning is a social process, and when children are genuinely engaged it is expected that they will be active and noisy.

Management principles	The child's perspective	Management strategies
Develop child-focused investigations.	It should be the children's questions that drive the investigations.	*Allow time for children to put forward their questions and to design their experiments.* Investigations may sometimes seem unscientific, or may not feel significant to adults. But children's assumptions about their world are being investigated, and their ideas need to also be tested out, before they can move forward with formulating a more scientific investigation.
Utilise the local surroundings and resources in the investigations.	Local contexts and resources are immediately relevant to children. Using these as the basis for investigating helps children meaningfully use what they learn in their everyday world.	*Allow space and time for utilising the outdoor area.* The local parks, industries, shopping centres, and family homes in the children's own community, are all important for identifying local problems, resources and solutions.
Help children to learn how to identify, plan and structure an inquiry.	Children who feel passionate about their investigation, because they are investigating their question, are more likely to engage with the inquiry process and through this are able to development inquiry skills.	*Over time, children develop their inquiry skills.* Central to an inquiry-based approach to learning science is children developing inquiry skills. Supporting children to recognise the importance of planning investigations, conducting fair tests, looking for evidence, evaluating evidence, etc., are important scientific inquiry skills, but also lifelong learning skills. Children's inquiry skills can be refined and developed over time. Giving children opportunities to work scientifically ensures they have the possibility to develop inquiry skills that become sharpened with practice and useful for determining and engaging in the complexity of their personal world.

The teacher's role

- *Preparation was important for these lessons so that the students were guaranteed of resource-rich, interesting, relevant tasks.*
- *During our lessons, I found the student were greatly affected by my interest participation, thoughts and questions.*
- *Lessons need to have a focus and desired outcomes, so that children are kept on task through questioning and extension of their ideas.*
- *I understand how my attitude and approach to science will greatly affect the children I teach!*

Figure 6.17 The role of the teacher is important in an inquiry-based approach to learning science.

Assessment in an inquiry-based approach to learning science

There are two parts to conceptualising assessment: the science content and the assessment of the inquiry skills. Although not discussed explicitly in this chapter due to space constraints, assessment should also look at how children are coming to understand science as a human endeavour.

Assessment of science content is driven by examining the differences between the before views and the after views. However, keep in mind that the younger the child, the more difficult it is to gain a full sense of their understandings if you are just relying upon using what they write or draw or make. Their physical skills will not be as developed as their oral skills. Consequently, it is important to also document children's thinking through other techniques, such as inviting the children to share their thinking informally with you as you move about the groups of children who are working; or more formally, but setting aside a time at the end of each lesson for children to report to the whole group on what they found out or were doing in that particular lesson. This latter approach is also useful for gaining a sense of how children are developing in relation to their inquiry-based skills.

Inquiry-based skills can be determined through observing children in action and making formal observations of them as they work and discuss their ideas and actions. Here it is important to also gather work samples from the children. Sometimes 'work in progress' can also be captured on a smartphone or other digital device and stored for later use when making judgements about children's achievements. Recorded conversations with children about their thinking can also act as a useful tool for gathering valuable data on children's achievements.

Figure 6.18 Smart phones and other digital devices are useful tools for keeping records, making observations and transferring data.

Here it is possible to specifically document how children go about:

1 Posing investigable questions.
2   Conceptualising and implementing their investigations.
3 Presenting their new understandings.
4 Reflecting on their own learning, where they work with data and evidence.

This approach to gathering work samples and children's work in action can also be directly helpful for children's understanding of science as a human endeavour.

Assessing the children's understanding of science as a human endeavour should consider:

1 Nature and development of science: this sub-strand develops an appreciation of the unique nature of science and scientific knowledge, including how current knowledge has developed over time through the actions of many people.
2 Use and influence of science: this sub-strand explores how science knowledge and applications affect peoples' lives, including their work, and how science is influenced by society and can be used to inform decisions and actions (ACARA 2014, p. 12).

Assessment is something that is clearly linked to the Achievement Standards in the Australian Curriculum – Science. In this document, achievement standards indicate the quality of learning that children would normally be expected to demonstrate by a particular point in their schooling.

What can be found in each year level of the curriculum is an achievement standard which comprises a written description of expected learning or achievement. For instance:

> An achievement standard describes the quality of learning (the extent of knowledge, the depth of understanding and the sophistication of skills) that would indicate the student is well placed to commence the learning required at the next level of achievement. The sequence of achievement standards across Foundation to Year 10 describes progress in the learning area. This sequence provides teachers with a framework of growth and development in the learning area (ACARA 2014, p. 12).

It is argued by ACARA (2014) that:

> Teachers also use the achievement standards, at the end of a period of teaching, to make on-balance judgments about the quality of learning demonstrated by the students – that is, whether they have achieved below, at or above the standard. To make these judgments, teachers draw on assessment data that they have collected as evidence during the course of the teaching period. These judgments about the quality of learning are one source of feedback to students and their parents and inform formal reporting processes (ACARA 2014, p. 19).

What is clear in the Australian Curriculum – Science is that work samples are an important part of gathering evidence of achievement. This is deemed so important that work samples are provided by ACARA for teachers to support them in making judgements about children's achievements. For example:

> Student work samples play a key role in communicating expectations described in the achievement standards. Each work sample includes the relevant assessment task, the student's response, and annotations identifying the quality of learning evident in the student's response in relation to relevant parts of the achievement standard. Together, the description of the achievement standard and the accompanying set of annotated work samples help teachers to make judgments about whether students have achieved the standard (ACARA 2014, p. 12).

An achievement standard for Year 1 is expressed as:

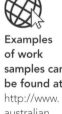

Examples of work samples can be found at http://www. australian curriculum. edu.au

> By the end of Year 1, students describe objects and events that they encounter in their everyday lives, and the effects of interacting with materials and objects. They identify a range of habitats. They describe changes to things in their local environment and suggest how science helps people care for environments. Students make predictions, and investigate everyday phenomena. They follow instructions to record and sort their observations and share their observations with others (ACARA 2014, p. 26).

An achievement standard for Year 5 is expressed as:

> By the end of Year 5, students classify substances according to their observable
> properties and behaviours. They explain everyday phenomena associated with the
> transfer of light. They describe the key features of our solar system. They analyse
> how the form of living things enables them to function in their environments.
> Students discuss how scientific developments have affected people's lives and
> how science knowledge develops from many people's contributions. Students
> follow instructions to pose questions for investigation, predict what might
> happen when variables are changed, and plan investigation methods. They use
> equipment in ways that are safe and improve the accuracy of their observations.
> Students construct tables and graphs to organise data and identify patterns. They
> use patterns in their data to suggest explanations and refer to data when they
> report findings. They describe ways to improve the fairness of their methods
> and communicate their ideas, methods and findings using a range of text types
> (ACARA 2014, p. 39).

The curriculum and website are valuable resources to support teachers in their
assessment of children's learning in science. Importantly, an inquiry-based
approach to learning is clearly linked to the strands of the Australian Curriculum –
Science, where inquiry skills are given as a key strand.

REFLECTIONS 6.7: CRITIQUING AN INQUIRY-BASED APPROACH TO LEARNING SCIENCE

Go back to your responses for 6.3 Reflections. Now reflect on your main
concerns about the prospect of using an inquiry-based approach to learning
science.

*Why do you think you have these concerns? That is, what experience, or lack
of experience, has influenced your concerns?*

Summary

In contrast to other approaches, an inquiry-based approach to learning science is primarily about working with children's inquiries and their conceptual change. As in an inquiry-
based approach to teaching science, the foundations for this approach are based on a
constructivist view of learning which for more than 25 years was considered the most effective approach to teaching by many science educators. The constructivist view of learning presents science as multifaceted and accessible to all. Working within this framework
emphasises the importance of exploring and engaging with children's initial understandings, encouraging them to assume a high level of responsibility for their own learning, and
the need to help children learn how to learn. The approach acknowledges that organising learning inquiries is not easy, and it must be planned for carefully and sensitively. An

inquiry-based approach to learning science presents many challenges, but its outcomes can generate many rewards for the teacher because the child and their interests are the focus of attention for teaching.

References

Alake-Tuenter, E, Biemans, HJA, Tobi, H Mulder, M 2013, 'Inquiry-based science teaching competence of primary school teachers: A Delphi study', *Teaching and Teacher Education*, vol. 35, pp. 13–4.

Australian Curriculum, Assessment and Reporting Authority 2014, Australian Curriculum – Science. Available at http://www.australiancurriculum.edu.au/ Science/Curriculum/F-6. (Accessed September 2014.)

Australian Government Department of Education, Employment and Workplace Relations 2009, *Belonging, Being and Becoming. The Early Years Learning Framework for Australia*, Canberra: Commonwealth Government.

Bianchi, J, Colburn, A 2000. 'Teaching the nature of science through inquiry to prospective elementary teachers: A tale of two researchers', *Journal of Research in Science Teaching*, vol. 37, pp. 177–209. (DOI 10.1002/ (SICI)1098–2736(200002)37:2\177::AIDTEA63.0.CO;2-Y.)

Chittleborough, G 2013, 'Using models in teaching and learning science' in C Redman ed, *Successful Science Education Practices. Exploring What, Why and How they Worked*, New York: Nova Science, pp. 183–202.

Haug, BS, Odegaard, M 2014, 'From words to concepts: Focusing on word knowledge when teaching for conceptual understanding within an inquiry-based science setting', *Research in Science Education*, vol. 44 no. 5, pp. 777–800. (DOI 1-1007/s11165-014-9402-5.)

Samarapungavan, A Patrick, H Mantzicopoulos, P 2011, 'What kindergarten students learn in inquiry-based science classrooms', *Cognition and Instruction*, vol. 29, no. 4, pp. 416–70.

Siry, C 2013, 'Exploring the complexities of children's inquiries in science: Knowledge production through participatory practices', *Research in Science Education*, pp. 1–24. (DOI 10.1007/s11165-013-9364.)

Vygotsky, LS 1987, 'Thinking and speech' in LS Vygotsky, *The Collected Works of L.S. Vygotsky, vol. 1, Problems of General Psychology*, RW Rieber and AS Carton eds, N Minick trans, New York: Plenum Press, pp. 39–285.

CHAPTER 7

Teaching for conceptual change: constructivism

Introduction

In the previous two chapters an *inquiry-based approach to teaching* (Chapter 5) and an *inquiry-based approach to learning* (Chapter 6) were presented through a range of working examples of children learning science. In this chapter we introduce an approach to science learning known as *teaching for conceptual change*. The focus of this chapter is on the pedagogy of conceptual change illustrated through the example of the physical sciences. In particular, we will explore conceptual change for the topics of electricity and light.

In this chapter we build upon the pedagogical content of the previous two chapters by examining conceptual change theory, discussing children's thinking about electricity and illustrating examples of children's work dedicated to this topic. This is followed by examples of children's thinking about light and information about teaching for conceptual change on that topic.

Here we examine the pedagogy of conceptual change for light in the context of the early years of school, and electricity for the continuum from Year 1 to the later years of school. As with the previous two chapters, the content strand of the physical sciences is introduced only as an illustration for presenting and critiquing the pedagogical approach detailed in this chapter. However, enough basic science content is given to help you with the preparation and planning of a unit on the topics of electricity and light.

How you feel about your learning matters

As shown in Chapter 1, there is an abundance of evidence that supports the view that how you feel when learning something matters. Teaching for conceptual change, with its focus on the learner, means that as a teacher you will need to be in tune with how your group of children are thinking and feeling about their learning of science. This is supportive of the Early Years Learning Framework (Australian Government 2009), which says in Outcome 3 that children should have a strong sense of wellbeing, where they take increasing responsibility for their own social and emotional wellbeing. The EYLF suggests that educators promote learning when they 'are emotionally available and support children's expression of their thoughts and feelings' (p. 21). Teaching for conceptual change focuses directly on this practice principle.

Constructivism

What is common to the approaches discussed in Chapters 5 and 6 is the theoretical foundation of inquiry learning, inquiry teaching and conceptual change. The theory that supports these approaches is known as constructivism.

Constructivism is a theoretical perspective that informs our thinking about the nature of teaching and learning. In this theory it is argued that humans make meaning from an interaction between their experiences and their existing ideas. Constructivism is one of the dominant modes of theorising teaching and learning in science education, particularly in primary education.

Constructivism focuses on the individual learner and how they make sense of their world. Constructivism underpins all the research that has been done on conceptual change, often named as misconceptions, alternative views or children's science. In teaching for conceptual change, it is important to find out what the child is thinking and to consider how their ideas influence any science they may experience.

Constructivism and conceptual change suggest that, once formed, children's ideas are very difficult to change (Roth, Goulart and Plakitsi 2013). It is argued that children who develop alternative views can hold on to their ideas right into adulthood, despite a range of contradictory and rich experiences in science.

Defining the nature of conceptual change

There are many views on the exact definition of conceptual change. Three dominant ways present themselves in the literature. They are:

- teaching for conceptual change involves strategies that bring children's conceptions in line with that of a scientist
- teaching for conceptual change captures the way scientists come to validate their scientific theories over time, where the process of conceptual change is valuable in its own right
- conceptual change takes place in social relations as children notice competing theories.

What is key for teaching for conceptual change is to continually determine what children know, and to work with the children's conceptions. The focus is the learner and what they think about the specific science concepts.

Children's thinking books

'Thinking books' are useful for finding out children's prior views and for encouraging children's questions, and for monitoring their thinking throughout a unit. The *Science for Children* website provides an example of a thinking book that can be downloaded and used with children. Thinking books encourage children to draw and write what they know about electricity and any questions they may have. In Figure 7.1 a child has identified what she knows about electricity and what she would like to find out about electricity.

Other ways of finding out what children think were detailed in Chapter 2.

Knowing in advance what kinds of things children ask about a topic is very helpful for planning – that is, pre-empting what they may ask. Some of the questions that have been asked by children include:

Example of a 'thinking book': www. cambridge.edu. au/academic/ science

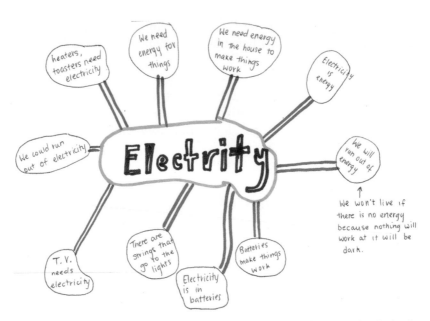

Figure 7.1 Thinking books are useful to find out what children know and to help them generate their questions.

- What is electricity?
- What did people do before electricity existed?
- How do they make electricity?
- Who made electricity?
- Can electricity kill people? If so, how?
- How does electricity travel?
- How does a torch work?
- How do batteries work?

Children's thinking about electricity

A lot of research has taken place into what children think about certain concepts in science. For instance, there has been over 30 years of research into children's thinking about electricity. Researchers have plotted children's thinking from the middle of primary school through to the end of secondary school (Roth, Goulart and Plakitsi 2013), and some studies have even been done into what university science teacher students think about topics in science (e.g. Balgopal 2014). Less is known about what infants, toddlers and preschoolers think (Sikder and Fleer 2014).

In this section we will explore what ideas children commonly express about electricity across the primary years, in the context of what we would want children to know about electricity. Figure 7.2 shows a broad overview of the ideas children have about electricity. Details of the views that primary-aged children have about electricity, and the questions they are likely to ask, are shown further below. This information will give you a starting point in planning for conceptual change teaching. For the purposes of long-term planning and resource collection before presenting a unit on electricity, the ideas outlined here might be helpful. What is key to teaching for conceptual change is knowing about these alternative views, and focusing on finding out exactly what science ideas are held by your group of children (see Chapter 2 for examples of how to find out their thinking).

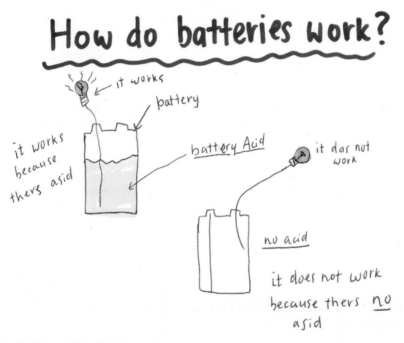

Figure 7.2 How do batteries work?

Figure 7.3 shows three common views. These are illustrated in Figures 7.3 (a), (b) and (c). Figure 7.3 (d) shows the scientific version of this same concept.

While Figure 7.3 gives a broad overview, it does not give us detailed insight into how children think and how we might support them with developing their ideas further. In particular, it says nothing about the pedagogy for conceptual change. What is important is considering children's thinking from their perspective – how they think about the topic of electricity in their everyday life and, as already mentioned, what kinds of questions they are curious about.

Table 7.1 shows what is expected to be taught about electricity in the Australian Curriculum – Science (Year 6), and what the research has identified about children's thinking on this topic across the year levels (F–Year 6). You will see that

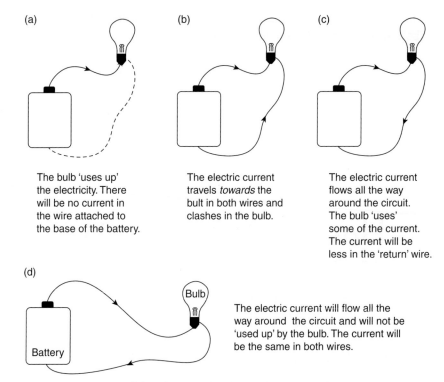

(a) The bulb 'uses up' the electricity. There will be no current in the wire attached to the base of the battery.

(b) The electric current travels *towards* the bult in both wires and clashes in the bulb.

(c) The electric current flows all the way around the circuit. The bulb 'uses' some of the current. The current will be less in the 'return' wire.

(d) The electric current will flow all the way around the circuit and will not be 'used up' by the bulb. The current will be the same in both wires.

Figure 7.3 An overview of the ideas children have about a simple circuit.

the thinking is not always consistent with scientific thought and the goals of the Australian Curriculum – Science.

Researching understandings about electricity

CAMBRIDGE DYNAMIC SCIENCE

Year 9, Module 4, Unit 10

In the previous section detail was provided about children's thinking about electricity. The research has shown that some of these ideas persist into adulthood (Campbell 2012). In planning for the teaching of conceptual change it is important for you to also research the concepts you are exploring with the children. A basic overview of some of the key ideas on the topic of electricity follows. This is just a 'starter kit' of scientific thinking about electricity.

   Electricity and magnetism: Having experiences with a range of components in electrical circuits gives children hands-on experiences with controlling electricity – for instance, when making a simple circuit, children use batteries, bulbs, switches, buzzers and bells. Kits such as Lego products provide many other components that can be used by children in the primary years when making their own robots, when making a powered lighthouse, or when using circuits for lighting up a Lego house. Of course there also exist logic gates, capacitors, transistors, diodes,

Table 7.1 Children's alternative conceptions about electricity across the school years

Physical sciences	Foundation year	Year 1	Year 2	Year 3	Year 4	Year 5	Year 6
	Young children think that electricity is a material that is contained in a battery. They use terms such as 'electricity', 'energy', 'power' or 'current' without making a distinction between them. Distance from the battery to the bulb is thought to be responsible for a weaker shine of a light bulb.			Children believe that a current is a kind of material called electricity. Electricity is often seen as a form of power that makes something go. Because of this, children often think a current gets used up or burnt up in a bulb.			Electrical circuits provide a means of transferring and transforming electricity. Energy from a variety of sources can be used to generate electricity. Children develop many different theories for explaining how a light bulb is illuminated – as shown in Figure 7.8 – clashing currents model, where a current comes from both ends of the battery and clashes together emitting light; a single wire or unipolar model, where the current just travels up one wire and is used up by the bulb; and a consumption model, where electricity travels from the battery to the bulb and back to the battery, but where some electricity is 'used up'.

relays and variable resistors. These latter components are less likely to be used in the primary years, unless special projects are planned, such as when constructing solar powered cars or boats. *What is important here is for children to have opportunities to make some kind of electrical measurement or observation so that understandings about the relationship between current, potential difference and resistance can begin to be introduced.*

Current and voltage: When we use the word current we are referring to the flow of electrons around a circuit. The flow of electrons can be measured using an ammeter. Electric current is measured in 'amperes' or 'amps'. Voltage is another important term that children may hear being used. Voltage is a measure of the energy that is available. The measure is called 'volts' and it is measured by a voltmeter. It is often described as 'the driving force that pushes electrons around a circuit'.

Electrical circuits: There are two different types of circuits that children are likely to set up when designing their own experiments or when, for example, 'wiring up a model house or diorama' as shown in Figure 7.4 or when making a circuit inside a tube to create their own 'home-made torch'. One is called a series circuit and the other is called a parallel circuit. In Figure 7.5, we see an example of a series circuit.

We now relate these science concept to a child's thinking in science – Anamika.

Figure 7.4 Our fantastic home has electricity!

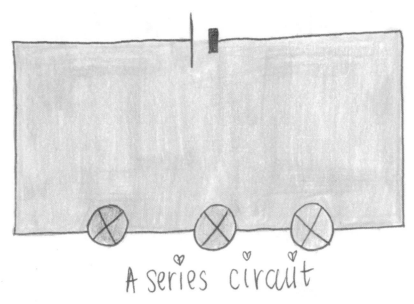

Figure 7.5 Anamika's designs of a series circuit for illuminating a diorama.

Anamika's understanding about electricity

Anamika has designed a series circuit into her diorama. In Figure 7.6 we see the symbols that are commonly used for producing circuit designs. In summary: the electrons are travelling around the circuit, and are carrying the energy but are *not* the energy itself. The electrons travelling = electricity, the energy carried = electrical energy.

Anamika learned that having the three bulbs across her diorama reduced the brightness of each of the individual bulbs. She tested this out by designing and then making three different series circuits as shown in Figure 7.7. She found that when more bulbs were added to her series circuit, they become dimmer. She felt this spoiled the effect she wanted.

Anamika solved the problem of the bulbs becoming dimmer by designing a parallel circuit. She found that a parallel circuit contains more than one loop. This meant that the bulbs could continually be added in parallel into the circuit, with each bulb having the normal brightness. But, she noted that the charge in the battery didn't last as long.

Measuring current: The problem of the dimmer bulbs bothered Anamika and, with support from her teacher, they decided to measure the current in her series circuit. Using an ammeter she decided to measure the current at different points along her circuit, especially between each of the bulbs. She found that the reading of

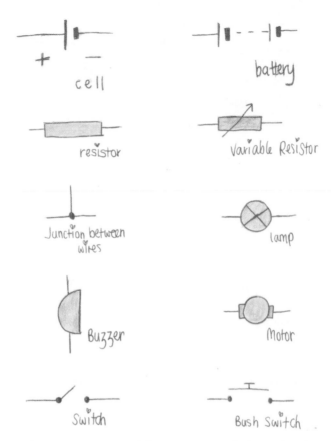

Figure 7.6 Anamika's representation of the common symbols used in drawing circuits.

the ammeter was identical, no matter where she positioned it. This investigation is important for helping Anamika to come to realise that the current is 'not consumed'. As we noted in the research into children's ideas about electricity, this is a surprising finding for many children because they believe the current is partially 'used up' as it passes through the first bulb.

Anamika decided then to measure the amps in the parallel circuit. To her surprise, she found that the current was not the same in all the parts of the circuit. The current that is put out by the battery divides up between the different branches of the parallel circuit.

You are probably wondering now how this can be. It seems counter-intuitive to what is observed. The concept of resistance helps us understand what is going on. We will now turn to the science concepts of resistance, transfer, power and batteries.

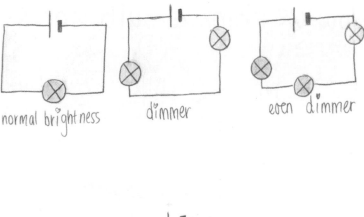

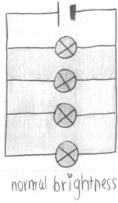

Figure 7.7 Anamika's series circuit observations and her design for a parallel circuit for illuminating a diorama.

Concepts about electricity

Resistance: The tungsten filament in a light bulb, as shown in Omar's drawing in Figure 7.8, is a difficult metal for currents to flow through, and as the current passes through the tungsten filament, the resistance causes the metal to heat and glow, emitting light. Energy is transformed into light (and heat and an imperceptible amount of sound) from electrical energy. Explained at the atomic level, the moving electrons in the current collide with all the atoms in the circuit. As they do this, the atoms vibrate.

Resistance is a measure of how difficult it is for electrons to flow through a particular material. For example, insulators have a very high resistance, conductors have a very low resistance and semi-conductors (as used in computer chips) are between these two extremes. Resistance is measured in 'ohms'. The name comes form a German physics teacher called Georg Simon Ohm.

Figure 7.8 Omar's diagrams of light bulbs.

Transfer is the 'movement' of energy from one location to another. For example, heat can be conducted, convected or radiated from one position to another. Energy transfer takes place.

We know that batteries have a fixed voltage. That is, the battery provides a certain amount of energy or 'push', which causes the electrons to move in one direction around the circuit. Therefore, when a battery is connected to a series circuit, the amount of current there is will depend upon the resistance in that circuit. The more bulbs with their resistant filaments, the more resistance there will be in the whole circuit (this is in addition to the resistance provided by the wire itself). This means that with high overall resistance in the series circuit, less current is put out by the battery. Also, fewer electrons are flowing per second to the battery.

The parallel circuit can be thought of as lots of series circuits added together, each with a bulb and their own resistance. This means that the battery puts out more current so that they all have enough current through them for each of the bulbs to give normal brightness. This can be explained by noting that the battery puts out an electrical field for each parallel circuit. Each loop in the parallel circuit has in effect one bulb, battery source and circuit of wire, and this means that in each loop the current and the bulb voltage will be the same as a series circuit of one battery, bulb and wires. The bulb will shine as brightly in the parallel circuit as the series circuit that has only one bulb.

There is an important difference between the parallel circuit and the series circuit. In the parallel circuit the current flowing in and out of the battery will be more than that of the series circuit. The wire from the battery feeds into the branches or loops in the parallel circuit. The current flows into each loop that has a bulb, and then the current flows back to the battery. This happens for each loop in the parallel circuit. It is like water coming from a main water source, running along a large pipe, and then branching out to other pipes, and then connecting back to into one large pipe and returning to the original water source. Obviously, more water will be in this parallel pipe system than in a single pipe system with no branches. This metaphor helps explain how more current is in a parallel circuit, and also why each bulb shines brightly.

Power: Children use the word power a lot when talking about batteries or electricity, but they do not always know what the term means in the context of science. A battery provides energy that causes electrons to move. This is what causes the current in an electrical circuit. Energy is measured in 'joules'. Many household electrical appliances, such as fans, heaters and electric kettles, are marked in 'watts'. This is most clearly shown on light bulbs, which are marked with a numerical figure, such as 60 watts. A wattage is a measure of power, and it is usually thought about in relation to energy transfer. For example a 60-watt light bulb will transfer energy to light and heat at a rate of 60 joules per second. In contrast, a 40-watt light bulb will transfer energy to light and heat at 40 joules per second. It is this energy transfer that is measured by companies that sell electricity to households and industries. So leaving on a 60-watt light bulb for a long period of time will cost a lot more than if a 40-watt light bulb is used instead.

Batteries: Children are very familiar with and interested in batteries, as many of the toys they play with use batteries to make them work. In addition, many electronic devices need to be 'charged' regularly. Understanding how batteries work is something that children may ask about.

Batteries create electricity through a chemical reaction. The main substance in a battery is called the electrolyte and this is a type of acid that can be dangerous to touch. The other two substances in a battery are called the cathode and the anode. The anode reacts with the electrolyte to produce an electron (negative charge) and the cathode reacts with the electrolyte wanting an electron (positive charge). The electric current happens through the movement of electrons between the wire that connects the anode and the cathode. Through this process, the chemicals break down over time, and this is what is meant by a 'flat' battery. Sometimes preschool children will think that a 'flat' battery is literally physically flat. Children think that the electricity is squeezed out of the 'hole in the battery' like a tube of toothpaste. The everyday use of 'flat battery' tends to give this image to children. Research by the author with young children has shown that preschool children need opportunities to test out this idea of a flat battery – if this is what they say about their understandings of how a battery works. Rather than measuring the electrical flow using an ammeter, a simple electrical circuit works well for supporting children to test if the 'battery is flat'. By connecting the battery to a bulb, children can check if the battery has lost its charge (is 'flat') and then check the physical appearance of the battery.

> ### REFLECTIONS 7.1: WORKING WITH CHILDREN'S IDEAS ABOUT ELECTRICITY FOR CONCEPTUAL CHANGE
>
> In considering the example of Anamika setting up and 'wiring' a diorama, how might you use the knowledge you have gained from reading the previous section to support her to develop scientific understandings of electricity rather than develop alternative views?
>
> What would you do if she says:
>
> - The electricity is being used up.
> - The battery is flat?
>
> What would you do if she asks:
>
> - How come these two bulbs (in series circuit) are so dull, but not the three bulbs in the other (parallel) circuit?
>
> How might you teach for conceptual change? How do you respectfully interact with children when they express alternative views?
>
> Write down your thoughts.

Respecting children's ideas

> The students responded well to my lessons because the activities were conducted in response to their questions. One student even came up to me after one of the lessons and said 'We like you because you make us feel important'. This was particularly heartening to hear (Year 6 teacher).

Teaching for conceptual change is highly respectful of children's existing knowledge and capacity to learn. However, respect for their existing ideas does not imply that the teacher necessarily regards the ideas as adequate or correct. The approach embodies a strong position on the role that the teacher must play in assisting conceptual change. One of the potential tensions or dilemmas for teachers – especially those new to the approach – is that, after their teaching of a topic, some children might not have changed their ideas about a topic greatly, if at all. Given what we know about conceptual change, this should not surprise us. But an anxious teacher might be tempted to then resort to didactic teaching. Importantly, teachers should be sensitive to the views the children are expressing, how they respond when children give weird and interesting ideas, which do not fit with what scientists explain about these concepts, and the child's self-confidence. Children's enthusiasm and curiosity about the world should always be prioritised by the teacher, as they guide them towards re-thinking the views they express, such as 'What interesting ideas …', 'Is this always the case?' or 'Do we see this always in situation X?' or 'What other ideas might we have about this?' or 'What do others think about this?' These suggestions are also relevant to the inquiry-based teaching and learning discussed in the previous two chapters.

REFLECTIONS 7.2: NEW SITUATIONS

Think of a fairly recent situation in your life in which you were confronted with a new setting (e.g. a new work situation or entering university for the first time) about which you knew very little. Trace how you developed knowledge about that new setting. In particular, think about the interactions you had with people that helped you make sense of the setting and develop knowledge.

What was your approach to constructing knowledge about the situation?
Did you have some prior knowledge of the situation and was this important?
Was this an effective way of learning for you in this situation? If so, what made it effective?

What I think is inside my torch:
battery
bulb
wires
electricity
switches.

Figure 7.9 Thinking book on 'What is inside my torch'.

In respecting children's ideas, teachers might have to exercise patience in achieving conceptual change. Such an outcome calls for careful planning of learning experiences to encourage new thinking.

Creating a need to change your thinking

If it is true that it is only the children themselves who can construct and reconstruct their understanding of the scientific world, then it is likely they must be dissatisfied with their existing ideas before they will do so. It is generally thought that teachers should recognise that children must have sufficient reason for discarding their current ideas (Danielsson and Warwick 2014). The new and alternative idea must be:

- intelligible – the new ideas must appear to be a consistent and coherent
- plausible – the new ideas must be reconcilable with their own existing ideas
- fruitful – the new ideas must be useful to them, or it must offer them a simpler but as satisfactory an explanation as they already have.

By now you will have concluded that teaching for conceptual change promotes extensive and intensive discussion among the children and between them and the teacher. Talk needs to be a core element of classroom and early childhood setting processes, and this will require sufficient time and the safety of a supportive learning environment. The early childhood setting and the classroom become a 'community of discourse' in which the teacher and children strive to make meaning together so that their joint understandings tend towards, or are consistent with, scientific views (Campbell and Jobling 2012). Teaching for conceptual change emphasises the need for the discourse to be explicitly metacognitive (thinking about one's own thinking); that is, the teacher and children will consider and comment on how they have constructed their initial understandings, what experiences in the classroom have challenged their thinking, and what they are uncertain about and why (Forbes and Skamp 2014).

In the case study that follows, we invite you to analyse the pedagogy of the teacher. How did she deal with conceptual change when teaching the concept of light?

Looking inside the classroom

A case study of teaching for conceptual change – children's thinking about light

In this section we present information on what views children might hold about the concept of light. We draw upon the longstanding research on children's thinking about light across the years. In the section that follows, we present content knowledge on the concept of light that is useful background reading. This is followed by a case study of the pedagogical practices of Bob, a teacher who worked together with a group of Foundation to Year 1 children. The broader topic of 'weather' was in his program. Bob decided that the concept of 'light' could enhance children's thinking about the weather.

Researching what children might know about the topic already – their alternative conceptions

In this section we begin by examining what the research has shown about children's thinking in science for the topic of light. In Table 7.2 is a summary of what is known about children's thinking about light. This table also shows what is expected to be covered on this topic, as presented in the Australian Curriculum – Science.

What do children need to know:

- Light travels in straight lines.
- You can block the path of light – causing a shadow.

Table 7.2 Children's conceptions across the school year for light

Physical sciences	Foundation year	Year 1	Year 2	Year 3	Year 4	Year 5	Year 6
		Light and sound are produced by a range of sources and can be sensed.				Light from a source forms shadows and can be absorbed, reflected and refracted.	
		Many children see light as 'normal' and think that darkness needs to be explained. Many children think of reflection as going from the eye to a mirror. Children are likely to explain a rainbow by saying that 'The water goes inside the light and then it explodes into colour'. Very young children often make no connections between the eye and the object, while older children often think vision is a passage from the eye to the object.		Some children think that there is a range of darkness or light. Children think that a hard surface is needed to reflect light. Many children think of colour as being a part of the object.		The progression from thinking of colour filters as 'things which add colour to light' to the concept to filters subtracting colour from ordinary light is difficult for children to understand.	

- When light comes into contact with a surface it can be: a) scattered, b) reflected, c) absorbed and d) partly scattered and partly absorbed.
- White light can be refracted into a spectrum of colours.
- Ordinary light is a mixture of all of the colours of the spectrum.
- Filters absorb all the colours except that which can be seen.
- A rainbow is an example of white light being refracted into the colours of the spectrum.
- Prisms are like raindrops.
- The Sun is always behind you when you look at a rainbow.
- The colour of an object is dependent upon the wavelength of the light it scatters. For instance, black objects scatter very little light and absorb light of all visual wavelengths.
- We can see objects because light from a source (e.g. the Sun) is reflected from the object to our eyes – allowing us to see.
- Light sources can be weak or strong.

Researching the concepts needed for teaching for conceptual change – building our own content knowledge about the topic to be taught

Bob's reflections

As I do not have a scientific background, having been unable to continue beyond Year 10 general science, I regard this teaching experience as an interesting challenge. Once the initial difficulties of deciding on a suitable topic that connected with the children were over, I felt enthusiastic but was a little apprehensive as to the development of suitable questions for investigation. However, the questions did arise readily and most difficulties which we had were unexpected and so I must allow for these in the future.

Finding out what the children in our class know

The children were observing the weather and collecting data. One of the children noticed a rainbow. Her screams of excitement attracted the attention of all the children in the class. Bob asked the children to talk about what they knew about rainbows in order to gain some insights into their understandings about the concept of light. Bob plotted their thinking onto a large sheet of butcher's paper in the form of a mind map. Bob noted: 'It was interesting to see the range of knowledge within the classroom. One child mentioned the words "refracted" and "reflection", while others only used colour words.' Bob put the mind map aside, for later use in assisting him in his evaluation.

What the children knew about rainbows:

- They are always curved.
- They have many colours.
- They seem to always move away when you try to get close.
- You can't touch them.
- They only come out after rain or a shower.
- They only come at certain times of the day.

The children wanted to know:

- What is a rainbow?
- Why does the rainbow move when you move?
- Why can't we touch a rainbow?
- How does it form?
- Why do rainbows have colours?
- How many colours are in a rainbow and what are they?
- What are the colours made up of?
- How long do rainbows last?
- Why are some rainbows big and some small?
- Why are rainbows semi-circles?
- Why do they come after rain?
- Why do we only see rainbows at certain times?
- Where do they normally appear?
- Can we walk through a rainbow?
- Why do 'rainbows' shine through a crystal?
- How does a rainbow go away?

Creating cognitive conflict – what might children not be so sure about and want to investigate?

Bob read a book on rainbows to the children in which a range of ideas were presented. He followed up the content by presenting them with a small colour wheel, where he was able to show them how the colours combined to become white light (Figure 7.10). This experience created cognitive conflict for the children. What seemed counter-intuitive was that:

- white light is made up of colours
- you can make white light by combining the colours through spinning a colour wheel.

Figure 7.10 How come the colours become white?

Children setting up the investigations

Bob talked to the children about these questions and as a group they decided to investigate the following questions:

1 What is a rainbow and how does it form?
2 What are the colours in a rainbow?

Children answering their questions

Question 1: What is a rainbow and how does it form?

Bob and the children decided they wanted to answer this question by seeing if they could 'make' some rainbows and by going to the library and researching about light.

Investigation 1: Making rainbows.
    Position a mirror inside a plastic box filled with water and put it opposite a window facing the Sun, juggle the position of the box and mirror and see if you can get anything reflected on to the paper.

Bob's reflections:

The children were very excited when large bands of colour appeared on the paper. Most groups had little difficulty once they discovered that they had to keep the paper from blocking the Sun's rays shining on to the mirror. The question 'Why are the colours moving like that on the paper?' was raised. I suggested they look more carefully and see if they could find the reason. Narran announced, 'It's because the water moves as we move the mirror, that's why.'
    The next investigation was to turn on a garden sprinkler one sunny day and to observe what happened. This was to have been carried out at home but shortly afterwards the sprinklers were turned on to the school oval to water in fertiliser. It was very timely and the children we quick to notice the resultant rainbow on the oval. They did comment on the size of the bow and were starting to realise why the size of rainbows varies.
    Our next observation was to see what happened if we stood a clear glass of water in the Sun so that the light could pass through it. We placed white paper under the glass. We observed small bands of colour on the paper but it was not very easily seen. The question was raised as to why the colours were so pale.

Figure 7.11 I made my own colour wheel.

Question 2: What are the colours in a rainbow?

Bob's reflections

As we saw these colours clearly during our observations – red, orange, yellow, green, blue, indigo and violet – we decided to explore colour wheels. The children made their own colour wheel. They placed colour cellophane over a light source, and they projected light through various combinations of colours.

Teacher reflections on the approach

Bob's reflections

The science unit was regarded by the children as a lot of fun and very interesting because it answered their questions.

The children gained a considerable amount of knowledge and understanding from the approach adopted.

The interactions and active involvement of each child ensured that no one was daydreaming at any stage.

I thought I needed further practice in eliciting better responses from the children.

I found that the very nature of this topic helped to avoid 'yes' or 'no' type responses.

The majority of the children's individual questions were covered during the investigations. They had developed a good understanding of the topic and were applying this knowledge when reviewing their original questions at the end of the unit.

The topic integrated well into our 'Weather unit' and the knowledge acquired in the science unit helped the children's understanding of the overall study of the topic of weather.

What assumptions underpin teaching for conceptual change?

REFLECTIONS 7.3: TEACHING FOR CONCEPTUAL CHANGE

Record what you think was being done in this situation by:

- the teacher, and
- the children.

What were the positive aspects of the teaching and learning?

What were the challenging aspects of the teaching and learning?

Bob's reflections

Bob indicated that there were some challenges to teaching for conceptual change on the topic of light. They were:

- *Inclement weather* – this delayed the progress of our investigations in the early states. *I didn't want to resort to artificial light because of the integration with the weather unit. This extended the duration of our study from three weeks to five weeks.*
- *Lack of adult assistance* – most of the parents work full time. Another pair of hand at least is needed in most sessions, especially for recording and photographing investigations.
- *Time constraints* – due to assembly, cancellation of athletics carnival due to rain, swimming program, band practice and team teaching of mathematics resulting in the tight scheduling of the investigations.
- *Shortage of equipment* – e.g. prisms for all the children to use.

Bob found many positive outcomes in teaching for conceptual change. They were:

- Very enthusiastic response from the children – this was really very rewarding.
- Finding out answers to the questions we set out to investigate.
- The development of a more questioning attitude to the world.
- Satisfaction of following the children's thinking and supporting them to think differently about light – that is, to follow children's thinking along the whole learning journey.

Teaching for conceptual changes needs good classroom management skills. We now examine this important area.

Classroom/centre management in teaching for conceptual change

Phasing into teaching for conceptual change

It is important that you do not involve the children fully in this approach without sufficiently educating them about it. It is possible that the class you begin teaching may not have had much experience of being in a classroom where the focus is on teaching for conceptual change. In this case, you will be courting disaster if you expect them, unprepared, to actively cooperate in all aspects of this approach. They need to learn new roles and new skills and, most importantly, to develop changed views about your role as the teacher. For instance, a student teacher reflected on this aspect the first time she introduced children to learning science through teaching for conceptual change.

In our initial foray, I asked the children to write down topics that they would like to think about in science. Next, I asked what kinds of questions would they like answers to. At first the children believed I was going to provide the answers!

There is a need for a phasing in of teaching for conceptual change approach. In Phase 1 you should endeavour to become more sensitive to the children's ideas and questions, and to collect their questions and select those for which activities are already published. You then limit the investigations to a few questions that many children have: you might carry out whole-class investigations or have groups investigate the same question. With increased confidence, in Phase 2, you could provide exploratory activities through which you help children to raise useful questions, refine these, and then help them to plan and to carry out their own investigations. You can then better help the children to develop sensible and useful conclusions from this work.

Selecting appropriate topics

Teaching for conceptual change with its emphasis on connecting with children's everyday experiences has implications for the topics you might choose to teach. As a guide to selecting appropriate topics, consider selecting those that have relevance to:

- everyday events
- children's existing ideas, and
- human relationships.

The last point includes the interest shown in science by parents and peers.

REFLECTIONS 7.4: DECIDING ON TOPICS

Consider the following content areas:

- spiders
- bricks
- bicycles
- desert life (for a class not located in a desert)
- flight into space.

Are they topics that you think might readily be taught using a teaching for conceptual change approach? If so, *make some sketches of how you could develop these topics in ways that lead to conceptual change.* If not, *how could you inject aspects* of teaching for conceptual change to learning science *into other topics?*

You could also use social media to discuss your ideas, and to find out what others think about each of these topics. As noted by Lewin (2013), 'One of the most powerful developments in recent years has been the growth of social media, enabling people to communicate and network more easily, as well as share their own resources with others. Micro-blogging tools such as Twitter can offer ways of sharing ideas, useful website and portals, as well as simply asking a question, often receiving responses from 'followers' within minutes. Hashtags are a form of tagging (representing a key feature) which enables Twitter users with shared interests (for example science education) to easily find relevant posts' (pp. 240–1).

Focusing the topic area for investigations

Given the degree of control that is accorded to the child in teaching for conceptual change, it is most important that the topic chosen has a definite focal point. Otherwise, it is highly probable that the investigations will become so far-ranging that learning will become superficial and not be shared across the classroom. Further, it might become very difficult for you, as the teacher, to manage, given the diverse demands made for resources and in terms of the base knowledge that you would need in order to guide the children effectively. An example of a topic that is almost certain to get out of hand would be 'water'. You might be inclined to choose such a broad topic because of your uncertainty about the process, wanting to ensure that there is sufficient scope for children's questions and activities. Our observations, and those of other teachers, lead us to urge you to plan more carefully.

A successful topic can be much more focused than you might imagine. While you might consider the topic 'spiders' as sufficiently focused, one preschool teacher narrowed it further to 'spider webs'. Questions generated from the teacher's conversations with the children were: 'What different sorts of webs are there?', 'How does a spider make a web?', 'What is the sticky stuff?', 'Do spiders use webs only to catch food?', 'Where do spiders make webs?', 'How strong are webs?', 'How do they get broken?', 'Do they get broken?', 'Why doesn't the spider get stuck in its web?'. From these questions there is ample scope for many hours of investigation, and this teacher developed a most effective set of learning experiences for these young children.

Further focusing is necessary when considering the questions children might have asked about a topic. For instance, one group of children in a Year 4 class studying 'space' raised some intriguing but difficult questions, including: 'How was space made?', 'Why is space black?', 'How big is space?', 'Why are there stars?'. You need to acknowledge the value of such questions, but you also need to consider whether the questions are answerable in their existing form, whether the class has the resources to investigate them and whether the children are able to work at the conceptual level of the question. You might need to negotiate with the children, to modify such questions or to suggest that the children concentrate on more manageable questions, such as 'Why does Mars look red?'

The process may differ, given different age groups. For example, with younger children the whole class could investigate one question.

Linking science to other curriculum areas

Teaching for conceptual change is ideal for making links to other curriculum areas, given its emphasis on the embeddedness of science in everyday life and society – where science is conceptualised as a human endeavour. In encouraging children to engage actively in setting the agenda for investigations, it is highly likely that questions will arise that cross curriculum boundaries. In other chapters (see Chapters 5 and 6) we show examples of how this can be done.

Assessment approaches for teaching for conceptual change

Teaching for conceptual change is clearly focused on continually monitoring what children know, what they are thinking and what conclusions they are drawing. This is foundational for formative assessment. What is key here is identifying exactly what concepts are important for children to know about. The Australian Curriculum – Science gives some guidance here.

In the content strand of physical sciences we can see the following areas that are important for light and for electricity (Table 7.3). They link well with the research into children's thinking in science discussed earlier. These particular curriculum statements are based on what might be covered at a particular year level (due to time constraints rather than children's ability to do more), rather than on what children might be interested in, thinking of or asking questions about. Summative assessment would follow their thinking as science is experienced in the classroom.

Table 7.3 Content to inform summative assessment of light and electricity

Physical sciences	Foundation year	Year 1	Year 2	Year 3	Year 4	Year 5	Year 6
		Light and sound are produced by a range of sources and can be sensed.				Light from a source forms shadows and can be absorbed, reflected and refracted.	Electrical circuits provide a means of transferring and transforming electricity. Energy from a variety of sources can be used to generate electricity.

Concerns about teaching for conceptual change

Concerns about teaching for conceptual change focus mostly on how to best create the conditions for conceptual change (Roth, Goulart and Plakitsi 2013). For instance, in extending your experiences of teaching for conceptual change on the topic of electricity – a topic we know is not readily tackled by many teachers – it has traditionally been suggested that you should *create conceptual conflict*.

This strategy allows children to initially share their understandings of a topic. Then the teacher confronts them with conflicting evidence or views that they are to explore. Subsequently, the children have opportunities to construct new or broader understandings and to use their new knowledge.

Original work by Keogh and Naylor: http://conceptcartoons. com/what-is-a-concept-cartoon-.html

One variant of this strategy makes use of concept cartoons, in which children are presented with competing but plausible views from individual children (original work was done by Keogh and Naylor). Such a cartoon could be presented to a group of children to explore and discuss.

What underpins both suggested approaches to creating conditions for conceptual conflict is the theory of constructivism (Fleer and Pramling 2005). Creating cognitive conflict, as espoused by Piaget, has had its critics over time (Roth, Goulart and Plakitsi 2013). Children's thinking in science has been shown to be:

- resistant to external suggestions
- deep within the child's thought
- age specific
- maintained in children's consciousness over several years
- the child's first answers.

This suggests that the child is a lone thinker in the world. The child is completely responsible for their own learning and that the child constructs knowledge for him or herself.

Conceptual conflict is also foundational to the socioscientific approaches to teaching science for much older children (Fleer and Pramling 2005). A socioscientific perspective sees children engaged in a variety of social dilemmas that they must solve. These dilemmas are usually conceptual, procedural or technological. Real world contexts create the conditions for engaging students in science learning as children discuss and debate the products or processes of science. Examples are usually controversial and often include cloning, climate change, genetically modified food, soil degradation and stem-cell research. From this literature we notice a growing number of studies that focus on how children learn science when a socioscientific perspective is featured. Some of these points were discussed in Chapter 5.

Through engagement in controversial issues, it is argued that children develop scientific literacy. Scientific literacy entails children being sufficiently informed to be able to make decisions about societal needs and practices. A focus on scientific reasoning and conceptual change of children is central. Examples include enhancing the quality of argumentation in school science (Osborne, Erduran and Simon 2004), and argumentation in science (Naylor, Keogh and Downing 2007).

As might be expected, a socioscientific approach to teaching science has not directly influenced research in the early years of school or the prior to school settings. Presenting scientific dilemmas to children in the birth to five year period has really only emerged in relation to environmental sustainability (e.g. Davies, et al. 2009) where research is focused mostly on what children think and how they might act, rather than investigating how through argumentation young children resolve issues or take a personal stand in relation to a socioscientific dilemma.

Summary

In the introduction to the three chapters, we said that in reading these chapters that you would find three common things for all the approaches:

- inquiries
- inquiry skills development
- constructivism.

You were invited to plot on the continuum if the science learning was *teacher-led* or *child-led*. Now that you have read each chapter, what have you noticed about how each approach begins?

You would have noticed that the example of the 5Es for an inquiry-based approach to teaching science was much more teacher-led than the other two approaches. You would have also noticed that what was unique about an inquiry-based approach to learning science was that the focus was on the child – the whole unit of work was geared around the child. The inquiries began from something the child had introduced as interesting to be investigated. In teaching for conceptual change, the role of the teacher was even more heightened. The teacher continually focused on moving the science experiences in ways that followed the children's thinking – s/he had to always be monitoring conceptual change. This meant introducing cognitive conflict at different points.

In examining the three approaches, what did you notice about the role of the teacher? Hopefully you would have seen that the teacher created the conditions in each of the three approaches for the children to take more responsibility in science. That is, the teacher did not position her or himself as the person with all the knowledge, imparting this knowledge to the children. Rather, the teacher supported the children to express their thinking, to come up with investigable questions, and to design experiments or experiences that would help answer the children's questions. Variation in how child centred this could be found across the three approaches, with more adult-led science experiences in the 5Es approach, and less in inquiry-based learning.

Table 7.4 Analysing the approaches

Approach	Pluses	Minuses	Interesting points
Inquiry-based teaching approach – the 5Es.			
Inquiry-based learning approach.			
Teaching for conceptual change – constructivism.			

In the introduction to this section you were also asked about what was learned when it was child-led and when it was teacher-led. What did you find? You might have noticed in the teacher reflections that a more child-led approach required a great deal of teacher management. You might also have noticed that in teaching for conceptual change, the teacher has to do a lot of research into what children might think about a topic and the scientific concepts they need to know to develop their thinking.

What is central for each approach? Analyse each approaches for positives, negatives and interesting points.

In this and the previous two chapters, constructivism was the key theory that framed each approach to teaching and learning in science. In the next chapter we draw upon a different theory known as cultural–historical theory to discuss a cultural–historical approach to learning in science.

References

Australian Curriculum, Assessment and Reporting Authority 2014, Australian Curriculum – Science. Available at http://www.australiancurriculum.edu.au/Science/Curriculum/F-6. (Accessed September 2014.)

Australian Government Department of Education, Employment and Workplace Relations 2009, *Belonging, Being and Becoming. The Early Years Learning Framework for Australia*, Canberra: Commonwealth Government.

Balgopal, MM 2014, 'Learning and intending to teach evolution: Concerns of pre-service biology teachers', *Research in Science Education*, vol. 44, no. 1, pp. 27–52. (DOI 10.1007/s11165-013-9367-9.)

Campbell, C 2012, 'Learning theories related to early childhood science education in C Campbell & W Jobling eds, *Science in Early Childhood*, New York: Cambridge University Press, pp. 24–37.

Campbell, C, Jobling, W eds 2012, *Science in Early Childhood*, Melbourne: Cambridge University Press.

Danielsson, AT, Warwick, P 2014, '"You have to give them some science facts": Primary student teachers' early negotiations of teacher identifiers in the intersection of discourses about science teaching and about primary teaching', *Research in Science Education*, vol. 44, no. 2, pp. 289–304. (DOI 10.1007/S11156-013-9383-9)

Davies, J, Engdahl, I, Otieno, L, Pramling-Samuelson, I, Siraj-Blatchford, J 2009, 'Early childhood education for sustainability: Recommendations for development', *International Journal of Early Childhood*, vol. 41, no. 2, pp. 113–17.

Fleer, M Pramling, N 2015, 'A cultural-historical study of children learning science: Foregrounding affective imagination in play-based settings', Dordrecht: Springer.

Forbes, A and Skamp, K 2014, '"Because we weren't actually teaching them, we thought they weren't learning": Primary teacher perspectives from the *MyScience* initiative', *Research in Science Education.* vol. 44, no. 1, pp. 1–25. (DOI. 10.1007/s11165-013-9367-9)

Lewin, C 2013, 'ICT and effective practices in science education: Lesson learned and future directions' in C. Redman ed, *Successful Science Education Practices. Exploring What, Why and How they Worked*, New York: Nova Science, pp. 227–44.

Naylor, S, Keogh, B, Downing, B 2007, 'Argumentation and primary science', *Research in Science Education*, vol. 37, no. 1, pp. 17–39.

Osborne, J, Erduran, S, Simon S 2004, 'Enhancing the quality of argumentation in school science', *Journal of Research in Science Teaching*, vol. 41, no. 10, pp. 994–1020.

Roth, M-W, Goulart, MIM Plakitsi, K 2013, *Science Education During Early Childhood: A Cultural-historical Perspective*, Dordrecht: Springer.

Sikder, S, Fleer, M, published on-line 2014, 'Small science: Infants and toddlers experiencing science in everyday family play', *Research in Science Education.* (DOI. 10.1007/s11165-014-9431-0)

PART 4

Inclusive Constructions of Knowledge Across and Within Communities and Cultures

In the two chapters that follow you will be invited to reflect upon how knowledge construction takes place across and within communities and cultures. This section of the book builds upon the second chapter where you considered how children think and develop understandings about their world.

The chapters that follow are: Chapter 8: Conceptual play and contextual and conceptual intersubjectivity: cultural–historical approaches to learning science and Chapter 9: Culturally sensitive teaching: sustainability and relatedness in our ecosystems.

What is common across these chapters is:

- cultural constructions of knowledge
- cultural-historical theory
- learning as a collective process rather than an individual construction
- inclusion.

As you read both chapters there are **key things to look for.**

One of the challenges you will face in reading this section will be in relation to how you conceptualise knowledge and particularly what you mean by the knowledge of science. Martin's (2008 cited in Chapters 8 and 9) critique of how Aboriginal knowledges have been positioned in Australia is helpful for conceptualising the philosophical and epistemological problem with which we must engage if we are to be inclusive of all forms of knowledge construction:

One contradiction exists in that Aboriginal knowledges can only be considered dichotomous to 'western scientific' knowledge. Another contradiction is identified as the lack of an overall conceptual framework within Aboriginal knoweldges, thus giving rise to some substantive, methodological and epistemological, and contextual differences. Substantive differences pertain to subject content and characteristics between Aboriginal knowledge and western science knowledge. Aboriginal knowledge is seen to be concerned with fulfilling immediate and short-term needs, whereas western science knowledge is somewhat removed from the everyday needs of *People* and is concerned with constructing generalisations (Martin 2008, p. 55).

As you think back to Chapter 2 and then read Chapters 8 and 9 consider the contradiction that is raised by Martin (2008). Document how you might position a range of knowledges, including Aboriginal knowledges, so that you do not create a dichotomy. Make sure you do not position one knowledge form against another or value one form above another. How can you present knowledge constructions in science so that all forms of knowledge construction are valued, while also meeting the requirements of the Australian Curriculum – Science (ACARA 2014), and the Early Years Learning Framework (Australian Government 2009)?

As you read **develop a model** of how you might bring a range of knowledges together so that you can understand what children bring into the learning environment, what is important in their community, and how they make sense of their world. Your model should explicitly consider inclusive constructions of knoweldges across and within communities. Draw your model here.

After you have read the chapters in this section using your model, go back and **critique** all the approaches to teaching science – transmission, discovery, inquiry and teaching for conceptual change. How inclusive are they of knowledge constructions? Armed with this understanding, now read the final chapter in this book. Use your model as an important tool for positioning yourself as a leader of inclusive knowledge constructions in science and in the knowledge construction of the community in which you are/will be teaching.

CHAPTER 8

Conceptual play and contextual and conceptual intersubjectivity: cultural–historical approaches to learning in science

Introduction

In this chapter we go beyond thinking about children's learning of science concepts as an individual construction and consider the learning of science as a social and cultural process in which the child is engaged. In this chapter our focus is not just on what the child knows and can do in science (constructivism), but rather how children collectively shape and are shaped by their social and material world through science.

In this chapter we specifically introduce a cultural–historical approach to learning in science. In the first part of this chapter we take a look inside a Year 3 classroom from the perspective of the teacher, as we follow how learning is socially mediated and culturally constructed. An integrated unit of work which features Earth and Space is presented through the diary of the teacher. This is followed by a brief presentation of learning on the same topic, but from the perspective of the preschool and Foundation year level children. Here, a range of work samples are presented to map how thinking emerges over time. Finally, a snapshot of what the topic of Earth and Space looks like for infants and toddlers is also presented. Together, these case examples show a continuum of pedagogical practice and learning of children from birth to eight years for the topic of Earth and Space. The content of this chapter links with the topic of Earth and Space presented in Chapter 3, where a transmission approach to teaching science is presented.

We finish this chapter with a discussion of what is unique about cultural–historical theory for explaining the pedagogy of science learning through conceptual play as a unique teaching approach for children aged from birth to eight years.

REFLECTIONS 8.1: THE EMOTIONAL WELLBEING OF THE LEARNER

In the EYLF educators promote pedagogical practices that position the young learner as feeling safe and supported in the learning of science when they:

Pedagogical practice	An example of this practice taken from the case studies
• acknowledge and respond sensitively to children's cues and signals *when working scientifically*	
• respond sensitively to children's attempts to initiate interactions and conversations *during investigations*	
• support children in times of change and bridge the gap between the familiar *science learning* and the unfamiliar *science learning*	
• build upon culturally valued child rearing practices and approaches to learning *science*	
• are emotionally available and support children's expression of their thoughts and feelings *in the context of science learning*	
• acknowledge each child's uniqueness in *how they think and act in scientific contexts*	e.g. *some activities will evolve as the unit progresses and children contribute to the shaping of the investigation*
• spend time interacting and conversing with each child *during science investigations* (Adapted from Australian Government 2009, p. 21).	

As you read this chapter and consider the case studies presented, examine the role of the teacher and see if they follow these important pedagogical practices when supporting children to learn science. Give one example of the pedagogical practice of the teacher for each of the indicators presented in this table.

The interactions that are organised in classrooms and centres during the process of teaching science are an important part of cultural–historical approach to teaching science. We highlight in **bold** the key features of cultural–historical theory in the case study that follows.

Looking inside the classroom – teacher diary

Karina focuses on building scientific relationships between her Year 3 children (eight-year-olds) and their preschool buddies (four-year-olds). She draws upon cultural–historical theory to support her pedagogical practices. What follows is Karina's diary on how she set up and launched a unit on Earth and Space. As you read, reflect on how she builds social and conceptual relations (as suggested in Reflections 8.1).

When developing a curriculum for individual schools, based on the Australian Curriculum – Science, some schools generate their own outcomes for assessment and reporting. At my school, a number of science concepts are integrated into one outcome, based on the Year 3 Achievement Standard. Our outcomes read as:

Students use their understanding of the movement of the Earth, materials and the behaviour of heat, to suggest explanations for everyday observations.

Through reflecting on this outcome, and the Australian Curriculum – Science, an investigations unit was created as our Term 4 focus. This unit is called: 'A Picnic for Every Season'. The idea behind this is that the planning of a picnic for each season of the year would demonstrate a significant depth of knowledge. If children can explain how to plan a picnic for each season, they would be demonstrating their understanding of how the movement of the Earth affects our seasons and the length of our days and therefore what time of day would best suit a picnic at different times of the year. **This is an authentic way of showing children that science is a human endeavour**.

If children can plan food for picnics in different seasons, they would be demonstrating their understanding of how to use materials to insulate food to keep it hot or cold. They would be showing their knowledge of the behaviour of heat in their preparation for the picnic.

My Year 3 class has a buddy class, the Preschool class (four-year-olds). I decided that an authentic overall activity would be **creating a children's non-fiction picture book to share with their buddies**. This book is called *A Picnic for Every Season*, and is part of the learning and assessment process for this Investigation.

Prior planning: I drew on the progression shown in the Australian Curriculum – Science for knowing about what learning might be expected, what learning might have already been achieved, and what learning will be planned for the future.

Table 8.1 Curriculum content for Earth and Space sciences

Year 7,
Module 3,
Unit 7

	Foundation	Year 1	Year 2	Year 3	Year 4	Year 5	Year 6
Earth and Space sciences.	Daily and seasonal changes in our environment, including the weather, affect everyday life.	Observable changes occur in the sky and landscape.	Earth's resources, including water, are used in a variety of ways.	Earth's rotation on its axis causes regular changes, including night and day.	Earth's surface changes over time as a result of natural processes and human activity.	The Earth is part of a system of planets orbiting around a star (the sun).	Sudden geological changes or extreme weather conditions can affect Earth's surface.

Source: ACARA | The Australian Curriculum | Version 6.0 dated Tuesday, 18 February 2014.

What follows is a diary of my work with my Year 3 class throughout our investigation unit 'A Picnic for Every Season'.

Before the term begins …

I made sure that I had a wide range of activities planned, but importantly, some activities will evolve as the unit progresses and children contribute to the shaping of the investigation

For a successful term of learning, there is much to do to prepare! So, in the week leading up to the start of term, these are some of the things I have done:

Play stations

I provided a range of materials that supported the children to play. The play materials were designed to support the children to role-play the science learning that they were investigating. **Encouraging children's play meant that the children could take abstract scientific ideas and play out key concepts in ways that mattered to them.** This also allowed science content and process to be explored in imaginative ways through role-play.

Wall displays

When children walk into the room, I like them to see things that give them clues about our investigation and spark their interest. One wall has a huge Sun on it (one metre diameter) and the question: If this is the Sun, how big is the Earth and how big is the Moon? Later we will draw the tiny Moon and small Earth to add to the display. There is also a 'Science Thinking Display' and a 'Science Word Wall'. Both of these are added to along the way.

Science table

Children love playing with interesting science toys. In my collection for this unit I have items like a plasma ball, a pendulum that draws in a tray of sand, some mini lava lamps, a slinky and such things. These are on a bench along the wall **for a child to play with and explore the concepts** together with other children. Later we will discuss these concepts and learn to explain what is happening when we use the toys.

Book displays

Books are an important resource for sparking ideas and researching answers to questions. On bookshelves and desk stands, I have placed lots of books about the seasons and weather, the Earth, Sun and Moon, electricity, experiments and other related topics. Children will make use of these during reading times and science times. **We will consult them when we need to find an answer and use them to spark interest and enjoyment.**

Week 1

Launching the investigation:

When I told the children that our investigation this term would be science-based and that the unit was called 'A Picnic for Every Season', one child called out: 'But picnics don't have anything to do with science!' (Robin, 13 October 2014). I was delighted to hear this! It shows what a great learning experience lies ahead.

For the first activity of the day, we head outside, which immediately excites the children. Each child has a marble. We discuss how when we hold up a small sphere like a marble, we can make bigger spheres look the same size. Other children walk away from the group holding different sized balls – a golf ball, a tennis ball, a basketball and a large fit ball. We call out 'stop' when their ball looks the same size as the marble we are holding up. This leads us into a discussion of the relative size of the Sun, Moon and Earth and the vast distances in space – **searching the internet and books for key information**. The children are really excited about these facts and the WOW factor of such big numbers and concepts!

Reflecting on what we know

We discussed what we knew about the Sun, Moon, Earth, heating, cooling, seasons, energy, conducting, insulating, etc. Children also record any questions that they have.

One of the resources I used is called 'Hexagons' (HOOKed on Education). This resource suggests that children be given a sheet of hexagons with key words from the unit on them (Sun, Moon, Earth, heating, cooling, seasons, energy, conducting, insulating, etc.). Children are asked to explain what the words mean and then arrange them showing how they think the concepts are connected. Children also record any questions that they have. The pictures on their strip include a symbol from the SOLO taxonomy.

'Hexagons' – HOOKed on Education: www. pamhook.com

After completing their reflection, children identify where they think they are at with their thinking, by placing a clip along a continuum, as shown in Figure 8.1.

Matilda said:

I have put my star clip on the picture, that means I just know a few things because I know a little bit, but not that much. For example, I know that cooling and heating could go with electricity but I'm not sure why. I have put Sun and Moon and Earth and seasons together because they belong together, but I want to know more about everything.

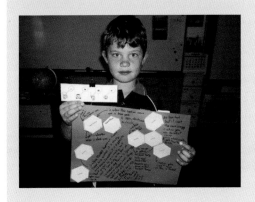

Joel said:

I have put my paper clip on the picture that means I know some facts and I know some of the ways that they connect with each other. I could combine ideas and make longer sentences about these words. I know what happens in the seasons and why they're my favourite like how spring is my birthday! So I explained things. But I'm looking forward to learning about conducting and insulating because actually I have no idea what they are.

Figure 8.1 Matilda and Joel share their hexagons.

Sharing our learning

A classroom display begins where we record ideas on large sheets of butcher's paper and join them together in different ways as we learn new things. Children can contribute to this **during class discussions** or independently as they find out new things. **As questions arise, they are also recorded on the display. A sense of the scientific thinking of the group emerges and this is something I actively encourage – talking, listening, sharing and coming together with a group investigation**. Some of the children's reflections are shown in Figure 8.2.

Figure 8.2 Hexagons of learning – our science word wall.

Week 2

Movement of the Earth

In keeping with a cultural–historical approach to teaching science, the children have the opportunity to **play and act out the movement of the Earth**! We do it as a class first, with just a few children being the Sun, Earth and Moon. Then, in groups of three, children take turns acting each part. We add words to a science word wall that we can now define, including spinning and orbiting. Children draw diagrams of what they have learned. We reflected on how our thinking was changing, as we engaged in science learning. Here are the comments we displayed:

Alyssa: I thought that the Earth went very slowly when it was spinning but now I know that it goes around so fast that we can't feel it.

Finlay: I thought that the Moon didn't move, but it just stayed in one place but now I know that it follows the Earth to orbit the Sun.

Joel: I thought that the Moon spun around so that we could see both sides but now I know that we only see one side of the Moon and never see the back of it.

Lili: I thought that there was no such thing as no gravity but now I know that there are places in space with no gravity.

Ruby: I thought the Sun went around the Earth and Moon but now I know that the Sun stays still while the Earth orbits it.

Bella: I thought that if there was no gravity, only humans would float, but now I know that everything would float away!

Sophie I didn't think that buildings and trees would float with no gravity.

Matilda: I thought that the Earth was bigger than the Moon and Sun, but now I know that the Sun is much bigger and the Moon is smaller.

Bailey: I didn't realise that you could fit one million Earths inside a hollow Sun.

Patterns in our world

Understanding that 'night and day' is an endlessly repeating pattern is an important concept. It helps children make sense of many everyday observations. The children were encouraged to record some ideas about patterns they observed that exist because of the pattern of night and day. **This supports the idea that science is a human endeavour.**

For example:

I'm awake, I'm asleep, I'm awake, I'm asleep …

Owls sleep, owls wake up, owls sleep, owls wake up …

Some flowers open, some flowers close, some flowers open, some flowers close …

We know from the accumulation of research into children's thinking in science (see Chapter 3) that children will have already developed views about Earth and Space.

What understandings do children have about Earth and Space sciences?

Night and day: Children tend to think about why it becomes dark at night time in four different ways.

1   The Sun is animate – the Sun hides behind the hills, trees, goes to a different country.
2   Covering theories – the Sun is covered by the clouds.
3   Astronomical movements – the Sun moves up and down as the Earth rotates, the Sun goes around the Earth once a day.
4   Rotational theory, but where the time taken varies – the Earth spins on its axis once a day, the Earth rotates in six minutes.

The planet Earth: Children's beliefs are shown in Figure 8.3.

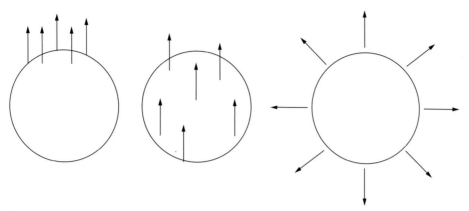

Figure 8.3 Three orientations of how the Earth is perceived by primary aged children.

The relations between the Earth, Moon and Sun: It is very difficult for children to understand the relative distance between the Sun, Earth and Moon, or their spatial arrangements. The idea of an Earth-centred perspective can persist throughout primary school.

Phases of the Moon: Mostly children think that the phases of the Moon are due to something covering the Moon, or something casting a shadow on the Moon. The most common idea is that the shadow of the Earth covers the Moon.

Seasonal changes: What most children think is that the seasons of the year are caused through the distance the Earth is away from the Sun. That is, they believe that winter happens because the Earth is further away from the Sun than in summer. Another view is that during winter the Sun moves to the other side of the Earth.

Week 3

Shadows

It can be surprising to discover that children in Year 3 still have weird and wonderful ideas about shadows – a concept that adults think is relatively simple to grasp. **As a whole group we began the week with a discussion about shadows** – their characteristics and cause. There was some discussion about shadows coming from us and there was some talk about the movie of Peter Pan that clearly contained some unscientific images of sewing on your shadow to your feet!

Jacqueline: 'I thought shadows came from your feet.'

We then went outside and explored shadows. We made shadows with our bodies and watched where the shadows fell and how they moved when we moved. We went outside at different times of the day to see the change in the angle of the Sun and how this changed where our shadow fell. Children made figures from foil that they positioned on a page, tracing the shadow at different times of the day. Everyone made sundials and learned about how this fits with the movement of the Earth and the times of the day.

Seasons

Thinking about time led us into learning about seasons. We were always making conceptual connections. The cause of the seasons being the tilt of the Earth is hard to grasp but the features of seasons and the opposite timing around the world were easier for them to make sense of. Small groups made posters about a season and shared their research with the class (see Figure 8.4).

We looked at how seasons are an everyday, scientific pattern. We also used our knowledge of the seasons to inspire collective artworks depicting trees through the seasons.

To integrate our learning, the children paired up and studied photos of picnics. The children asked important everyday questions, such as: 'What can we tell about the time of day in this picture?', 'How?', 'What is the season?', 'Why?' This made children really focus on things like the length of shadows, clothing, leaves on trees and so on. We prepared a display board.

Summary posters

To summarise our learning so far, children created posters about 'Spinning in Space'. They were given suggested headings if they wanted to use them and encouraged to use words, diagrams and pictures to explain their learning.

Week 4

This week saw us move into a new but related area of study, the study of energy. We first revisited our original hexagon headings and **thought about what we already knew and shared our questions. We talked with each other, constantly sharing and thinking together. What everyday understandings did we have? What scientific understandings did we need to know about?**

Kinds of energy

As a discussion starter, we did some simple experiments that showed some of the different kinds of energy. For example, we boiled water in a clear kettle to see heat energy in action. We dropped different-sized balls into buckets of water to show potential and movement energy. We looked at clips and read some books about energy. We played with energy by being still and active ourselves as 'Kinetic kids'. Children did some artwork about this.

Friction experiments

In teams, children explored friction and how it relates to energy. They completed a circuit of simple experiments that they had found on the internet – 'Handy experiments with friction'. We recorded the results of these experiments and began exploring the

Matilda said:

I learnt a lot. I learnt that the Earth is spinning so fast that we can't feel it. I saw what this meant when you (teacher) spun the bucket of water so fast that the water stayed in the bucket and didn't spill.

I liked getting into activities with shadows. I thought that shadows were like Peter Pan's shadow that got sewn to his shoes in the movie. Now I know that shadows are made because an object blocks the light so there isn't light where the shadow is.

My favourite fact is about the sizes, that a million Earths could fit in the Sun and four Moons could fit in the Earth and that means that four million Moons could fit in the Sun.

Joel said:

When I first started there were things I didn't know but I've learned about more. Now I know more about shadows and seasons. I never knew the Earth was on a tilt to make the seasons and so we are closer and further away from the Sun. I love the facts about a million Earths fitting inside the Sun. Now I also know it isn't day everywhere at the same time.

I learnt a lot by listening well and doing everything really enthusiastically because I really was interested and I even looked stuff up at home. I was so enthusiastic like I found the best for a shadow so that I could work out about them and how the light is blocked to make the shadow.

Figure 8.4 Matilda and Joel share their findings.

ways in which scientists write about their experiments. We discussed scientific processes that are important in experiments, such as keeping things the same and changing one thing, making sure it was a fair test and so on. Children found it hard to understand the word 'fair' in the science context. **We noticed that science as an important human endeavour was invented by humans to help them explain their world.**

Here are some of the children's comments about their experiments:

Bailey: I had different results for every station which showed me that different things change the amount of friction.

Robin: I realised it was important to count the beats each time so that we kept the time the same.

Ruby: Rubbing my hands makes friction, which is why it keeps me warm in winter.

Sabrina: Friction wears your shoes out faster and rubbing them on concrete really ruins your shoes.

Amy: I think that rubbing sticks to make fire is good friction and helped Aboriginal people.

Erin: There was less friction in the cold water and with hand cream but more on the carpet. My hands got really hot then.

Electrical energy

We next looked at electrical circuits and torches, to learn about electrical energy and how it works. Firstly, children drew diagrams of how they thought a light bulb would light up or how a torch would work. They date-stamped this and recorded the time. Then, in small groups, children tried to make a light bulb work. **The excitement in the room as group after group 'got it' was tangible! It was as though they had invented the light bulb personally, such was their delight in making it work**. Children then added to their diagrams and recorded the time gain. They loved seeing how their thinking had changed in just a couple of hours. It made learning very visible for them, which is always an empowering experience for children.

Week 5

Conductors and insulators

The children were very interested to learn about conductors and insulators, as these were the two words that they knew least about at the start of term – terms that some of the children had raised, but without a sense of understanding them. Some of the children found different activities, and as a group we set about doing several experiments to show how some materials conduct electricity and then looked at the conduction and insulation of heat. Children wrote about what they had done and learned. We did experiments about insulators and conductors particularly in the context of food, exploring how and why we keep food hot or cold. **Once again, science was revealed to the children as an important human endeavour that improves the quality of their lives.**

Week 6

Molecules and energy

When investigating heat, we got into discussions about molecules and the way they react to heat. This also led into discussing the energy of hot water and how things can change. Children learned about solids, liquids and gases.

Matilda said:

I've learnt that a thermos is an insulator so it doesn't let out heat or cold. It has layers to keep it in. The ice cubes didn't even hardly melt all day. When we had hot water in something that is insulated it stayed hot for a long time. It was really hot in the thermos and a bit hot in some kinds of cups but other cups got cool faster because things want to be the same as the air around them.

A metal spoon is a conductor so it does let the heat through. When something is hot the molecules and atoms travel faster but then it is slower if it is cold. So the metal spoon got hot fast when we put it in the hot water but the plastic one was slow to get warm.

Joel said:

I've found out now that conduction means that heat travels through and the wax paper cup is not good at conducting. It is a good insulator because the heat doesn't spread through and that is why people use this kind of cup to get hot drinks at a café.

I also learned that a thermos helps things stay really cool or really hot. Even ice stayed as ice all day in our classroom. So you could do that in summer or in winter you'd have hot chocolate.

I know a lot more than I did at the start now that I did the experiments.

Figure 8.5 So what did Matilda and Joel learn about conductors and insulators?

Experimenting time

We then conducted experiments where children heated and cooled different substances: water, butter and honey. They completed reports about the experiment and the results, which we discussed as a class.

We repeated the process of the experiment with a mini experiment on melting a chocolate drop.

Finally, the children had to design their own experiment to do with heating and cooling. They were given an icy pole (the kind in a plastic tube) each and the choice of how to create an experiment. **They were able to work in groups so as to have multiple icy poles to use.**

They shared their investigative questions:

Cameron: I want to know if putting sunscreen on the ice block packet will make it melt slower than if I don't put sunscreen on the packet.

Alyssa: I want to know if it takes longer to melt the icy poles if we put them in different places like in a school bag or on the bench or in my desk tray.

Sarah: I want to know if my hat will stop the icy pole melting even when it is in the Sun.

Matilda: I want to know the fastest way to melt the icy pole, if it is in hot water or the Sun or other places.

Although seemingly simple, these experiments were the children's favourite part of science. The necessary resources were easy to provide, yet children found it great fun to heat and cool these things – especially because they got to eat melted chocolate and drink slushy icy poles!

Children wrote explanations about how heating and cooling changes things, to demonstrate their understanding of these processes.

Week 7

Summing up: In our final week, we engaged in activities that drew together our **learning through a range of social processes.**

Making books

Firstly, children completed **group-made books called** *A Picnic for Every Season.* These books had pages for each season that children illustrated and tables to complete about a picnic in each season. They had to consider what kind of picnic they would have in each season: the time of day and why, the location and why, the food and why. They had to explain how to keep the food hot or cold. This task really engaged their thinking and helped them integrate the learning from across the topics.

Picnic inventions

Once the booklets were completed, children chose their favourite picnic and engaged in a Design–Make–Appraise process (see Technologies curriculum). Their task was to invent something to improve a picnic that only used items found in the children's environment – items such as natural things found in nature, and things that may have been taken on a picnic, like paper plates, straws and containers. The children invented some weird and wonderful items, such as heating ovens, footwear, **toys for small children** and various insulating containers.

Group presentations

Lastly, children **worked in groups to create a presentation for the class**. Children wore a thinking hat, each representing the colours of thinking styles. As a group they needed to include ideas from the perspectives of the different hats and include as much information as they could. They were allowed to present their ideas in any format they chose.

Some groups became life-sized circuits. Some made posters. Some did a short play. The most creative, however, was the group that made up a rap. Imagine five children rocking to a beat that one of them is keeping with imitation rap sounds. Picture a lead singer saying the first line and a few chorus singers responding with each second line.

The words are as follows:

When water is hot it turns into a gas.

Steam it's called, let's get on with our rap.

When something's hot, the molecules move,

Now let's get on with our groove.

When you freeze honey, it stays runny,

Now, we think that is really funny!

When you put dye in hot water to drown,

It goes all the way down.

When dye goes in a hot, hot cup

It also goes all the way up.

Ms Harris is awesome; she is rad

That must mean we're totes mad!!

Now we're done with our rap …

Yay!

(Hats thrown into the audience.)

This energetic and entertaining rap was a delight to watch – and we had repeated performances for everyone who walked into our classroom! Although not the whole breadth of the unit, it certainly demonstrated some key understandings and the joy of learning about science!

Final thoughts from Matilda and Joel

Matilda: I thought that science was really fun because the experiments were yummy, especially melting chocolate. I liked learning new stuff about space like the sizes of the Sun, Moon and Earth. I learned most by actually doing the experiments and working in my science group. We were allowed to talk to each other, so my group helped each other with their ideas. I can now write or draw something about all the words on the hexagons that I started with. And I know how the ideas go together, like how the Sun is so, so hot and that is a fact and we know that fact when we want to go on a picnic. So we won't go on a picnic in the middle of the day in summer and we would put chocolate or watermelon in a cold bag with ice. But in winter the middle of the day might warm you up and you would want some hot chocolate in a thermos. So I liked understanding how these ideas go together to help us.

Joel: Science this term has been awesome. We got to do science in a way that was fun. Eating chocolate helped me remember about melting and freezing! My group made a rap at the end. We had thinking hats that are like caps and, because cap rhymes with rap, we made a rap. You can make the caps look really cool by being sideways or backwards so that helped everyone like our rap and think it was cool. This was a fun, cool way to show what we had learned. And I know more than the rap words too. Like all about the seasons and the different clothes and food and weather and how the tilt of the Earth makes the seasons in different parts of the world. There is a lot that I have learned about.

In reflecting on how Karina builds social and conceptual relations in her classroom (Reflections 8.1), what did you notice?

Karina's diary is rich with teaching ideas, but also pedagogical practices for supporting the children's sense of themselves as knowledgeable about their world (discussing what children already know), being able to make a valuable contribution in class (designing their own experiments), and feeling emotionally safe when expressing their ideas with others. Karina also creates a sense of community in her classroom. This is central for a teaching program that draws upon cultural–historical theory, where:

1   Learning science is social process.
2   Science learning is a collective process.
3   Learning science must be personally and socially meaningful.
4   Assessment of science learning is a collaborative process between child and teacher.

Karina's diary provides insights into aspects of a cultural–historical approach to teaching science. We see that the pedagogy foregrounds learning as a social and cultural process. In the next section, we introduce another case example that features night and day, but which highlights the cultural artefacts that the children produced alongside of the pedagogical practice that elicited them.

Looking inside the classroom – the child's perspective

Preschool and the Foundation year of school: We now return to the teacher we introduced in Chapter 3 – Bob. In that chapter, Bob taught Earth and Space to his children using a transmission approach to teaching science. However, in a subsequent year Bob felt he would like to teach this topic through a cultural–historical approach. As with Karina, Bob set up an experience to find out what his children knew about the topic through engineering group discussions. When using a transmission approach (Chapter 3), finding out children's prior ideas is not a pedagogical feature of that approach, therefore Bob did not do this. In using a cultural–historical approach Bob provided experiences to the children which would allow him to find out how their thinking was developing throughout the unit. Bob, provided opportunities:

- to observe, question, develop and represent understandings
- for sustained interest, and enhanced learning through engaging families
- to participate in spaces designed especially for children, allowing multiple entry points into exploring 'big ideas' in science
- for connecting science learning to things that matter to children and have high social value (see Cowie and Otrel-Cass 2011).

This has also been named by Cowie and Otrel-Cass (2011) as 'horizontal learning'.

The unit of work that follows is based on a belief that 'children can engage with and develop proficiency with sophisticated science ideas when teachers provide a variety of multimodal learning opportunities that expand on their existing and developing ideas and experiences' (Cowie and Otrel-Cas, 2011, p. 285). The case study that follows shows many multimodal examples of children's work. As was observed in the unit of work taught by Karina, Bob's cultural–historical approach to teaching science is also focused on:

1　Learning science is a social process.
2　Science learning is a collective process.
3　Learning science must be personally and socially meaningful.
4　Assessment of science learning is a collaborative process between child and teacher.

These key principles are illustrated through work samples and teaching objectives.

1　Learning science is a social process

Objective 1 – Finding out children's ideas:

- Draw the world at day time. Draw the world at night time. Show me night time and day time in the world.

Objective 2 – Finding out about children's thinking about the shape of the Earth, Sun and Moon:

- You are up in a rocket. Draw the Earth, Sun and Moon. What would they look like? What shape would they be?

Science content knowledge: Every 24 hours the Earth turns on its axis once. This is what causes day and night. At any one time half of the Earth's sphere is in sunlight (day) and half of it is in darkness (night).

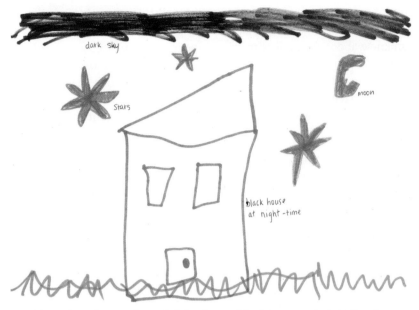

Figure 8.6 Laura's understanding of night time – 'Black houses at night time'.

Figure 8.7 Understandings about the Sun.

2 Learning science is a collective process

Objective 1 – A means of answering the question 'Why do we need the Sun?', plus demonstrating comprehension of information from the Big Book: The Sun is always shining somewhere:

- Draw a picture that shows me why we need the Sun.

3 Learning science must be personally and socially meaningful

Objective 2 – To measure children's knowledge retention. Drawing how night and day happens after two and a half weeks:

- Draw a picture of the world on the front and back of a piece of paper. Pretend you are in a rocket in space. Show me how night and day happens.

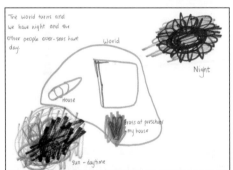

Figure 8.8 Katie representing night and day (at the beginning of the unit and at the end of the unit).

These two images (Figure 8.8) were produced on the front and back of the same piece of paper in order to help children with their thinking about how it can be night time and day time in different parts of the world. This technique allowed the children to show both day time and night time simultaneously on their one piece of paper (back and front of the paper)

Objective 3 – Find out the views children have about night time:

- Draw the world at night time and show/tell me what happens to the Sun. Why can't we see it? Where does it go?

Objective 4 – Introducing 'perspective' to children. We spoke about the Sun being far away and looking small:

- Draw a picture to show me the houses that are far away and the preschool that is close to us.

Figure 8.9 text labels:

Sun

The preschool looks bigger than the houses because we are near it.

little tree (far away)

little grass

Figure 8.9 Introducing 'perspective' to children.

Background science content knowledge: The Sun is at the centre of the solar system. The Earth, Moon and Sun are part of that solar system. The Earth orbits the Sun, taking one year to complete one orbit. The Moon is a natural satellite for the Earth. It takes one lunar month to complete one orbit of the Earth. Understanding the spatial relationship of the Earth, Sun and Moon is important for children to know before they attempt modelling the whole solar system.

4 Assessment in science is a collaborative process between teacher and child

Objective 1 – After views of night and day. End of the fourth week of teaching:

- Draw the Sun and the Earth and show me how night and day happen.

What is evident from the work samples shown in this case study of Bob teaching the unit on Earth and Space is that the children had many *different* views of night and day. These views are not surprising because what children observe in the sky is counter-intuitive to scientific thinking about Earth and Space.

It took centuries to develop scientific understandings about Earth and Space. This topic is a good example of how certain forms of knowledge cannot be just

On this side is the
sun. It is day time.

On this side
of the world
is the moon.
It is night time.

Figure 8.10 What Chandra knows about night and day at the end of the unit.

'discovered' by children (see Chapter 4), but require contexts and social conditions that draw children's attention to valued forms of knowledge, which represent the best-known explanations at the time of Earth and Space. A cultural–historical perspective of Earth and Space would suggest that all knowledge, including scientific knowledge, is a human construction. The knowledge does not just exist 'out there to be found', but is created by humans and is passed on from one generation to the next. Sometimes existing theories are refuted because they no longer provide an adequate explanation for all contexts and situations. New scientific theories are then needed. There are many examples found in the history of science. For example, the Egyptian scientists A. D. Ptolemy (140 AD) put forward the Ptolemaic system theory to explain the Earth's position in the solar system. He argued that the Earth was the centre of the solar system. He stated that all the planets circled the Earth. This was known as a geocentric view. Polish scientist Nicolaus Copernicus (1473–1543), German scientist Johannes Kepler (1571–1630) and finally Italian astronomer Galileo Galilei (1564–1642), with his supporting observations using a telescope, over time moved thinking from a Ptolemaic system to a heliocentric theory to explain the Earth's position in the solar system (as opposed to a geocentric view).

In order to fully appreciate the continuum of learning science for the topic of Earth and Space, we now turn to a snapshot of science learning for infants and toddlers, which also draws upon cultural–historical theory.

Looking inside the classroom: infants–toddlers perspective

Infants and toddlers working and playing scientifically: In the context of family day care, childcare and playgroups, there are many opportunities to study the foundational concepts associated with Earth and Space. In particular, educators can point out to infants what is visible in the night sky, but also what can be seen in the sky during the day. Noticing the Moon, particularly the different phases of the Moon, is not only something that can be a deliberate focus of attention during adult–child interactions at night, but also something that can be observed during the day. The Moon is often visible during the day. Noticing the Moon contributes to building an understanding of night and day.

Toddlers in family day care, childcare and playgroups also have opportunities to notice important parts of night and day. Discussing the Sun and Moon, by drawing pictures of them (adult and child together), by finding images of the Sun and Moon on the range of websites now available, and by discussing the Sun as a star, build foundational understandings for later study.

The science of Earth and Space for such young children focuses on children's everyday lives. Drawing children's attention to scientific explanations of what is happening around them is central to a cultural–historical conception of play, learning and development.

These experiences of the infants and toddlers described in this section, and also those of the preschool children discussed in the previous section, link directly with the outcomes in the EYLF.

REFLECTIONS 8.2: SCIENCE LEARNING AND THE GENERAL OUTCOMES DETAILED IN THE EYLF

Examine the suggested learning outcome of 'Children as confident and involved learners' and map which of these fits with the experiences shown in the case studies discussed here so far.

Outcomes	Learning experience that promotes this outcome
Children develop dispositions for learning, such as curiosity, cooperation, confidence, creativity, commitment, enthusiasm, persistence, imagination and reflexivity.	
Children develop a range of skills and processes, such as problem solving, inquiry, experimentation, hypothesising, researching and investigating.	
Children transfer and adapt what they have learned from one context to another.	
Children resource their own learning through connecting with people, places, technologies and natural and processed materials (Australian Government 2009, p. 34).	

In the next section we give more detail about the concepts from cultural–historical theory that have been used to inform science learning in the case studies discussed here. This theory is different from the theory of constructivism that supported the teaching and learning approaches discussed in Chapters 5–7. We introduce cultural–historical theory because its focus goes beyond the individual learner's thinking in science, and foregrounds the learner's thinking in the context of social interactions.

A cultural–historical perspective on learning in science

The studies that have dominated research in science education have predominantly focused on finding out what individuals think about a particular science concept, such as force, day and night, energy, etc. From this body of research, theorists have built learning models of children's alternative thinking to Western science (e.g. Fleer and Robbins 2003). The research that has been undertaken to find out what individuals think about topics, such as night and day has been framed from a constructivist perspective (see Chapter 7). It is suggested that these everyday or alternative concepts are developed by children during everyday interactions with the world. This longstanding science education research suggests that everyday concepts get in the way when teaching science concepts in schools (e.g. Fleer and Pramling 2015). This research, dating back to the 1980s, was deemed innovative and thought to be useful for changing the nature of science teaching in schools. In contrast, Zapata (2012) has argued for reform in science education so that teachers recognise 'that knowledge is constructed through social acts and culturally embedded' and that this will 'provide opportunities for the experiences of women, minorities and currently marginalized members of society to present their views on resources for research' (p. 797) and, in the context of this chapter, resources for teaching science.

As discussed in the previous chapter, constructivism was an important theoretical driver in this research and the subsequent pedagogical work that resulted. In recent times, researchers have found that this research has not substantially progressed scholarship in science education or dramatically changed learning outcomes for children, and new directions have been sought (e.g. Andree and Lager-Nyqvist 2013; Plakitsi 2013). Two different ways of conceptualising pedagogy have emerged. The first is called a socio-scientific approach and the second is known as a cultural–historical perspective. The former was discussed in the context of inquiry-based approaches to teaching and learning (Chapters 5–7) and is not discussed here. The latter cultural–historical approach allows for re-analysing or re-conceptualising the observations of children's thinking in science so that more than the individual child's ideas are considered. A cultural–historical approach considers how children collectively shape and are shaped by their social and material world through science as one form of knowledge construction.

Looking into the context, rather than just considering the concept

As introduced in Chapter 2, a cultural–historical perspective on learning and development comes from the work of Vygotsky (see *The Collected Works*, volumes 1–6). It is also called sociocultural theory by some researchers and educators. The legacy of Vygotsky's writing has been the interest generated in understanding the social, cultural and historical contexts in which children and adults find themselves. Of significance is Vygotsky's view that in order to understand the individual, one must also understand the cultural–historical context in which the individual exists (Vygotsky 1987).

Cultural–historical theory draws our attention to the social and material context as a source for the development of the child's scientific thinking. Here we think about:

- how social relationships shape children and how children shape their social relations
- community values
- family beliefs and practices, and
- the past practices that have laid the foundations of what participants pay attention to in their communities.

An increasing number of researchers in science education have considered the potential of Vygotsky's work (e.g. Chen, Masur and McNamee 2011; Fleer and Pramling 2015; Roth, Goulart and Plakitsi 2013; Zapata 2012), even though studies on what individuals think about particular science concepts are still published. For instance, Carter (2007) has argued in her analysis of the literature that, 'Taken together, this research argues the need for science education to go beyond imparting scientific conceptual knowledge and skills and advocates critical participation in a world dominated by science conceptualized its sociocultural and political interests' (p. 7). Longstanding research by Fleer and Robbins (2003) has shown that, when a cultural–historical perspective is taken, the researchers spend longer in the research context, mapping the movement of children's thinking, rather than simply recording an end point. They argue that going in to find out what children think, and leaving as soon as their thinking has been determined, is like a 'hit and run approach', yielding 'hit and miss results'. For example, in the context of the concept of Earth and Space discussed in this chapter, it is pertinent to note a broader set of ideas than just Western science to explain Earth and Space, which may take time to determine, as noted by Carter (2007):

> All cultures create their own stories or cosmologies that not only help explain but also provide a sense of wonder and awe about the universe and their place within it. This more inclusive view of science sees it as any systematic attempt to produce knowledge about the natural world and makes room for other local/indigenous, indeed multiple, and previously excluded conceptualizations of scientific knowledge.

> Hence, scientific knowledge has arisen from local contexts and in response to local needs … Western science can thus be understood as a particular form of local knowledge tradition, shaped by and reproductive of, the culture and society in which it is articulated (p. 11).

Teachers who draw upon cultural–historical theory do not simply focus on concepts, they also seek to examine the social contexts and engagements in which conceptual processes take place. As such, teachers who draw upon a cultural–historical approach for learning in science do not just ask about children's cognitive processes, but rather they look beyond concepts and seek to find the levels of social engagement in which learning is taking place.

Knowledge construction through building contextual intersubjectivity

In Chapter 2 we considered how communities build localised knowledges to explain the world in which they live. There we introduced a range of ways of connecting with communities, so that as a teacher you can respectfully gain insights into valued forms of knowledge and better understand the worldview of the community in which you will be teaching. This section builds upon this introduction.

In the context of developing a robust research methodology for foregrounding Aboriginal knowledges, Martin (2008) has put forward an approach that repositions those who were once the subject of research, as the ones to be doing the research. This work has relevance for us as teacher-researchers, finding out how best to connect with the local communities in which we teach. She says that what is needed is to:

- decolonise
- build a research agenda
- build research capacity.

In the context of connecting with the local community, this means positioning ourselves as learners when in someone's community. We do not seek to move in with more highly valued forms of knowledge, such as Western science, but build a relationship with the community.

Decolonise: In line with Martin's (2008) work, we do not seek to colonise, but rather to create the space for communities to decolonise. This means their knowledge systems and ways of constructing knowledge are valued, respected and given space within the curriculum. As Hamlin (2013) has argued 'educators must begin with the scientific knowledge inherent within' the communities in which they teach. These understandings 'contextualize science curricula' so that the curricula is 'purposely designed to meet the nuanced cultural needs' of those in that community (p. 759).

Build a research agenda: In building new curricula so that it does not colonise the knowledge system inherent in that community, it is important for educators to co-construct the agenda for gathering knowledge about that particular community. In reviewing the literature, Hamlin (2013) raises the following questions:

What research is needed?

Who is the research for?

What difference will the findings of the research make for that community?

Who will undertake the research?

Who is likely to benefit from the research?

We can add to this by drawing inspiration from the work of Martin (2008) where she asks:

Has permissions been gained for doing the research from the community?

Is knowledge being appropriated from the community?

Hamlin (2013) in citing McKinley (2007, p. 221) from New Zealand, says that it is extremely important to 'find a place in our curricula and classrooms for indigenous knowledge – a place that recognizes and protects indigenous information, understanding and wisdom. This will add to our scientific knowledge and methods' (p. 764). This begins to address the appropriation and misuse of knowledges that are located in local communities.

Finding out about the worldviews and ways of constructing knowledge within a community is not simply about going into the community and asking questions. Hamlin (2013) states that, 'This process requires teachers to participate and experience community activities to learn about the socio-political, historical, and global contexts in which their students and families live' (p. 765).

Build research capacity – as a two-way process: Martin (2008) in referring to the building of research capacity is talking about Aboriginal peoples generally. However, Martin's methodology is also relevant for the teacher entering the community. In order to build the right sort of research capacity for finding out about the community in which you will be teaching, it is important to build trust. By being a part of the community you signal trust. For instance, Hamlin (2013) says:

> When Indigenous families see their children's teachers participating in community events, it provides a space for community members to begin to develop a sense of trust of these same teachers. This developing trust is an important component needed to promote respectful exchange of ideas and knowledge between teachers and Indigenous community members (p. 764).

In co-producing curriculum knowledges for Indigenous and non-Indigenous children, both non-Indigenous teachers and Indigenous teachers from outside of the community develop a strong sense of contextual and conceptual intersubjectivity. Intersubjectivity means that teachers generate curricula that are meaningful, and respectful of the construction of knowledge within that community. Communities also generate concepts to explain and predict their social and material world. What are the ways in which families and educators induct their children into what matters for them in their communities and how does this relate to the learning of science?

Cultural–historical theory acknowledges that communities build knowledge based on their own needs, and this knowledge is intergenerationally shared. That is, families and communities also build intersubjectivity with each other and pass on valued forms of knowledge to their children. But how are concepts culturally constructed in the first place?

In the next section, we move from contextual intersubjectivity to conceptual intersubjectivity. The idea of conceptual play is introduced to show how teachers and children can and do play with science concepts in the process of building intersubjectivity.

Knowledge construction through building conceptual intersubjectivity

What is meant by scientific conceptual play?

The idea of scientific conceptual play (see Fleer 2011) is to give time and space for children to play with concepts, resources and ideas in science. Conceptual play brings together both a personal and a cultural construction of knowledge. In this form of knowledge construction, scientific concepts that are promoted by the teacher are always embedded in what matters in particular communities.

In the early years of school and in preschool, the teacher gives space and time for children to play with ideas and resources, but does so within a scientific framework. Emotions, imagination and creativity are supported as children play with ideas, concepts and resources (Fleer and Pramling 2015). The adult–child interactions are focused so that children do not have to discover scientific explanations (see Chapter 4) for what they are experiencing or playing, but rather a level of intentionality with concepts on the teacher's part is evident. This is in keeping with the EYLF (Australian Government Department of Education, Employment and Workplace Relations 2009) where teachers are expected to engage in intentional teaching, and not just leave children to discover concepts by themselves.

In the Foundation to Year 6 level, children are given time and space to play with everyday concepts whilst also being introduced to scientific concepts (see Vygotsky 1987). It is just as important at this level for children to engage with scientific ideas in a playful manner as it is in the early childhood period. Older children also need the opportunity act and think creatively in science. It is the role of the teacher to enter into shared and sustained scientific conversations with children as they play, create and imagine in scientific ways for real world purposes.

Conceptual play captures this pedagogical practice, where children engage with everyday concepts and scientific concepts simultaneously. The relations between everyday and scientific concepts are discussed in the next section.

A cultural–historical reading of how concepts develop

Vygotsky (1987) suggested that concept formation should be thought about at two levels. First, concepts should be considered at the everyday level. That is, concepts

Figure 8.11 How do you keep warm in the water?

are learned as a result of interacting directly with the world. Through children's interactions with the social and material world they develop intuitive understandings of how to do things, such as putting on a jumper when they feel cold, or taking off their jumper when feeling hot. Children will say that they feel hot or cold, but are less likely to tell you about the science behind their actions. That is, young children are unlikely to express a scientific understanding of insulation. Knowing about how to keep warm or how to cool down are important everyday concepts. Vygotsky argued that these everyday concepts lay the foundations for learning scientific concepts. But everyday understandings of concepts cannot be transferred to other situations. For instance, knowing that a jumper keeps you warm may not be useful if you are learning to surf. The question is then, how do you keep warm in the water? Having an understanding about the scientific concept of insulation is useful for knowing how a wetsuit works. Being locked into everyday understandings limits what children can do, because they act intuitively rather than with scientific understanding. Learning science concepts supports children to think as they navigate through the world in which they live.

Paired with the idea of everyday concepts is Vygotsky's (1987) theory of scientific concepts. Here he conceptualises scientific concepts, not just as Western science, but any concept that is abstract, such as learning to read print. He suggested that learning science concepts at school, away from the context in which such concepts are used, gives little meaning to children about how a particular concept, such as insulation, can help them. That is, when children learn about the concept of insulation by putting different materials/fabrics around jars with hot liquid in them, in order to determine which stays warm the longest, this experience says little about children's real world experiences. However, real world experiences,

Figure 8.12 Learning scientific concepts away from their everyday use does not change practices in everyday life.

such as when using an insulated lunch bag or when trying to work out how to keep icy poles from melting when going on an excursion matter to children. These are authentic experience related to children's needs and interests.

Vygotsky argued that when children develop everyday or basic concepts, these experiences lay the foundation for higher order thinking. For example, having lots of experience with different types of blankets or jumpers, and talking about how they insulate or keep your body heat in, lays the foundation for talking about insulation. In this context, it makes perfect sense to a child to learn about insulation (scientific concept). Learning about insulation can transform the child's everyday experience. It is transformative, as the child can transfer this knowledge to other contexts. It is a higher-order concept (or as Vygotsky said, a higher mental function) that provides important understandings across a range of everyday contexts – such as insulation in housing, insulation of lunch boxes, insulation of fridges and insulated drink containers. According to cultural–historical theory, higher mental functions are always culturally produced and used. Learning science is therefore a cultural practice that we as humans have invented as a valued form of cultural knowledge that we pass on to our children, and which our children use and develop (as well as refute) further.

Both everyday concept formation and scientific concept formation are interrelated. An everyday concept that develops from day-to-day life practices creates the possibility for the development of scientific concepts in the context of more formal

Figure 8.13 Knowing about insulation helps you ask better questions when buying surfing gear to keep you warm in the water.

experiences. A scientific concept prepares the structural formations of a child's thinking so that there is a new way of conceptualising an intuitive everyday experience (Vygotsky 1987). That is, as children bring together their working everyday knowledge of 'keeping warm' and their scientific knowledge of 'insulation', they transform their everyday practice. Children need to develop both everyday concepts and scientific concepts.

Hedegaard and Chaiklin (2005) suggest that the most powerful learning contexts are those where the professional keeps in mind the everyday concepts and the scientific concepts when planning for learning. Hedegaard and Chaiklin (2005) have called this the *double move* in teaching. As teachers, we create many different types of learning contexts for children – some of these are opportunities for building everyday concepts, and some are contexts that suit the introduction of scientific concepts. What is important here is the double move on the teacher's part – where everyday concepts and scientific concepts are always conceptualised together as part of social practice, so that a child's thinking and practice can be transformed.

In the preschool context this is captured through the idea of conceptual play. However, there are some challenges (Blake and Howitt 2012). For instance, there is research by Sakellariou and Rentzou (2012) in Greek preschool science which suggests that while teachers note the importance of high quality teacher–child interactions for supporting science learning, they found that the teachers 'favour more an uninvolved approach to children's play rather than getting involved into children's dramatic play' (p. 130), where it might be possible to build scientific opportunities.

Figure 8.14 Using science in everyday life transforms how we think and act.

This is in line with findings by Blake and Howitt (2012), who note that 'Children are innate explorers and researchers, yet facilitation is required to encourage scientific characteristics and develop sound skills' (p. 297), yet their research showed that many opportunities in purposeful play were lost as adult involvement was limited. In contrast, Siry and Kremer (2011) have shown how preschool teachers in Luxembourg broaden scientific interactions in the early years by providing support through 'peer-to-peer interaction in the co-construction of science concepts', allowing 'children to learn *from*, and *with*, each other' (p. 643).

Digital technologies supporting learning

Using digital technology for producing an animation creates the conditions for children to work both with their everyday understandings, while explicitly thinking about the science concept. An animation allows the child to deliberately showcase their scientific thinking as they make a model of something, and animate it in order to illustrate the concepts in action, thereby bringing together everyday and scientific concepts. For example, children can create a digital model of the Earth and other planets going around the Sun; they could also show the life cycle of a frog or caterpillar, or even show how an electric circuit works. You will find a range of examples on the websites in the margin box. This website shows how scientific concepts can be animated in two different ways:

1 *Teacher-made resources* for children to teach specific science concepts.
2 *Child-created animations* to show concepts in action (see the *Science for Children* website for an example of a six-year-old showing how playing in a playground gives experience of the concept of force through push and pull).

Animated science examples: www. slowmation. com
Concept of force in the playground: www. cambridge.edu. au/academic/ science

Hoban (2011) has named this process 'slowmation'. This term has been abbreviated from 'slow animation', which is a simplified way of making stop-motion animation. The animation is played slowly at two frames per second, enabling the creators to narrate the slow-moving images to explain a science concept or tell a story (Hoban, 2011). The child just needs a digital tablet and materials for making the models. The idea is that a diorama is created in which a scene is created, and photographed. An object in the diorama is then moved slightly, and the same scene is photographed. The object is moved again, and photographed. This occurs until the sequence of steps that illustrate the concept in action has been completed. All the photographs are then brought together, creating the effect of motion. This animation is then narrated as though it were a documentary with a voiceover of the moving images. Music can be added, as can text.

Hoban, Loughran and Nielsen (2011) have shown the making of the animation as a five-step process. These steps are useful for teachers to use, and also to use with children. They include:

1 Researching (researching the concepts).
2 Storyboarding (step by step lay out of how the objects will be introduced and moved).
3 Modelling (making the objects to be introduced, including text).
4 Photographing the scene using a digital tablet or device.
5 Narrating the animation (putting a narration over the string of photographic images).

Both 3D and 2D objects can be used, as shown in Figure 8.15. Fleer and Hoban (2012) have argued that in early childhood, intentional teaching is supported by the use of slowmation because the teacher is working explicitly with science concepts through creating an animation.

Leading change in science education

Professor Gary Hoban has pioneered the research about and the approach for using slowmation in both primary schools and early childhood settings. In his research he has been able to show how the process of using slowmation helps

Figure 8.15 Slowmation in action by children.

both children and teachers to learn science concepts more deeply. Through his work, he has been able to reserach new pedagogical approaches for the teaching of science. Although his work is theorised predominantly from a constructivist perspective (see Hoban and Nielsen 2010), we have chosen to include it in this chapter on cultural–historical theory because when conceptualised as a tool for bringing together everyday concepts and scientific concepts (see Fleer and Hoban 2012), it is possible to see how conceptual play is supported.

Cultural–historical curriculum

In drawing upon cultural–historical theory for engineering many different opportunities for dialogue about curriculum, as we saw in the case example of Bob, Siry and Kremer (2011) argue that:

> conceptualizations about such complex topics [mini beasts, dinosaurs, weather, metamorphosis] are often quite rich, and as we go beyond their everyday experiences we can try to build upon what they know *and* what they imagine to move towards

investigating the science concepts themselves. Finding out what children know is a valuable tool in designing curriculum in a way that address the theories they already have, either through direct experience with the phenomena, or through the media (p. 654).

In researching curriculum development in New Zealand for physics teachers, Fernandez, Ritchie and Barker (2008) write that curriculum can be conceptualised and written with a progressive teacher in mind: 'Our ideal idea of teaching is very interactive with kids, and puzzling over things; being prepared to say "Can't understand that", "Don't know", "I'll find out", or "What do we think could be happening"' (writer one, cited in Fernandez, Ritchie and Barker 2008 p. 206). Both the concepts and the process of researching these concepts can take an authentic pathway, as teachers' frame learning using the pedagogical device of a double move, following a cultural–historical approach to teaching science.

Goulart and Roth (2010) use cultural–historical theory for framing and introducing the idea of collective curriculum design. In their study of preschool children in Brazil, they examine how teachers collectively designed science curriculum with children. In their research, they present the example of a teacher who has provided children with a list of science topics for them to classify and discuss as the foundations for building their own program of learning – this is similar to what Karina discussed as her entry point for the topic of Earth and Space. It is through dialogue that collective design emerges. For example: 'A conflict emerges with the word "plant." Where should it be fit …?' (p. 552). Goulart and Roth (2010) argue that the curriculum emerges through a process that they have called *participative thinking*. 'Participative thinking means being conscious of the world and transforming it based on the understanding associated with this consciousness' (p. 557). Goulart and Roth (2010) further argue that collective curriculum design is possible when:

- the structure is a dialogue
- the teacher provides a starting point to open up discussion that is meaningful to the children, e.g. cards with words on them
- recognition of the children's culture is foundational
- the teacher is a participant in the design process
- working with and being comfortable with uncertainty – as the teacher cannot predict the outcome
- all interactions and decisions are negotiated.

Children's agency in shaping the directions of the curriculum are central to Goulart and Roth's (2010) collective curriculum design process: 'Both teacher and children are open to listen to and to be touched by the artifacts and the words created by others' (p. 559).

Summary

This chapter challenged you to re-position children's alternative views or prior knowledge not simply as an individual construction, but as part of children's everyday life. This was captured through the idea of conceptual and contextual intersubjectivity. It was argued that everyday concepts represent the foundations of scientific concepts, at the same time as scientific concepts are foundational for helping children make meaning of everyday practices. What was key was children's meaningful social engagement with others as they developed everyday and scientific concepts as mutually constituting processes in the context of their community. Here science knowledge was shown to be a cultural construction, and pedagogical practices and curriculum design were found to be negotiated, fluid and collectively engineered.

References

Andree, M, Lager-Nyqvist, L 2013, 'Spontaneous play and imagination in everyday science classroom practice', *Research in Science Education*, vol. 43, pp. 1735–50. (DOI 10.1007/s11165-012-9333-y.)

Australian Curriculum, Assessment and Reporting Authority 2014, Australian Curriculum – Science. Available at http://www.australiancurriculum.edu.au/Science/Curriculum/F-6. (Accessed September 2014.)

Australian Government Department of Education, Employment and Workplace Relations 2009, *Belonging, Being and Becoming. The Early Years Learning Framework for Australia*, Canberra: Commonwealth of Australia.

Blake, E Howitt, C 2012, 'Science in early learning centres: Satisfying curiosity, guided play or lost opportunities?' in KCD Tan & M Kim eds, *Issues and Challenges in Science Education Research: Moving Forward*, Dordrecht: Springer, pp. 281–98.

Carter, L 2007, 'Sociocultural influences on science education: Innovation for contemporary times', *Science Education*, pp. 1–17. (DOI: 10.1002/sce.)

Chen, J-Q, Masur, A, McNamee, G 2011, 'Young children's approaches to learning: A sociocultural perspective', *Early Child Development and Care*, vol. 181, no. 3, pp. 1137–52.

Cowie, B, Otrel-Cass, K 2011, 'Exploring the value of "horizontal" learning in early years science classrooms, *Early Years: An International Journal of Research and Development*, vol. 31, no. 3, pp. 285–95.

Fleer, M, 2011, '"Conceptual Play": Foregrounding imagination and cognition during concept formation in early years education', *Contemporary Issues in Early Childhood*, vol. 12, no. 3, pp. 224–40.

Fleer, M, Hoban, G 2012, 'Using "slowmation" for intentional teaching in early childhood centres: Possibilities and imaginings', *Australasian Journal of Early Childhood*, vol. 37, no. 3, pp. 137–46.

Fleer, M, Pramling, N 2015, *A Cultural-historical Study of Children Learning Science: Foregrounding Affective Imagination in Play-based Settings*, Dordrecht: Spinger.

Fleer, M, Robbins, J 2003, '"Hit and run research" with "hit and miss" results in early childhood science education', *Research in Science Education*, vol. 33, no. 4, pp. 405–32.

Fernandez, T, Ritchie, G, Barker, M 2008, 'A sociocultural analysis of mandated curriculum change: The implementation of a new senior physics curriculum in New Zealand schools', *Journal of Curriculum Studies*, vol. 40, no. 2, pp. 187–213.

Goulart, MIM, Roth, W-M 2010, 'Engaging young children in collective curriculum design', *Cultural Studies of Science Education*, vol. 5, pp. 533–62.

Hamlin, ML 2013, '"Yo soy indigena": Identifying and using traditional ecological knowledge (TEK) to make the teaching of science culturally responsive for Mayua girls', *Cultural Studies of Science Education*, vol. 8 no. 4, pp. 759–76.

Hedegaard, M, Chaiklin, S 2005, *Radical-Local Teaching and Learning: A Cultural-historical Approach*, Aarhus, Denmark: Aarhus University Press.

Hoban, G, Loughran, J, Nielsen, W 2011, 'Slowmation: Engaging preservice elementary teachers with science knowledge through creating digital animations', *Journal of Research in Science Teaching*, vol. 48, pp. 985–1009.

Hoban, G, Nielsen, W 2010, 'The 5Rs: A new teaching approach to encourage slowmations (student generated animations) of science concepts', *Teaching Science*, vol. 56, no. 3, pp. 33–7.

Martin, K 2008, *Please Knock Before You Enter: Aboriginal Regulation of Outsiders and the Implications for Researchers*, Brisbare: Post Pressed.

Plakitsi, K ed 2013, *Activity Theory in Formal and Informal Science Education*, Rotterdam: Sense.

Roth, W-M, Goulart, MIM, Plakitsi, K 2013, *Science Education During Early Childhood: A cultural-historical perspective*, Dordrecht: Springer.

Sakellariou, M, Rentzou, K 2012, 'Greek pre-service kindergarten teachers' beliefs and intentions about the importance of teacher–child interactions', *Early Child Development and Care*, vol. 132, no. 1, pp. 123–35.

Siry, C, Kremer, I. 2011, 'Children explain the rainbow: Using young children's ideas to guide science curricula', *International Journal of Science Education and Technology*, vol. 20, pp. 643–55.

Vygotsky, LS 1987, 'Thinking and speech' in LS Vygotsky, *The Collected Works of L.S. Vygotsky, Vol. 1, Problems of General Psychology*. RW Rieber, AS Carton eds, N Minick trans, New York: Plenum Press, pp. 39–285.

Zapata, M 2012, 'Substantiating the need to apply a sociocultural lens to the preparation of teachers in an effort to achieve science reform', *Cultural Studies of Science Education*, vol. 8, pp. 777–801. (DOI 10.1007/s11422-013-9513-8.)

Acknowledgement

Special acknowledgement is made of the Year 3 case study that was so skilfully taught and written by Karina Harris.

CHAPTER 9

Culturally sensitive teaching: sustainability and relatedness in our ecosystems

Introduction

In this chapter we introduce a culturally sensitive approach to teaching science with a focus on sustainability and relatedness. Specifically, we discuss the multitude of interrelated ecosystems that make up life and living for all things on our planet in the context of Martin's concept of relatedness (Martin 2008). We introduce a broad range of ways that the ecosystems may be conceptualised, and highlight the differing worldviews that should be respected and celebrated. We focus on:

1 Citizen Science.
2 Place-based education.
3 Culturally sensitive teaching.

We begin this chapter by looking at how children from five to 12 years imagine their future in the context of their environment, followed by a discussion of research into children's thinking about ecosystems. We then turn to a discussion of culturally sensitive ways in which we as educators can enter into a community and work with the worldviews of the people living there. Here we discuss how to engage elders, and other respected community members, in order to find the appropriate ways in which we can learn about how the environment or Country is conceptualised for that community, but in ways that foreground relatedness. This could mean walking this path with local Indigenous elders or it could mean engaging newly arrived (as well as established) families from a range of communities from around the world. It is now commonplace to have culturally and linguistically diverse urban communities in Australia (e.g. African families, Asian families, Middle Eastern families, etc.). The intent here is to build upon the existing thinking of children, their families and the community in which they live, or one that they still connect with even though they now live in Australia. We link back to some of the ideas introduced in Chapters 2 and 8, where the cultural construction of knowledge was considered. We move forward by conceptualising this process as being jointly constructed between the educator and the community. We invite you to think about how you and the children you teach can simultaneously value cultural and scientific ways of knowing which may or may not be complementary.

HAVE YOU EVER WONDERED ABOUT …?
CONTEXTS OF SCIENCE

Did you know that a special fungus called Ghoul Fungus breaks down the bones of dead animals? This fungus only grows near old bones. This species can be described as having a large cap that is sticky, cream to pink-brown in colour, with pink-brown gills (see Negus 2014).

Fungi are fascinating because they are neither plants nor animals. Fungi have challenged scientists because of how they behave and what they are made from. Fungi are invisible most of the time. Fungi reproduce by spores. They do not depend on the Sun for their energy source. Unlike green plants, they do not photosynthesise. Mostly they are made up of microscopic threads (hyphae – the group is called mycelium) that weave their way through the host material (e.g. soil, dead trees, bones and even living organisms). These threads are made up of chitin, which is similar to the exoskeletons of some sea creatures and insects. Young (2013) describes fungi by discussing the difference between fungi and plants:

'Plant cells have protective walls that are largely constructed of a hard substance called cellulose, the principal component of wood. A fungal mycelium is very different in that the walls of the hyphae are constructed out of a type of protein belonging to a general class of chemicals call chitins. Like cellulose, chitins can be physically quite strong, and the shells of crabs and prawns are based on a type of chitin (p. 3)'.

Young (2013) asks, 'Does this mean that fungi are more closely related to animals than to plants?' (p. 3). He responds by saying no. But this does show that fungi are not plants either.

In Chapter 2 we discussed the common classification of organisms into animals and plants, and the organisational framework of the world into living and non-living. They each represent a particular scientific classification system. They mirror particular worldviews. There are other worldviews. We begin in Research activity 9.1 by examining children's worldviews of their future environment.

RESEARCH ACTIVITY 9.1: CHILDREN'S WORLDVIEWS OF THEIR FUTURE ENVIRONMENT

Children were asked to imagine themselves 50 years into the future when they were old enough to be grandparents. They were asked to think about what their environment would be like. What views might children have? Ellen aged 12 and Alex aged five share their thinking:

'In the future maybe the ozone holes get bigger, and so roughly half of the ozone has disappeared, and so instead of having summer, autumn, winter and spring, you have ozone seasons. In the ozone season it's cold and you know it can also be warmish, and like you know then the average heat will be 40 degrees Celsius' (Ellen, 12 years).

'... we've got a very, very, big tree that's very old in my yard, but it doesn't belong to us – it belongs to the world' (Alex, 5 years).

Both children have well-formed views about their environment. Ellen is worried about the ozone and what this might mean for climate change. This is consistent with the literature which suggests that children do worry about their environment (Yazdanpanah 2013). She also has some mixed understandings about the science concepts for explaining her worries. Her thinking opens up opportunities for teachers to give agency to Ellen through learning how to better understand climate change with science concepts.

Alex understands at a very young age that the environment is not something that is owned by people, but rather he and the tree are part of an interrelated ecosystem. Alex has an ecocentric worldview. Young and Elliott (2014) explain that an 'ecocentric world view is about understanding that the Earth is made up of both living and non-living parts that are all interlinked though multiple systems and relationships' (p. 2). Martin's (2008) concept of relatedness also helps explain Alex's worldview.

Interview proforma: www. cambridge. edu.co/ accdemic/ science

In Figure 9.1 is an example of a pro forma that you could use to interview three boys and three girls of different ages about their ways of thinking, acting and relating about sustainability. Invite children to write or/and draw their ideas. Examine their responses. What do you notice? A blank copy of the proforma can be found on the *Science for Children* website.

In Figures 9.1 to 9.3 are shown examples of children's responses to the research described in Research activity 9.1. Across four different communities (both urban and rural) it was found that very young children positively discussed their environment. However, the older the child, the more negative the response. This is illustrated in the figures. For instance, Sarah's (eight years) was very positive, stating that 'The world will be clean with no rubbish – there will be lots of birds, fish, flowers and trees'. Hannah (10 years) stated that 'I think the world would change and there would be more cars and buildings'. Alicia (12 years) wrote a diary discussing

What I think about the future

Imagine that it is 50 years in the future and you are old enough to be a grandparent. What do you think the environment will be like? Use this page to draw a picture or write a story that tells YOUR IDEAS about the future and the environment.

"the world will be clean with no rubbish – there will be lots of birds, fish, flowers and trees."

Figure 9.1 Sarah's (eight years) worldview about sustainability.

that 'Everything has changed. All the birds and animals have totally vanished off the Earth'. How do these results compare with your research? Did you find a gradually more negative view for older children or something different? What might explain these findings?

REFLECTIONS 9.1: PLANNING FOR CHILDREN'S LEARNING

In Research Activity 9.1 you were introduced to Ellen's thinking about the environment in the context of considering a worldview on sustainability. If you were to support Ellen in her thinking, what might you need to do? Reflect on this for a moment. What science content would she need to support her with thinking about sustainability so that she had agency? What understandings about the ecosystem would she need to know about? How should she be positioned within that ecosystem? Write down your own ideas about planning for science learning that takes account of her scientific ways of knowing nature.

What I think about the future

Imagine that it is 50 years in the future and you are old enough to be a grandparent. What do you think the environment will be like? Use this page to draw a picture or write a story that tells YOUR IDEAS about the future and the environment.

I think that the world would change and there would be more cars and buildings. There also might be more schools and more nature. e.g. more plants. I think they should have more recreation, and on farms there should be more trees. and plants. because animals need shelter and shade. There might be more skyscrapers. I also think sheds could improve by making them bigger.

Figure 9.2 Hannah's (10 years) worldview about sustainability.

Dear Diary,

Everything has changed. All the birds and animals have totally vanished off the Earth. We no longer have trees to flush all the air. Now we use a stupid machine for air. All the nice blue sky is covered with smog from all the chemical acid and machines we are now using. When I was young the Earth was fine the way it is, and I don't think it should have changed. All the new machinery and things have caused World War 3. I bet that is the reason why all the birds got wiped out. Fortunately the place I live in is not that destructive, because it's in the middle of nowhere. These days it is very very quiet and I wish it had not changed.

End diary

Figure 9.3 Alicia's (12 years) worldview about sustainability.

Figure 9.4 Teachers support preschool children's thinking about sustainability.

Teacher thinking about sustainability

What are your thoughts about sustainability? Zeegers and Clark (2014) in their research with pre-service teachers have shown that many students come into teacher education programs with an enviro-centric bias. For example:

> I thought I did okay with regard to 'living sustainability' by having short showers, saving water, using public transport, not wasting food, recycling. However, the whole embodied energy concept made me realize that other things I do, such as buying bottled water, buying clothes made overseas/all ways (sic) updating things when new version is released (i.e. phones, laptop. tablet, etc.) may in fact counter the things that I deem are good or in the right direction in terms of sustainability (p. 250).

How does this student's thinking compare with your understandings and views on sustainability? It is argued by Zeegers and Clark (2014) that it is important for teachers to have a balanced view of sustainability, arguing for social, environmental and economic perspectives. For example:

> ... sustainability ... that is about growth is not sustainable. I see clearly now how society is based upon growth. We are addicted to it. We cannot achieve sustainability until we determine no-growth systems. This relates to all parts of the triple bottom line:
> • Social – we cannot continue to consume so much and grow our populations.
> • Environment – we are bound by the limits of the environment. We only have one planet and it is not growing in size or fertility.

- Economic – is bound by the limits to society and the environment (primarily reductions in consumption). (pp. 248–9)

As will be shown in the remainder of this chapter, one of the key ideas for learning about sustainability is system thinking and the concept of relatedness. We see systems thinking in the key concepts that were introduced by Zeegers and Clark (2014) in their teacher education program:

- Earth as a system
- sustainability, health and wellbeing
- sustainable energy
- sustainable building
- food security
- sustainable waste management
- climate change.

Systems thinking can also be conceptualised through the concept of ecosystems. We now turn to this concept.

Native Australian bees:
www.aussiebee.com.au/
trigona_
carbonaria.html

Figure 9.5 Working with Council: 'We were very fortunate recipients of the Brisbane City Council Lord Mayor's Community Sustainability and Environmental Grants Program. About the beehive … This beehive contains native stingless bees. These bees, *Tetragonula carbonaria*, are the southernmost stingless bees in the world'.

Science content knowledge – ecosystems

Year 7, Module 1, Unit 4–5

An ecosystem explains how all domains of life and living process are interrelated. All living things interact with other living things in the context of the non-living environment. In Figure 9.6 are some central concepts from Western science which encompass the following concepts:

Interdependence:

- living things all depend upon one another
- all living things and the material on the Earth are interdependent.

Competition:

- an environment can only ever support a finite number of living things
- there will always be competition for the finite resources in an environment
- each species has characteristics that support its survival in its environment (e.g. shape of bird beaks is directly related to food source).

Cycling of matter:

- living things are always returned to the environment through the process of breaking down into simple substances (i.e. decay)
- green plants take in simple substances and convert these into plant matter, and they convert light energy into plant matter
- a food chain describes a sequence of living things that feed on one another
- the transference of material occurs when the body of a living thing is used by another living thing as food
- the chemical changes in living cells also produce waste products and these are excreted into the environment, acting as a food/material source for other living things.

Respiration:

- in the cells of living things is the site where food substances interact with oxygen, 'new' substances are formed and energy is transferred, the 'new' substances are carbon dioxide and water; this is called respiration.

Pollution:

- some environmental changes are harmful to the environment; changes in materials within an ecosystem, such as human activity, can have a devastating impact on an ecosystem
- pollution can affect living things
- pollution is described as any material that builds up faster than they can be recycled back to a raw state.

Another way to build a systems view around a child is to study with children what is in their lunch boxes, and to investigate where the food scraps and wrappings

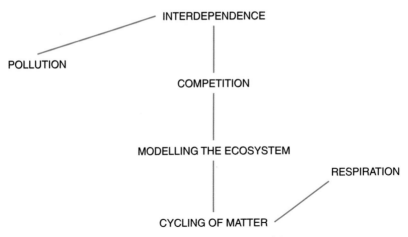

Figure 9.6 A model to build conceptual understanding of the ecosystem.

go and what happens to them. This begins to develop a system view of the things that surround children, in the context of the things that are important to them, such as packing and eating their lunch each day. We see in Figure 9.7 how one child has mapped what happens to the contents of his lunch box. In Figure 9.8 we see another child who has mapped the waterways in her community because she knows a creek runs through the local rubbish tip where the scraps from her lunch box go. She begins by looking at the drains in her school, and then walking around her community to gain a better insight into how all the waterways are interconnected. She then studies where the waterways begin and builds a map of what she has learned.

Figure 9.7 Mapping what we do with our lunch scraps and wrappings.

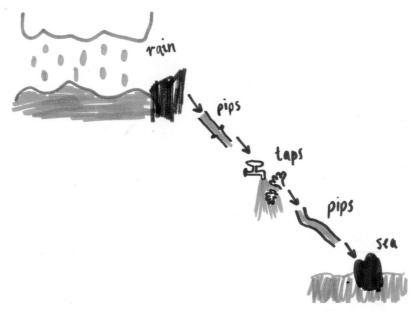

Figure 9.8 Following the waterways in our community.

These images give insights into the 'chain' but not the 'cycle' of matter. In the next section, we look inside an early childhood setting and see how the human body can also help children build a system view as a foundation for thinking more broadly and ecologically in other contexts.

Looking inside an early childhood setting: infants, toddlers and preschoolers working and playing scientifically – a systems view of the human body

Ecosystems as discussed in this chapter are global and holistic. But a system worldview can also be conceptualised on a smaller scale. A system view of a single organism, such as the human body, is also helpful to know about. For example, in a teaching sequence on children's understandings of their body the teacher invited the toddlers to draw around their bodies and then to draw what they thought was inside of themselves. For the five-year-olds, the teacher asked that they draw a picture of themselves and what they thought they looked like from the inside. Not only did the children not know about the organs in their bodies, but they also believed that food, after being swallowed, floated around in any area of the body (perhaps the expression 'hollow legs' does little to assist children with developing scientific understandings of themselves). In addition, their everyday experiences with cuts, scratches and bruises tend to reinforce a view that blood is below the surface of the skin, filling the spaces inside the body (like a bag of blood). The primary function of blood and how it travels throughout the body, being dispersed and collected through a system of veins and arteries, were ideas not considered by many of the children. Having a system view of the human body is important for young children, as it helps them to better understand how their bodies work. It is also important when children are sick and need to identify to a nurse practitioner or doctor details of what is hurting or making them feel ill. Knowing the names of body organs, and being able to name these when in an emergency health situation, can lead to better care. Understanding the body as a system lays an important conceptual foundation for systems thinking that can connect more broadly when talking about the universe as a system.

There are other systems that are important to children in schools, such as their playground, lunch-ordering systems or rubbish collection and recycling processes.

Pedagogical practices for supporting sustainability in early childhood education

The EYLF advocates for children to 'develop dispositions for learning such as curiosity, cooperation, confidence, creativity, commitment, enthusiasm, persistence, imagination and reflexivity' (DEEWR 2009, p. 32). Intentional teaching promotes the active engagement of the adult and the child in an expansive conversation about the things in their learning environment. In the context of sustainability, Edwards and Cutter-Mackenzie (2013) found in their cultural–historical research into pedagogical play types for supporting biodiversity that open-ended play was the least likely approach for promoting teachers to engage in intentional teaching on sustainability. Their study found that a more purposeful approach to play was more successful. A summary of their results is shown below, where the pedagogical strategies used by teachers are listed:

Pedagogical strategies for supporting *a purposeful approach to play*:

- step the children through the process
- share a book
- explain to the children about careful observations
- position science, such as worm farms, so that all children have access
- provide posters on science information, such as mini beasts
- discuss the posters with the children
- demonstrate while children work
- sort
- provide information
- explain procedures, modelling step by step
- look for existing knowledge
- question – What do you know about …

- discuss, observe, look, feel, share
- use tools such as magnifying glasses
- draw – draw an insect using fine black markers
- show – digital microscope for observing pond water
- draw – what you see under the microscope, cross referencing to books
- group reflection
- sing songs about science, e.g. worms (extracted and edited from Edwards and Cutter-Mackenzie 2013, p. 34).

The results provide a broad selection of practices that are already found in many preschool environments. However, bringing them together as a pedagogical practice for purposeful play opens up more possibilities than can be found in traditional approaches to play and learning. Elliott and Davis (2009) note that despite the advocacy of Early Childhood Australia, many early childhood teachers do not engage in teaching of sustainability. They suggest that teachers are held back because of their belief that because their programs provide rich outdoor environments, that they are already engaged in sustainability through children 'playing in nature'. They also suggest that most teachers believe that concepts of sustainability are beyond young children's conceptual ability.

Figure 9.9 Please take care of Eloise's birds in their nest.

Elliott (2014) through her extensive research into strategies for promoting and embedding a culture of sustainability into an early childhood centre, found that the following pedagogical practices supported the teaching of sustainability and management:

- Ensure children, staff and families are central to the co-construction of curriculum, including how sustainability is embedded within it.
- Be aware of and respect multiplicities of meaning and values … Practice shared decision making and collaboration so that choices are respected and people do not feel pushed into decisions, but rather the implications of choices are considered and made transparent.
- View sustainability challenges as opportunities for creativity, innovation and working together.
- Create opportunities for commitment and sustainable leadership at various levels.
- Acknowledge children's rights to participate in decision making that impacts on their future by engaging with sustainable practices and solutions.
- Invite children to ask questions, find answers and create change through ethical dilemmas, understanding the Earth's systems, and consideration of and relationships with animals, people, plants and the land.
- Use a diverse range of approaches for engagement; be responsive to individual skills and interests, and local issues.
- Create an atmosphere of open discussion, debate and negotiation.
- Engage in external relationships and partnerships for expertise and support.
- Practise respectful, responsible and reciprocal relationships (Elliott 2014, cited in Young and Elliott 2014, p. 12).

These pedagogical practices link directly with the work of Martin (2014), where Indigenous perspectives on sustainability and relatedness are more than knowledge of biodiversity.

In the next section we take a look inside a classroom where the children studied the birds that shared the school playground with them. This project links with important work being done in South Australia on Citizen Science (see Zeegers, Paige, Lloyd and Roetman 2012).

Looking inside the classroom: Year 4 children investigating the birds in their playground

Exploratory activities

The children walked around the school playground early in the morning and noticed a range of birds.

Before views

Figure 9.10 What Michelle knows about birds.

Children's questions

Birds	Bats
Wings	Wings
Beak	Teeth
Feather	Fur
Live in trees	Live in caves
Nest	Hang
Eggs	Baby born alive
Seeds	Milk from mother
Nuts	Fruit
Good eyes	Nearly blind
Eats worms, meat	Eats fruit, insects

Figure 9.11 Jenny thinks through the different features of birds and bats to answer the question Why isn't a bird a bat?

Investigations

Figure 9.12 Freya draws about the birds she saw when investigating the school playground.

After views

Kookaburras eat frogs and snakes and cheese and meat.

The laughing kookaburra is a giant among the kingfisher of the world. Its laughing call has made it one of Australia's most famous birds. Kookaburras usually laugh long in the early morning and the late afternoon. Usually the whole family laughs together. They are telling each other 'This is our country. Keep out.' Kookaburras have other calls. It is their way of talking.

Figure 9.13 Leslie and Anne write a report on kookaburras.

Reflection

In this snapshot of what took place in the classroom through the work samples of children, it is possible to gain some insight into how children's thinking evolved over time. In Figure 9.14 we see how Henriette modelled the relationship she found between the shape of the birds' beaks and their food. But how do we as teachers create the conditions for moving children from simply observing birds

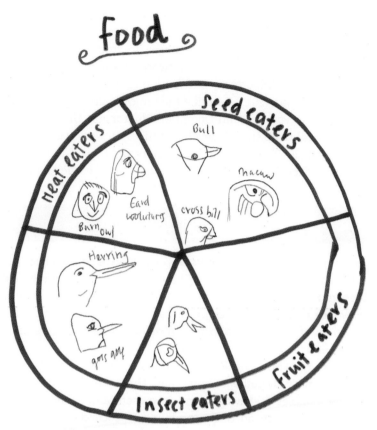

Figure 9.14 Henriette prepares a chart which shows the relationship between the beaks of birds and the available food sources.

through to building models that show relationships between the characteristics of organisms and their environment? What is the narrative that went with the work samples? What do you think took place? What was the story of the playground? What was the children's collective story for investigating the birds in their playground?

Citizen Science

The *case study on birds* illustrated above was undertaken directly in a Year 4 children's playground. This provides an interesting and motivating context in which to study science. The scope of the ecosystem is therefore contained, and does not take account of the migration of birds across the planet, or connect with other parts of the children's ecosystem, such as their backyard. The project is focused on the education setting and does not reach out into the community. How might you expand this case study? What might be the next step in broadening the scope of the children's investigations?

**Citizen
Science**
Bird
project:
bird.cornell.
edu

Zeegers, Paige, Lloyd and Roetman (2012) describe an innovative program known as *Citizen Science* that brings together teachers, children and urban ecologists across a whole state of South Australia to study wildlife. *Citizen Science* positions children as part of a broader network of amateur scientists or urban ecologists, who make an important contribution to the study of wildlife. Zeegers, Paige, Lloyd and Roetman (2012) describe the project called Operation Magpie, an offshoot of Operation Possum, and Operation Bluetongue. Urban ecologists with the support of a local radio station developed this statewide study. Zeegers, Paige, Lloyd and Roetman (2012) supported the teachers and their children who became involved in this project. The project can be found at: bird.cornell.edu.

REFLECTIONS 9.2: CITIZEN SCIENCE

The project of supporting the teachers was described as constructivist because it used the approaches described in Chapters 5–7. As you read the extracts from Zeegers, Paige, Lloyd and Roetman's (2012) research presented here, think about why their research has been presented in this chapter, nestled between the case study of the playground bird investigation, and the discussion on place-based education.

Zeegers, Paige, Lloyd and Roetman (2012) state that Operation Magpie sought to systematically gather scientific data about the sightings of magpies, to study the magpies' behaviours, and to present and submit this data to the urban ecologists on an online proforma. The children participated in gathering scientific data on bird sightings over six weeks. Science was being taught through an environmental lens and building eco-literacy. Their study also focused on teacher learning. Zeegers, Paige, Lloyd and Roetman (2012) stated that, 'the approach to professional learning in this study established a community of practice that provided a sustained and supported learning experience for the teachers' (p. 28).

The pedagogical strategies that were described by Zeegers, Paige, Lloyd and Roetman (2012) and the teachers who were involved in the study included:

- drawing magpies before the children started their investigations, and again afterwards, noting the differences
- using binoculars to study the birds
- studying stuffed birds
- using ornithological texts to identify bird species
- supporting children to ask questions about the birds
- five-year-olds co-writing a daily blog about the children's observations and experiences
- 'magic spots' where the children could sit quietly and observe birds featured, as did going on excursions to local parks specifically to find magpies.

Explicit teaching of observation skills and accurately collecting data were noted by the teachers. Zeegers, Paige, Lloyd and Roetman (2012) state that children needed to be workshopped on 'observing (looking and listening), the ability to use new equipment such as binoculars and stopwatches, the ability to collect and use data and, for some, the translation of the data into graphs and charts' (p. 35).

The teachers reported that the children engaged in observing birds in a broad range of contexts, became authorities in their own right on bird watching, and shared their observations with scientific accuracy. Families became involved and were genuinely impressed by what their children were learning. Importantly, Zeegers, Paige, Lloyd and Roetman (2012) state that:

> It has previously been found that many children, particularly those living in urban environments, do not connect strongly, if at all, with their natural environment and this can lead to what is termed a 'nature-deficit disorder, resulting in human alienation form nature' (Louv 2008, p. 36). In this study of the teachers' responses indicated that focusing on an iconic animal species that was readily found in and around schools and homes motivated and engaged them and their students (p. 37).

What is key about *Citizen Science* is that the urban ecologists give back to the community. The children observe and gather data and these data are passed on to the urban ecologists, who in turn analyse the data more broadly, and their findings are then returned to the community through detailed reports. It is a bilateral relationship for gathering scientific data and undertaking research (see Chapter 8 for a broader discussion of research methodologies).

Citizen Science also opens up the possibilities for hearing about the stories that are told about particular species that are being observed. These stories can connect together the particular species being observed, so that a more related conception of nature and Country can emerge.

We now turn to a theoretical concept of place-based education for illustrating how children connect with not just the places in which they live, but also their schools, people and spaces within their communities.

Place-based education

Yazdanpanah (2013) argues that caring for the non-human environment and nature is central to the idea of place-based education. One way to establish a place-based approach in science education is to share stories about what happens in the community, where all parts of that community are interconnected. Place-based education offers insights into the relationship between culture and environment (Somerville, Power and De Carteret 2009). It is suggested by Somerville, Power and De Carteret (2009) that we all have connections with the places we grow up in, and working with a feeling of connection with a place is usually through a narrative of ourselves, and that place. This constitutes a story. Place-based education therefore can be thought of as:

- a story of our relationship to a place or places
- embodied and local
- a contact zone of cultural contestation.

Place-based education can include delicate and fragile lands, an urban community, a local river system or even the city centre of a large capital city. Stories of place are important because they reposition humans as part of nature – as interrelated. This forms the basis of both Indigenous and scientific ways of knowing nature, as discussed in Chapters 1 and 2, and is foundational for understanding culturally sensitive teaching. We now turn to this approach to teaching.

Culturally sensitive teaching

Relatedness: Martin (2008) has theorised the *concept of relatedness* as a powerful concept for explaining the forms of connectedness that exists within Aboriginal communities. For example,

> … understanding of the contexts, the conditions and agents that exit within our world that has been and will continue to be encoded, expressed and preserved by us in many forms such as literature, film, performance and art. It is particularly preserved in the Stories and through these we confirm ourselves … (p. 65).

The dimensions of a worldview that Martin (2008) has theorised focus on:

The Ancestral Core: The Ancestral Core gives identity to the people. The law and the stories told, are formed and expressed by the Creators and the Ancestors.

The spirits: The spirit is the worldview of the people. The spirit 'filters the power of the Creators and the Ancestor to ensure their messages are received' (p. 66).

The Entities: Entities include the land, the people, the animals, the plants, the skies, the waterways and the climate. One part of the system of relations is no more important than another part.

The Filter: The Filter protects and sustains the relations of all the Entities. The connections are a form of relatedness.

The concept of relatedness includes a 'set of conditions, processes and practices that occur amongst and between the Creators and Ancestors; the *Spirits*; the Filter and the Entities. This relatedness occurs across contexts and is maintained within conditions that are: physical, spiritual, political, geographical, intellectual, emotional, social, historical, sensory, instinctive and intuitive' (Martin 2008, p. 69). Martin (2008) states that relatedness can be found among or between entities. For example, relatedness could be among people, or it can be between people and other entities such as plants or animals. When relatedness is between people, then it is experienced as being Ancestral. For instance, through clans or family, relatedness guides peoples' lives. Martin (2008) says relatedness is more than a metaphor. Some forms of relatedness are stronger, such as relatedness to areas of Country, which connect more strongly to some family groups or clans. Some of these are known as sacred sites or story sites. Relatedness is also reciprocated, because Entities look after people and people in turn look after the Entities.

Ways of knowing, ways of being, and ways of doing form the three *knowledge bands* as described by Martin (2008).

Ways of knowing foreground knowing who your people are, knowing where your Country is located, and knowing how you are related to the Entities. Finding out the Stories of relatedness, which are both communal Stories and individual Stories. Together they map the person's identity.

Ways of being encompass ways of knowing, where respect for relatedness is central. Ways of being is about knowing oneself to be a part of, not above, all the Entities of the world. Ways of being exemplify three conditions. Being:

1   Respectful.
2   Responsible.
3   Accountable.

Ways of doing is explained by Martin (2008) as living relatedness. Immersion is not just physically enacting something, but it is also spiritual, social, intellectual and emotional. It is about being among the Stories. This means maintaining self-identity, autonomy while experiencing and living relatedness. Martin (2008) gives the following example of a willi-wagtail:

> The willi-wagtail, a small black and white bird that communicates by chittering and using its small body to tell its Stories. For us, the willi-wagtail is a messenger. When the willi-wagtail is excited and chitters fast, spreads it tail feathers and swings its tail from side to side, the message is more urgent. To 'interpret' its messages, the process is to come alongside, to immerse oneself in relatedness to the willi-wagtail and separate from one's embodied thoughts, words and language. Because the willi-wagtail assumes you can speak its language, it will repeat the message but will also grow impatient with each repetition until some acknowledgement or reply is given. Yet, it is just a message, it is never a full Story with all the details of who, what, where and when. Thus pausing and immersing oneself in relatedness, other messages come forth to confirm, or clarify the message form the willi-wagtail … In coming amongst, you learn more bout this process of Ways of Doing by applying it in the range of contexts in which you live. It is highly contextual and involves engaging consciously and subconsciously in relatedness through processes of observing, discerning, filtering, applying reflecting, sharing and confirming (p. 79).

Martin (2008) gives insight into the importance of relatedness in knowing, being and doing. Her theoretical insights give just a taste of the complexities of the worldview that is part of her own identity as a scholar, and as an Aboriginal women. To gain an appreciation for the depth of her research, it is important to read her work. It is only possible to include a snapshot of her research in this textbook.

However, what is important here is acknowledging, respecting and finding the ways to bring into the primary and early childhood settings the breadth of knowledge discussed here.

Planning for inclusive pedagogy

In the previous chapters, we discussed the idea of the cultural construction of knowledge. We have foregrounded the need to observe, plan and implement approaches to science that are inclusive of all knowledges. However, a range of frameworks and pedagogy were discussed. We reintroduce the work of Hamlin (2013), who provides an approach to finding the ways of connecting with communities so that differing knoweldges are made available to educators for supporting a more inclusive curriculum framework and pedagogy.

Table 9.1 Planning an inclusive classroom/centre and pedagogy

Pedagogical principles	Pedagogical practices	Scientific learning
Build authentic and meaningful relationships with community.	Process of learning from community members assumes you prioritise the needs of the community.	*Question to ask:* What science knowledge does the community want their children to learn?
Identify the funds of knowledge found in the community (see Licona 2013).	Begin by participating and informally observing in the community. Find the right contexts – such as open air markets, local sporting venues, shopping centres, church groups, community action groups, etc.	*Question to ask:* What science learning is already supported or taking place in the community? How involved are children and what role do they take in these activities?
Document the funds of knowledge.	Make observations in local contexts.	*Question to ask:* Ask about the practices, e.g. 'What is the white chalky substance women buy at the market. What is it used for?'
Short interviews of key community members to empower community members about their own knowledge and use of science within their communities.	Teacher with the assistance of a community member should use the recorded observations to interview a respected community member. Begin by sharing a story about what was observed and ask for clarification.	Begin with 'what questions' that can lead to 'how questions'.
Teacher is welcomed into the world of the community, and the teacher in turn welcomes the community into the classroom.	Present new material to community for feedback and possible change.	Create curriculum that links to the local funds of knowledge in the community.

Leading change – Priscilla Reid-Loynes

It is also important to draw upon the expertise from the professional community. Those with cultural knowledge can and do support teachers in building relations with community and with Country. For instance, Priscilla Reid-Loynes is a Goomeroi Yularoi woman, whose traditional homelands are in north-west New South Wales. She is an early childhood and primary teacher currently working as an independent Indigenous education consultant. Within her consultancy role she specialises in early and primary years product design and development, curriculum and professional development and mentoring. This year she has taken on a new role as sessional lecturer at RMIT in higher education for early years education and continues her work as the visiting teacher sharing culture through Indigenous pedagogies at Somers Bush Kinder in the Coolart Wetlands (Boonwurrung Country, Mornington Peninsula). Since her Elders have worked as activists, she continues this role as she aspires to honour children's voices of past, present and future generations. Priscilla *learns with Indigenous pedagogy* within the early years environment and shares her knowledge so that we can all be *Learning with Country. Learning with Children, Families and Communities* (see http://web.education.unimelb.edu.au/yrc/honoring_child_Equity_conference_2014/speakers.html).

Priscilla says that in working with preschool children, she just does not come in for one quick lesson, to show children Country. Rather, learning about Country is about experiencing and listening to Stories of relatedness, as discussed by Martin (2007). Learning about Country is about entering into, and being a part of Country, as told through an Indigenous Elder or with the permission of a custodian of that community. Being in Country means also giving back to Country. It is through the exchange of receiving from Country and giving back to Country that relatedness becomes established for young children.

According to Priscilla, being in Country means to walk in Country through the eyes of the Aboriginal or Torres Strait Islander. It means to share in, and be a part of that walk through the Stories told. **Being** in Country as explained by Martin (2008) is about being respectful, responsible and accountable in Country. The Stories heard will explain this relatedness. Some of these Stories will be both communal Stories and individual Stories.

Through Country, children experience ways of knowing, ways of being, and ways of doing. These form the three *knowledge bands* that explain Country (Martin 2008). This is important knowledge that is gained through being in Country.

As an Indigenous education consultant introducing preschool children to Country, Priscilla visits many preschools across Australia, as either an Aboriginal woman from that Country or with the permission of the Elders of that Country. She shares her own Stories with children, and it is through being in Country with the children sharing her Stories, children experience and learn about yarning. Sometimes yarning is about just being and not saying anything at all. Being in Country in this way takes time.

Priscilla has developed a pedagogical approach for learning about Country that is in keeping with the concept of relatedness as described by Martin (2008), and reflects a culturally sensitive approach to teaching science, as discussed by Hernandez, Morales and Shroyer (2013) (see Chapters 2 and 8). As educators, you need to build relationships with your community so that you can open your pre-school or classroom door to allow your children to experience Country in the ways described by Priscilla.

Summary

In this chapter we have examined a range of ways of building inclusive pedagogy so that ways of knowing, ways of being and ways of doing (Martin 2008) are respected when planning for and teaching science in a range of educational settings. In the introduction to this section, you were invited to think about different knowledge forms and world-views and how they could be brought together. Are you now in a position to achieve this? What approaches to teaching science do you think allow you to do this? You were also asked in Reflections 9.1 to consider the extracts from Zeegers, Paige, Lloyd and Roetman's (2012) research and to think about why their research has been presented in this chapter, nestled between the case study of the playground bird investigation and the discussion on place-based education. What specific features of Citizen Science make the approach more cultural–historical than constructivist do you believe? Martin's (2008) work on relatedness explains aspects of the pedagogical features. Similarly, the development of a community of practice also signals that learning is collectively, rather than individually constructed. Together, these begin the journal of teaching for sustainability in a culturally sensitive way.

In the next chapter you will be invited to take a stand, and to critique the approaches to teaching science that have been presented and to decide which approaches (and why) you believe you will use.

References

Edwards, S, Cutter-Mackenzie, A 2013, 'Pedagogical play types: What do they suggest for learning about sustainability in early childhood education?', *International Journal of Early Childhood*, vol. 45, pp. 327–46.

Elliott, S 2014, *Sustainability and the Yearly Years Learning Framework*, Mt Victoria, NSW: Pademelon.

Elliott, S, Davis, J 2009, 'Exploring the resistance: An Australian perspective on educating for sustainability in early childhood', *International Journal of Early Childhood*, vol. 41, no. 2, pp. 65–77.

Hamlin, ML 2013, '"Yo soy indigena": Identifying and using traditional ecological knowledge (TEK) to make the teaching of science culturally responsive for Mayua girls', *Cultural Studies of Science Education*, vol. 8 no. 4, pp. 759–76.

Hernandez, CM, Morales, AR, Shroyer, MG 2013, 'The development of a model of culturally responsive science and mathematics teaching', *Cultural Studies of Science Education*, vol. 8, pp. 803–20. (DOI 10.1007/s11422-013-9513-8.)

Licona, MM 2013, 'Mexican and Mexican-American children's funds of knowledge as interventions into deficit thinking: Opportunities for praxis in science education', *Cultural Studies of Science Education*, vol. 8, pp. 859–73. (DOI 10.1007/s11422-013-9513-8.)

Louv, R 2008, *Last Child in the Woods: Saving our Children from Nature-deficit Disorder* 2nd edn, Chapel Hill, NC: Algonquin Books.

Martin, K 2008, *Please Knock Before You Enter: Aboriginal regulation of outsiders and the implications for researchers*, Brisbane: Post Pressed.

Negus, P 2014, *The Magical World of Fungi*, 2nd edn, North Fremantle: Cape to Cape Publishing.

Somerville, M, Power, K, de Carteret, P eds 2009, *Landscapes and Learning: Place studies for a global world*, Rotterdam: Sense.

Yazdanpanah, G 2013, 'Developing a more critical approach to the teaching of environmental education' in C. Redman ed, *Successful Science Education Practices. Exploring What, Why and How they Worked*, New York: Nova Science, pp. 93–111.

Young, AM 2013, *A Field Guide to Fungi of Australia*, Sydney: UNSW Press.

Young, T, Elliott, S 2014, *Ways of Thinking, Acting and Relating About Sustainability.* Canberra: Early Childhood Australia.

Zeegers, Y, Clark, IF 2014, 'Students' perceptions of education for sustainable development', *International Journal of Sustainability in Higher Education*, vol. 15, no. 2, pp. 242–53.

Zeegers, Y, Paige, K, Lloyd, D, Roetman, P 2012, '"Operation Magpie": Inspiring teachers' professional learning through environmental science', *Australian Journal of Environmental Education*, vol. 28, no. 1, pp. 27–41.

Appendix

Resources for teachers for building sustainability and relatedness

There are a range of resources that support teachers in building knowledge of sustainability and relatedness. Five examples are provided.

Indigenous knowledge and sustainability

Information about sustainability and Indigenous knowledge can be found at: http://www.unesco.org/education/tlsf/mods/theme_c/mod11.html.

A series of modules are provided to build your understanding about:

1   The wisdom of the elders.
2   UN Declaration on the Rights of Indigenous Peoples.
3   Why is Indigenous knowledge important?
4   Living by Indigenous knowledge.
5   Indigenous and formal education.
6   Enhancing the curriculum through Indigenous knowledge.
7   Reflection.

Building relatedness

Talking up Our Strengths: Images of Strength and Resilience in Aboriginal and Torres Strait Islander Cultures, prepared by the Secretariat of National Aboriginal and Islander Child Care (SNAICC), the national peak body for Aboriginal and Torres Strait Island children and families:

http://www.snaicc.org.au/_uploads/rsfil/02762.pdf

Centre for Environmental Education Australia

The Centre for Environment Education (CEE) Australia Incorporated is a not-for-profit association devoted to the development and implementation of innovative environmental education, communication and action programs in Australia and the Asia Pacific region. See:

http://www.ceeaustralia.org

Outdoor and environmental education centres

The outdoor and environmental education centres seek to support teachers and communities to deliver highly effective outdoor and environmental education programs where sustainable future and valuing biodiversity are promoted:

http://education.qld.gov.au/schools/environment/outdoor/

Sustainable education

This website lists a range of resources for promoting sustainable education, including a Sustainability Curriculum Framework – a guide for curriculum developers and policy makers – and a series of publications:

http://www.environment.gov.au/sustainability/education/publications.

Making a difference – children as activists

There are many websites available that support children to make a difference. Three examples are provided that give agency to children. Prepare your own set of links by evaluating sites and bookmarking them for easy use when teaching. Three examples are provided:

1   'Kids for saving the Earth' is a website that supports children and their teachers to act sustainably and in an environmentally responsible way. Topics include mining,

endangered species, recycling, toxic waste, rainforests, forests and more. Resources of ideas, such as http://www.kidsforsavingearth.org/ecoactivities/wrapgreen.pdf, can be found at this website – http://www.kidsforsavingearth.org.

2   'Creating a sustainable future for education' is a site that lists a series of challenges that teachers and children can do together. It can be found at: http://www.green educationfoundation.org/teacher-resources.html.

For example the

- Green building program
- Green thumb program.Although the teaching notes are prescriptive, some useful questions can be found that are helpful, such as:

  Conduct an energy audit. Ask:
  – Which rooms utilise the least energy? Why?
  – Which rooms utilise the most energy? Why?
  – Which rooms have the highest number of standby power locations?
  – What stands out as areas where energy is wasted?

3   The Stephanie Alexander Kitchen Garden National Program supports teachers and communities to work with children to grow and harvest their own food in their local community.

The site can be found at: http://www.kitchengardenfoundation.org.au.

PART 5

Leadership in Science

This is the final part of the book. In the chapter that follows you will be thinking about your own personal pedagogical framework for teaching science. As you read this chapter, think about yourself now as a beginning teacher, then into the future as an experienced teacher, and finally as a leader in science teaching. Although the book concludes with Chapter 10, your journey into science teaching has only just begun.

CHAPTER 10

Becoming a leader of science: situating yourself

Introduction

The preceding seven chapters have provided you with an opportunity to explore seven quite different approaches to the teaching and learning of science. Now we examine the differences, similarities and relationships among these approaches to help you develop your own framework for teaching science. In this chapter we will present several important guiding principles that should influence the construction of this framework. By adopting a framework based on these principles and different approaches, you will be able to position yourself to become a leader of science in your school or early childhood setting.

REFLECTIONS 10.1: COMPARING THE SEVEN APPROACHES TO TEACHING SCIENCE

After exploring teaching by using the different approaches, one student teacher commented about them as shown in Figure 10.1.

The approaches
It's hard to choose one approach to teaching science. The approach you take depends on the lesson you aim to take. I would not use one approach only, as it deprives the students of varied study approaches and therefore would restrict their learning and decrease student motivation. Vary the teaching approaches and I believe you will enhance learning and interest. Each teaching approach is as valuable as the other.

Figure 10.1 Approaches to teaching science.

It is important at this stage that you reject none of the approaches out of hand and that you accept none of them uncritically. You can now consolidate your understanding of each by carrying out a systematic comparison of the seven approaches, highlighting both critical differences and aspects that are shared among them. You started this process at the end of Part 2. Collectively, the reflections you made and will make through the content of this chapter will help you to develop a broader view of the possibilities for the use of these approaches for teaching science.

REFLECTIONS 10.2: COMPARING APPROACHES

Refer to any notes you have made concerning the teaching approaches, to help you consider both the positive and problematic aspects of each. For each of the seven teaching approaches – transmission, discovery, inquiry for teaching, inquiry for learning, teaching for conceptual change, cultural–historical conceptual play and culturally sensitive teaching–list:

- the advantages and strengths of the approach
- the disadvantages and problems of the approach
- how planning might look in the approach
- how technical language is developed in the approach
- how assessment might look and be judged in the approach.

You may like to consider the inquiry-based approaches together, drawing on the analysis you did when you read the three chapters in Part 2.

Draw up a table (see Table 10.1) that enables you to readily compare the advantages and disadvantages of the various approaches. It may be even more productive if you can carry out this exercise in a small group of student teachers so that you can share your perceptions.

Table 10.1 Analysing the teaching approaches

	Transmission	Discovery	Inquiry – teaching	Inquiry – learning	Conceptual change	Cultural–historical conceptual play	Culturally sensitive teaching
Disadvantages/problems							
Advantages/strengths							

You may wish to draw upon social media to set up a discussion forum to help further your understandings through other technologies. For instance:

'... there are many other generic apps which teachers (and learners for that matter) can use to create resources through collating video links, web links, images and photographs ... Smartphones an tablets can be used in numerous other ways such as capturing data (video, photograph, GPS, logging data via probes or othe sound apps). GS tracking data can also be combined with visualization tools such as Google Earth' (Lewin (2013, p. 241).

Do you recognise that, in using any of the teaching approaches discussed, there are going to be certain advantages for both teacher and children, but that these must be weighed against the disadvantages? A central issue in your summary analysis of the approaches is likely to focus on the degree of structure for the children and for the teacher. While this can help provide guidance and a degree of certainty, the disadvantage is that it could impede effective learning. Other common areas in your summary might include the level of child motivation and the demands on the teacher in terms of required knowledge and management of the learning group.

To extend your understanding of the seven approaches, consider what relationship each approach has to the others. Until this stage we have treated them as analytically separate frameworks for teaching. However, like all models, this is a simplification.

REFLECTIONS 10.3: COMMON GROUND

Consider the seven teaching approaches and attempt to identify how they are related to one another. What overlap is there among the approaches and what do they have in common? Highlight key features that demonstrate the relationship between them. Decide which of the seven approaches are closest to one another; for example, we have already aligned three together for you based on constructivism (Part 2).

Illustrate your ideas in a labelled diagram or chart. (You could use circles,

Figure 10.2 The relationship among teaching approaches.

bar graphs or other means.) Share this work.

We recognise that teachers and student teachers have different learning prefer-ences, teaching preferences, competency levels and other concerns in adopting a particular approach. We believe it is important that you be given the full opportu-nity to construct your own framework, and it could take several years before you have developed a well-established sense of what works for you.

Selecting and constructing a personal framework

You are now at the point where you are encouraged to make a selection from the approaches as you have understood them. In particular, consider how you might teach a group of children in the near future and if you have a science practice teaching situation or you are already teaching this is a choice you have to make.

In constructing your framework at this stage, you have several options avail-able. You could:

- choose one of the seven approaches
- modify one of the approaches in significant ways
- combine two or more of the approaches
- decide that you will employ all of the approaches at different times for dif-ferent topics.

How will you make the decision? There is a complex range of factors that you should take into account. These factors might include:

1   Your level of confidence in managing children in a classroom or early child-hood setting.
2   Your familiarity and rapport with the children you are to teach.
3   Your level of understanding of one or more of the approaches.
4   The experiences that the children already have in science, including with their families.
5   The learning organisation that exists in the classroom or early childhood set-ting – for example, cooperative learning, free play.
6   Your sense of competence in teaching science.
7   The support you might receive from your associates, another teacher or parents.

These factors focus on the context in which you will teach and your perceptions of your own competence at this stage of your development. However, there are two other critical and related factors:

8   Your conception of the nature of science.
9   The learning outcomes in science that you have decided are desirable for the children.

If we hold a particular view of science, we are likely to emphasise learning outcomes that are consistent with that view. For instance, if we perceive science to be a well-established body of knowledge constructed by experts, it is likely that we will favour a transmission approach to science. However, if we want to underline the everyday, human qualities of science, it is likely that we will be attracted to an inquiry-based approach and culturally sensitive teaching. It is helpful to consider that the different approaches portray different facets of science (see Figure 10.3).

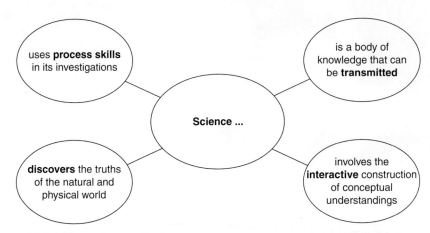

Figure 10.3 Different facets of science.

The choice of teaching approaches can be difficult, and you could experience some tensions in weighing the different factors. You want to succeed in whatever you implement, but you must be true to what you believe about science and desirable outcomes. Also, you want to learn from the experiences of teaching, which implies moving out of your safety zone. Reflections 10.4 might help you to systematise your decision-making about the approaches that you could incorporate into your framework. Here you bring together your analyses from the previous chapters about the nature of science that underpins the approaches you have reviewed.

REFLECTIONS 10.4: LISTING CONCERNS AND ISSUES

Record your consideration of each of the seven listed factors (1–7).
    Take these into account in making a choice of approaches. Comment on those factors that are the overriding influences on your choice. *What are the conflicting concerns or issues?*
    If you have the opportunity, talk this over with other students. Bring these ideas together with your thoughts on 8 and 9.

Figure 10.4 What do the approaches allow and what do they limit?

The place of each approach in teaching science

We strongly hold the view that there is a place for each of the teaching approaches in supporting children's learning in science, assuming the approaches are used effectively.

Science is a complex area, and a framework for teaching science should reflect that. As noted in the previous chapter (Chapter 9), we are increasingly recognising the diversity of children in our schools and centres, in terms of their life experiences, capabilities, interests and learning styles. Furthermore, we are attempting to achieve a range of learning outcomes with the children. All of these matters imply the need for flexibility and ingenuity in the teaching of science.

There is a strong case for using different approaches at different times in different contexts and in attempting to achieve different learning outcomes. Some of the central justifications for each approach are suggested below.

Transmission

In Chapter 3, a number of justifications for using the transmission approach were put forward. These include those areas where the nature of some topics makes it very difficult to teach without relying heavily on transmission. However, the challenge in such a situation is to also involve the children as actively in their own learning as possible – for instance, by organising complementary hands-on activities. Another important use of a transmission approach is as a strategy at the start of a unit: you might consider it important to share some key information before children begin their own investigations. For instance, discovery activities of the type encountered during Chapter 4 in the topic 'Sound' might be considerably enhanced if you, as a teacher, ensure at the start that children have a clear understanding of the relationship of vibrations and sound.

Discovery

There is an important place for discovery learning of the type that is relatively unstructured and almost *playful*. After all, this is what some scientists do during phases of their work. In contrast to a tightly disciplined strategy, adopting a 'What if?' approach can lead to very useful questions and aid understanding – for example, 'What if we drop this object from twice the height, will it break?', 'What if we tried to pedal our bike on a slippery surface?'. It is clear that the exploratory phase of an inquiry approach has these features of play, but you might also consider from time to time giving discovery of this kind a special emphasis. For such an approach to be effective, as we have seen, it is essential that you have a dialogue with the children in such activities. It would be valid to point out to pupils that this is the type of activity scientists use sometimes to help them generate questions and find answers. But we need to promote awareness that when scientists make discoveries, they do so with a strong background framework of knowledge and understanding.

Following are the reflections by one student teacher after she had taught a small group of children using the discovery approach.

The children had a fantastic time conducting the food experiments. They were excited because the experiments belonged to them: it was their ideas that formed this lesson. I wanted to show the children that science wasn't 'hard work done by those geeky guys in white coats and glasses'. I wanted to show them how science is a part of our daily lives and a subject that everyone can be actively involved in. I know I succeeded at this task when a child approached me and declared: 'I thought that Science was just Chemistry stuff. This is so fun! I want to be a scientist when I finish school.'

Inquiry-based approaches

In science education it is important to develop and to refine children's observations, classifications, planning investigations and other important skills, so you are justified in developing a topic with a clear focus on inquiry skills. As children asked questions that they were interested in investigating, and went about undertaking these investigations using a guided approach, a raft of inquiry skills needed to be used and developed. The level of child ownership over the whole inquiry process is what distinguishes an inquiry-based approach to learning and an inquiry-based approach to teaching. The models presented in Part 2 were structured for easier comparison. However, in reality, the particular group of children you are teaching, with their differing enthusiasm and questions, in addition to your level of comfort with following and guiding the inquiries, is more likely to determine the inquiry approach you adopt.

Constructivism: teaching for conceptual change

Teaching for conceptual change is much more common in schools than it used to be. As with inquiry-based approaches, conceptual change teaching explicitly builds on what children know and think in science. However, the focus is on only beginning with the children's questions. It lends itself to a vast range of topics, which must be linked to children's experiences and interests. However, if it were used all the time, it may create problems in terms of covering a curriculum where schools or centres have set topics they want taught – the pathway of the learning may not move in that direction when following children's interests and questions. Similarly, in some schools and early childhood settings, topics may be prescribed across the whole school/early childhood setting, making it difficult to follow children's interests, which may go beyond what is prescribed for a particular year level on a particular topic. For example, the topic of electricity is not covered in full until Year 5 in the Australian Curriculum – Science. However, young children when exploring light might become very interested in electricity during their investigations. The theoretical framework of constructivism is foundational for teaching for conceptual change, as well as the inquiry-based approach to learning and to teaching.

Cultural–historical theory: conceptual scientific play

A cultural–historical approach to the teaching of science invites a genuine connection with children's personal experiences and cultural practices, while also taking into account what communities and society deem to be important science content knowledge worthy of study. A personal, institutional and societal perspective dominates in this approach where intentional teaching is important (Australian Government Department of Education, Employment and Workplace Relations 2009). This has the advantage of teaching in a culturally sensitive way and for bringing together everyday understandings with scientific understandings. This is captured through the idea of conceptual play. The disadvantage is that there are many different cultural practices and traditions in the Australian community. How is it possible for one teacher in one classroom or early childhood setting to consider the broad range of cultural diversity that is brought into the teaching–learning context? This is challenging for an early career teacher and requires a level of management and conceptual analysis of all the children. In this approach the teacher should think about a cultural–historical approach to teaching science as a journey, and over time to build the necessary cultural competence needed for engaging all children when teaching science. Reflect on the data you gathered: the outcomes and process, and when you operationalised this model. Was it easy or difficult to adopt a cultural–historical approach where conceptual play is foregrounded?

Culturally sensitive teaching

Culturally sensitive teaching includes the five thematic categories of content integration, facilitating knowledge construction, prejudice reduction, social justice and academic development. The model of culturally sensitive teaching acts as a tool for science learning where positive teacher–child relationships are developed, teachers hold high expectations of their children, they draw upon real-world contexts for framing science learning and build upon what children already know about their world. Indigenous ways of living in nature, rather than just a focus on Western science, is promoted through culturally sensitive teaching. Advocacy is promoted both by teachers, but also for children who are given a real sense of agency through their understandings and worldview being respected, validated and expanded. Rogoff's (2003) three lenses (as introduced in Chapter 2) can help you to focus on culturally sensitive teaching through thinking about the individual, the interpersonal context in which the individual is acting and thinking, and the cultural–institutional context that shapes and is shaped by the children and adults located in it.

> ### REFLECTIONS 10.5: MY PERSONAL FRAMEWORK FOR TEACHING SCIENCE
>
> *Following your consideration of the many possible factors that can affect your teaching framework, where do you now stand? What approaches or combination of approaches are you tending towards?*
>
> Talk about your ideas with another student.

Key principles for effective teaching

There are several principles that are critical in teaching science, irrespective of the particular approaches in your framework. They are summarised here.

Take account of children's ideas in planning and teaching

As shown in this book it is very important to take into account what children bring to each science learning experience. This point is best illustrated through student teacher reflections. The following evaluation was made by a student teacher following her teaching of a small group of children.

The lesson has definitely proved to me that the children need to be experiencing new information in order to stay interested. I unknowingly planned a lesson that strongly focused on concepts on which some of the children already had well developed ideas. It did result in some children losing interest – Cindy loses interest, becomes distracted easily and disruptive to others when she is bored. Cindy already had a good understanding about how plants grow from seeds. I tried to use her as a peer teacher, but this was ineffective.

This proves to me that it is important to get an understanding of where children's thinking is before lessons are planned.

At the end of this plant lesson I quizzed the children about their knowledge of animals, to ensure I was planning a lesson for next week that would include new information for everyone.

Another student teacher's reflections were as follows:

I had asked my group the previous week what they were interested in and would like to know about plants, so I planned the lesson according to their responses. I have seen that the three of them are all interested in dinosaurs so I structured their learning of plants around that topic, with great success I am happy to say!

It is interesting to see the wonderful theories and naive views the children have. I sometimes forget they do not know as much as I do. At the same time, though, I feel it is important not to underestimate children because they are clever and full of surprise!

Clearly develop a rationale and set of learning outcomes

As well as your own rationale for teaching science, it is also important that you can justify a specific science content area, such as a particular theme or topic that you have developed. A student teacher who planned a program for a Year 3 class stated as part of her justification for her choice of topic:

The primary reason why I chose to teach about worms was to demonstrate to children that even the most simple, smallest, ugliest and seemingly useless things in nature are actually quite complex, well designed and have an important part to play in our world. I want children to gain an understanding of just how amazing our world really is.

In addition to a well-founded rationale for a program, you should state a carefully developed set of learning outcomes. You must develop a clear view of the outcomes for a specific program or unit you wish to see in children's behaviours and understandings. You should carefully consider what each unit encourages children to learn about the nature of science.

The following reflections were written by another student teacher after a lesson with her small group of children.

- The planning of this lesson – the way it turned out was not intentional. I must have got caught up in designing what I thought were fantastic worksheets and forgot the most important aspect of lesson planning. That is: Is it meaningful? Is it at an appropriate level of understanding for these children? Will it be fun? I now look back and think to myself, what was I thinking?
- If nothing else, this proves to me that I really like the outcomes of lessons taught with a discovery approach. I will be planning discovery-based lessons for the three weeks on reaction and change and will try to involve as much practical/hands on work as I possibly can because it is the preferred learning style of my three children.
- I have set out to achieve broadening my children's concepts of science and scientists and I hope that this has occurred. I haven't exactly tested for this, but I do know that wherever and whenever I have been able to add bits of information on scientists and science of particular fields, I have. Whether the children have taken this on board or not, I am unsure.
- I wanted to promote risk-taking to these children, particularly in their writing. This proved to be quite difficult; writing itself is physically challenging for them still. Verbally these children will take almost any risk required of them, and I hope I have helped to develop these skills.

Develop children's learning within appropriate contexts

With a commitment to developing scientific literacy for all students, we must take account of the contexts in which different students live, whether these are the home or the wider community (Hamlin 2013). This underlines the need to recognise in our planning and teaching the special needs of girls and boys, and of children from different ethnic and racial groups. For these groups, we need to examine the suitability of the teaching approach, topics, content to be chosen and assessment strategies. To ensure that the science is accessible for children from culturally and linguistically diverse backgrounds, it is possible for you to use a wide range of strategies (see Chapter 9). This has been illustrated particularly for the case of Indigenous children in the context of the dominance of Western science. Culturally sensitive teaching recognises the importance of accepting the existence of a broad range of explanations about the world. With such an approach, the teacher avoids demeaning Indigenous cultural beliefs.

The experiences and viewpoints of disadvantaged groups in science should be incorporated into programs for the benefit of all children. For instance, children's knowledge and understanding of and respect for the environment are important viewpoints for all. Many topics in science can provide deeper and richer insights into children's lives that should be introduced in holistic ways. This provides a richer context for children's learning. Similarly, it may be challenging in the context of perceptions of science being male dominated, as shown in Chapters 1 and 9, for you to highlight female contributions to science. Changing worldviews is always difficult. Both Indigenous understandings of the world and the lack of recognition of female contributions to science could be used to teach about different aspects of the nature of science.

Early in this book you were asked to recall your own experiences in science at school, and any sense of alienation from science is probably a consequence of experiencing a relatively decontextualised science course. We urge you to avoid presenting science as separate from the social, cultural, environmental, political, economic and personal contexts (as discussed in Chapters 1 and 9). It is not sufficient simply to point out the applications and implications of science (a traditional secondary teaching strategy to link science to life). Context implies something much broader: science is to be contextualised from the outset in the learning environment. It is important to choose a context that is familiar and non-threatening to all learners in their everyday lives.

REFLECTIONS 10.6: A CONTEXT FOR SCIENCE

For each of the following science topics, create a context suitable for the group indicated. State the reasons why you advocate a particular learning context for a classroom.

Topic: Group.

Friction: Year 4 girls.

Seeds: Year 3 Aboriginal children.

Sight: Preschool children where English may be their second or third language.

Growth in children: Year 6 boys who are uninterested in human topics.

Children should engage with concrete objects and materials

It is now commonplace to hear teachers speaking of the need for hands-on experiences for children in learning science. However, this is no guarantee for effective learning. To know that children are experiencing 'hands-on science' does not inform you about many key aspects of the teaching or learning approaches being adopted, as we can have hands-on experiences in each of the seven teaching approaches demonstrated in the preceding nine chapters. It is also becoming common to hear talk of 'hands-on/minds-on science', which is possibly an improved slogan.

> ## REFLECTIONS 10.7: 'HANDS-ON SCIENCE' AS A SLOGAN
>
> Some teachers have readily accepted 'hands-on science' as an improvement on the situation where children do not engage in such activity. Argue the view that this is not necessarily the case. How might 'hands-on/minds-on science' be considered an improved slogan? Return to your notes made in Chapter 4 for some guidance.

The opportunity to manipulate objects and materials does not ensure particular learning outcomes if they are not carefully planned for and if the manipulation is not linked to children's thinking. However, such an opportunity is an important feature of any effective teaching approach. The stimulation gained, the recognition of relevance of an object to one's life and the opportunity for control over learning are some of the positive elements of incorporating hands-on experiences. Endeavour to build them into each and every topic in the science you teach.

Encourage children to construct their own meanings in science

The central idea of constructivism is that children (and adults) construct their own meanings in science, and this idea is now incorporated into many curricular statements. A challenge for teachers is to incorporate the idea into those teaching frameworks that have not typically given it a central place; that is, the approaches of inquiry, conceptual change, culturally sensitive teaching, cultural–historical, transmission and discovery. If this were to be done, all classrooms would become dynamic arenas for the discussion and reformulation of ideas and differing conceptions of the scientific world. To create such an environment may be one of the most challenging but also one of the most rewarding activities you could undertake. Similarly, culturally sensitive teaching, which draws on cultural–historical theory, invites us to pay attention to the learner as a participant in the real world (not just our simulated classrooms). It also encourages us to explore how social situations give meaning and motivate children to engage in learning. Taking this view means that we will think about teaching and learning from a community perspective, and not just what an individual thinks.

Encourage children to ask their own questions

Part 2 provided a broad range of ways by which children's questions can be used to begin, guide or frame scientific inquiries. Using children's questions can be justified for the following reasons:

- curriculum grounds – children's questions provide a guide to content that is most likely to engage children

- pedagogical grounds – questions offered by children are revealing of their present understandings
- philosophical grounds – question asking plays a central role in science and, through learning to ask questions, children will appreciate what it means to think scientifically
- psychological grounds – children's questions provide a purpose to their learning and allow them to learn at a pace appropriate to their development.

We have discussed how encouraging children to ask questions often injects elements of excitement and the unexpected into teaching. You will probably welcome that!

However, keep in mind that question asking is only one way of interacting with children. You will need to find out what interactions are familiar or work best with the particular group of children you are working with in your classrooms/centres. This is particularly important when considering that not all children come from backgrounds where question asking is encouraged or supported. For some cultural communities, asking questions is about questioning the authority of elders, and therefore viewed as disrespectful. Question asking is also difficult to generate in early childhood settings, particularly for infants and toddlers whose language is still developing.

Encourage children to become more sensitive to the environment

In Australia there has been a substantial growth in awareness of the need to respect and care for our environment. With a new emphasis on environmental education and sustainability, the classroom situation is conducive to the teaching of science making its contribution to such awareness. It will be easy for you to integrate an environmental theme in many science topics. Developing an ecological understanding through science learning will be a very important contribution. Respecting and caring for plant and animal life is an essential aspect of science education; this could be encouraged on excursions in the bush, and should be in evidence when animals are brought into the classroom (see MacDonald, Miller, Murry, Herrera and Spears 2013). Cruel treatment of any animal, no matter how small and seemingly inconsequential, is unacceptable.

Children should learn through rich educational activities

Much of the preceding discussion of principles for effective teaching of science could be summarised as the need to construct rich learning challenges for the children. You might find the following list of elements useful.

- Are the experiences accessible to everyone when you begin the unit of science?
- Are the children positioned to make decisions?
- Are a range of questions being used, such as, 'what if' questions?

- Are children encouraged to work with their own methods and approaches to learning?
- Are classrooms and early childhood settings full of rich discussion and communication?
- Is curiosity, surprise and genuine interest featured?
- Is there a sense of enjoyment?
- Are the experiences and contexts extendable?

Guidelines for implementing a teaching approach

In addition to these broad principles to inform your teaching, a number of more focused guidelines can assist you in achieving successful outcomes as you implement and trial an approach, especially if this is a new one for you.

Work with children as a co-investigator and co-learner

At the outset, recognise that your knowledge of a science topic or area may be limited, and that, inevitably, you will be asked questions for which you do not have answers. There is much research to indicate that many teachers worry about what they see as the inadequacy of their science knowledge for teaching. It is probably one of your concerns as well.

While you will need an adequate base of science knowledge to plan any topic and to guide children's investigations, it is a realistic and sound pedagogical approach to work alongside children, learning as they do. With this attitude, you clarify your own understandings of the topic as you interact with the children. You also extend your knowledge of the science involved. Children gain a great deal from appreciating that you are a learner, and that they can help you learn new ideas!

Adopting such an approach allows you to share the wonder and delight of children as they explore their world. As teachers, we should share our own sense of wonder about life and the universe. Science can enhance our appreciation of the beauty and awesome nature of our existence.

The following points were made by a student teacher after teaching a small group of children each week for a semester.

- Lessons that I plan must be interesting, relevant, resource rich and allow for high child participation.
- Social interaction and discussion are critical for children to construct knowledge and must be a significant part of lessons.
- An inquiry approach to teaching tends to be a powerful teaching tool as it encompasses the other teaching styles, and can be modified in lessons that require more of one element than another.

- Teaching needs to consider the great diversity of children, in respect to both their current conceptions and learning abilities.
- Various assessment strategies are needed to check that children are learning vital concepts. Thinking books enable both teachers and the students to visualise preconceptions, what new concepts have been formed and what still needs investigation.
- I need to be an active co-learner with the children.
- I will often need to move out of my comfort zone to try different teaching approaches, and then evaluate both my own learning and that of the children!

Consider the children's previous experiences of science education

A critical question in your planning is: how much responsibility can the children assume for their own learning? This partly depends on their previous learning of science in school or early childhood setting, and especially on the responsibility they have been allowed and encouraged to assume in the classroom or early childhood setting. The answer also depends on the extent and effectiveness of the children's work in groups. A sudden change in the approach to science might produce much excitement, but might bring other problems of management and pedagogy. You need to attempt to envisage and plan for these.

In one interesting case of children experiencing a different approach, a student teacher was implementing an inquiry-based approach to learning on the topic of 'skeletons' with a Year 1/2 class. She reported:

The children are not used to an inquiry approach to learning science. They were quite inquisitive as to why I wanted to find out what they knew – one child asked 'Why do you want to know what we know?' What does one say to that? I told them that I was sure they knew heaps about skeletons and that the class was going to make a list of all of them.

REFLECTIONS 10.8: RESPONDING TO CHILDREN

Consider the situation described above. Imagine you are the teacher whom the children questioned. *What would you have said to them as a response?*

Decide on a realistic level of risk-taking

Earlier in this chapter we discussed factors that will influence your choice of an approach, and it is likely that some of these centre on the degree of risk involved for you. One area of risk-taking is the choice of topic. One student teacher decided to develop a unit on electromagnets to challenge herself, as she said she knew nothing about them. After much preparation in building working models and reading, she developed a highly successful program. Another student teacher reported on another unit on 'worms'.

[W]hen I first began to prepare this unit I knew very little about worms and I purposely chose to teach 'worms' for this reason. I believe that it is important for teachers to take risks and to make the effort to teach to children subjects which they themselves might not feel comfortable with.

We strongly endorse the latter comment. Children's education in science should not be limited by a teacher's preference for certain topics although, unfortunately, this has been quite common. These student teachers took major risks, but developed and implemented highly effective teaching programs.

However, many other student teachers and teachers might want to choose a topic with which they feel confident and knowledgeable as a starting point. This might make good sense: when you have developed sufficient confidence you might decide to branch into areas about which you know less. The choice must depend on your own level of confidence and your judgement about the dynamics of the classroom or early childhood situation.

Support children's learning of new roles

You need to explain and to model for the children new roles and new approaches to learning. If they are not accustomed to asking questions in science (which will be the basis of the children's investigations), do not assume that they will ask such questions readily. You need to model the process and provide sufficient stimulation to generate questions. These can emerge from a range of hands-on activities carefully set up by you to initiate a unit. In the case of very young children, take up their statements and transform them into questions. With sufficient practice and stimulation, the children are likely to ask more questions. This is particularly important in early childhood settings.

You need to model and to support children in similar ways for other aspects of investigating, including the planning of investigations, sharing their own emergent understandings, recording their ideas and observations and reporting to others. Classrooms and early childhood settings should become dynamic and supportive communities of learners.

We suggest that you do not overestimate what children are able and motivated to do, but do not underestimate them either. Be optimistic about what children are capable of doing and achieving – it is likely that you will be pleasantly surprised.

Ensure that children learn science in a safe environment

There can be particular hazards in teaching some science topics that you will need to consider. Do not assume that because you have used some substances in high school they are allowable in primary classrooms. Education departments have guidelines on hazardous chemicals, so consult these or ask experts if you are considering using such materials in the classroom. Boiling water is especially dangerous, and you alone should handle this if it is necessary in the classroom. Other potential dangers include heavy weights, sharp objects and projectiles. Investigations involving flames are best restricted to a teacher demonstration. In electricity investigations for children, use only dry-cell batteries, and on no account let children use the mains electricity supply. It is essential that rules of behaviour be well understood if children are handling potentially hazardous items, and you need to monitor their activities carefully. Through such care you are helping the children to learn how to safely handle some of the dangers in our everyday environment or to avoid them.

Plan your approach to assessment and evaluation

It is most important that you plan how you will assess children's learning and evaluate your effectiveness before you begin the teaching of a topic. Assessment needs to be built into the very heart of your teaching approach; it should not be an

Figure 10.5 Planning for Elvin's learning and development: building on what he knows and can do in science.

afterthought. As discussed in earlier chapters, assessment can itself make a contribution to children's learning. Throughout all the chapters there is a range of suggestions as to how you can assess children's achievement of your planned learning outcomes. Evaluation of the success of your approach includes assessment of the learning, but extends to other aspects of your teaching. Again, evaluation must be planned if it is to be really valuable to you.

A synthesising activity

To help you develop skills in applying key features of this chapter, develop a skeletal plan for teaching the same topic, using each of the seven approaches discussed here. This challenge gives you a sense of how differently a program could look and be experienced by both teacher and children.

REFLECTIONS 10.9: TEACHING AND LEARNING OPTIONS

Visualise a group of students, deciding on the setting of the school or centre, children's cultural background, ages, gender, and previous experiences of science teaching and learning. Then select one of the following topics (or put forward one of your own):

- Sun
- snails
- wood
- rain.

For each of the seven teaching approaches in turn, develop a plan of the main features of a program to be developed around the topic. Include in your initial plan how to initiate the topic, what learning outcomes you desire, the role of the teacher, some ideas for activities and ways the children's work might be assessed.

When you have completed the five plans, compare them. Do you see clearly how different the children's learning experiences would be for the same topic using the different approaches?

Becoming a leader of science

Once you have researched the approaches (both through the literature in this book and through undertaking your own research in classrooms and centres), you will be in a position to argue for the particular approach you are adopting or modifying.

Teachers also need to look to the future and think about how they can continue to grow their understandings and competence.

The area of science for children is one in which you have many opportunities to exercise leadership. If you are an experienced teacher, you are aware of this opening. As a pre-service teacher, you might not think this is possible for many years. However, recent graduates who have had an effective introduction to science education in their teaching course have quite often been invited to take on leadership activities in the school of their first appointment. Preschools offer similar opportunities for leadership. This is not surprising, as there is a large proportion of teachers who did not experience science education as a significant part of their initial teacher education. Even if they did, it is quite possible that your knowledge and understanding of developments are more advanced. Therefore you might well have the opportunity of in-servicing colleagues. You are fortunate to be doing this in an environment in which there are a number of positive and supportive developments in science for children.

Leading change in science education

Professor Peter Fensham as a distinguished science education researcher has led the field of science education at the international level for over 40 years. As an Australian, he has actively engaged in science education reform around the world. He continually analyses the current curriculum context, always seeking to improve the science learning of the community, and through this has actively contributed to the development of education programs in science. He has been an advocate for change in science education research, moving the field away from a purely quantitative approach to gathering data, stating publicly at conferences that much of this research has not changed the level of science learning in schools. He has always argued that science education research should make a difference to pedagogical practices, and through this change the quality of the child's experience in science education.

RESEARCH ACTIVITY 10.1: THE POSSIBILITIES FOR TEACHING SCIENCE IN PRIMARY SCHOOLS AND EARLY CHILDHOOD SETTINGS

Leading change in schools so that science is actively experienced each week is challenging. Zapata (2013) interviewed practising teachers about what possibilities they saw for the teaching of science in their primary schools. She asked:

1   How would you describe what you currently teach?
2   Do you teach science as part of your daily classroom structure? Elaborate on how long science is taught and how many times a week?

3 What guides your teaching of science? Elaborate on how strictly you adhere to the curriculum materials provided or whether you use other resources.

4 How much freedom do you feel you have to implement some of the methods and strategies you learned as you were preparing to become a teacher?

This study was done in the context of the United States, where greater conformity exists in relation to lesson plans – which explains the phrasing of question three.

When on field placement, undertake a small study of the teachers in your centre or school. Ask these questions. Perhaps phrase question three as follows:

What guides your teaching of science? Elaborate on how strictly you follow the curriculum approach and sequence of content as set out in your school or whether you are free to select your own science content?

Bring the data together into a grid as shown in Table 10.2. What do you notice?

Table 10.2 What possibilities are there for teaching science?

	Teacher 1	Teacher 2	Teacher 3
How would you describe what you currently teach?			
Do you teach science as part of your daily classroom structure? Elaborate on how long science is taught and how many times a week.			
What guides your teaching of science? Elaborate on how strictly you follow the curriculum approach and sequence of content as set out in your school or whether you are free to select your own science content.			
How much freedom do you feel you have to implement some of the methods and strategies you learned as you were preparing to become a teacher?			

In the research of Zapata (2013), she found an interesting diversity of views among teachers (positive or doubtful) and restrictions or enablers for the teaching of science in their schools. For example, a Year 2 teacher of Caucasian background said: 'I do not teach science. It is not really emphasized as that important in my school. As long as students are reading something science related once a week that is fine.' *How do you feel about that?* 'Well, I don't know I learned enough science to teach science. I am already pressured to make sure they are reading and writing.'

(p. 793). This is a consistent finding across Australia. The amount of science taught in primary schools has been of concern (Tytler 2007). There is an expectation of teaching science each week, and the curriculum is designed with this expectation in mind (ACARA 2014). Another Year 4 primary teacher of Haitian background in Zapata's study (2013) said: 'I teach science twice a week and once a week students go to the science lab with the science teacher' (p. 794). A Year 3 teacher of Hispanic background said: 'I teach science once a week for 30 mins. *Do you think 30 mins once a week is enough?* It is for me because I don't feel comfortable teaching science' (p. 794). In contrast, a Year 1 teacher of Hispanic background said:

> My science is scheduled three times a week during the last half hour of the day. I use the pacing guides to guide my teaching of science. I do not use the textbooks or workbooks provided because I feel they are extremely boring. I did try them before and my students got nothing out of them. Many of my students have trouble reading, so having them read about science is even more confusing for them and does not foster any love of the subject. *What do you use instead of the textbooks?* 'I use a lot of online resources in order to introduce and practice concepts with my class. The students love the videos on "brain-pop" and I feel that videos do a good job of explaining things in kid-friendly terms as well another resource that I love is "discovery education". I also try to incorporate as many in-class labs as possible.' (Zapata 2013, p. 795).

Sometimes teachers have a lot of autonomy to make decisions about what approach to teaching science they adopt. A Year 1 teacher (Caucasian) and a Kindergarten (Hispanic) teacher discuss this autonomy:

> I feel that I do have a lot of freedom to implement any methods and strategies that help my students learn. My principal and science coach love the hands-on approach and science is a subject that lends itself to that approach generously. Unfortunately, I have found that I lose a lot of my science time because it is scheduled at the end of the day. I also try to find 'teachable moments' throughout the day that relate to science. If one comes up, I try to take some time to explain it and incorporate it into whatever subject area we are studying (Zapata 2013, p. 796).

> I do teach science every day. We talk about weather, seasons, and also growing plants. I have the freedom to teach pretty much what I want. Depending on the week and what is scheduled. I teach science for 30 mins (Zapata 2013, p. 796).

As a teacher of science there are many things to consider, including participating in professional learning, team curriculum development, communicating science to the general community and reviewing the resources available in the centre, school or community for supporting science learning. These dimensions of the professional practice of teachers are introduced below:

- *Professional development of teachers*: your own teaching could be a model for others. Sharing your ideas at staff meetings is another means of convincing those teachers reticent about teaching science that it is a satisfying and important area of education. Show other teachers how science can effectively be incorporated into curriculum areas in which they do feel competent. If workshops are developed as part of a professional development day, you should be able to make valuable inputs to these.

- *Policy and curriculum development:* your school or centre is required to develop its own policy on teaching and learning – for schools it is likely to be explicit about science education, while in an early childhood setting it maybe be integrated more into a sense of investigating (rather than science specifically). The development of the school or centre curriculum is likely to occur within a systematic framework document. With your knowledge of developments and general understanding of issues in science education, you could play a leading role in such tasks.
- *Promoting science education in the community:* another challenge is to develop support among the school or early childhood community for science for young children. You are encouraged to develop a sound rationale for the inclusion of science in education. You should be able to talk with members of the school and early childhood community about the importance and relevance of science for the whole education of a child. Convincing families of this also depends on their opportunities to observe effective science in action in the school or early childhood setting. You might organise science events to which families are invited, and the national Science Week, which involves the Australian Science Teachers' Association, could be an effective context for such events.
- *Resources:* reviewing and ordering relevant resources in science for the school or early childhood library is another valuable contribution you could make. The organisation and purchase of materials and equipment are important potential uses of your expertise.

You now appreciate that there is a wide range of ways in which to influence the direction and development of science in a school or centre. It is highly likely that your expertise will be welcomed.

Summary

The development of an appropriate framework for the teaching of science is complex. A number of personal and contextual factors must always be considered in the decision-making process. Relevant to the choice of approaches are the planned learning outcomes, contextual factors in the classroom, and the extent to which you are willing to take risks.

Each of the approaches to teaching science has a legitimate place and will emphasise different facets of the nature of science. Whatever teaching framework is constructed, there are several core principles that should underpin it. Such principles revolve around the goal of actively engaging children in science, and providing them with a secure and challenging learning environment. Now that you have reflected on the seven different approaches to teaching science, you are well on the way to becoming a leader in science in a school or early childhood setting.

References

Australian Curriculum, Assessment and Reporting Authority 2014, Australian Curriculum – Science. Available at http://www.australiancurriculum.edu.au/Science/Curriculum/F-6. (Accessed September 2014.)

Australian Government Department of Education, Employment and Workplace Relations 2009, *Belonging, Being and Becoming. The Early Years Learning Framework for Australia*, Canberra: Commonwealth of Australia.

Hamlin, ML 2013, '"Yo soy indigena": Identifying and using traditional ecological knowledge (TEK) to make the teaching of science culturally responsive Mayua girls', *Cultural Studies of Science Education*, vol. 8, no. 4, pp. 759–76.

Lewin, C 2013, 'ICT and effective practices in science education: Lesson learned and future directions in C Redman ed, *Successful Science Education Practices: Exploring what, why and how they worked*, New York: Nova Science, pp. 227–44.

MacDonald, GL, Miller, SS, Murry, K Herrera, S, Spears, JD 2013, 'Efficacy of ACA strategies in biography driven science teaching: An investigation', *Cultural Studies of Science Education*, vol. 8, no. 4, pp. 889–903.

Rogoff, B 2003, *The Cultural Nature of Human Development*, Oxford: Oxford University Press.

Tytler, R 2007, *Review. Re-imagining Science Education: Engaging students in science for Australia's future. Australian Education Review*, Camberwell, Victoria: Australian Council for Educational Research.

Zapata, M 2013, 'Substantiating the need to apply a sociocultural lens to the preparation of teachers in an effort to achieve science reform', *Cultural Studies of Science Education*, vol. 8, no. 4, pp. 777–801.

Index